IMAGES
of America

DOWNTOWN ST. PAUL

On the Cover: Downtown St. Paul's Seventh Street was a busy place on this summer day in 1922. (Courtesy of the Minnesota Historical Society.)

IMAGES
of America

DOWNTOWN ST. PAUL

Iric Nathanson

ARCADIA PUBLISHING

ISBN 978-1-4671-0246-9

Published by Arcadia Publishing
Charleston, South Carolina

Printed in the United States of America

Library of Congress Control Number: 2018941135

For all general information, please contact Arcadia Publishing:
Telephone 843-853-2070
Fax 843-853-0044
E-mail sales@arcadiapublishing.com
For customer service and orders:
Toll-Free 1-888-313-2665

Visit us on the Internet at www.arcadiapublishing.com

To Marlene.

Contents

ACKNOWLEDGMENTS

During this past year, I was able to draw on the expertise of the many people who helped make this book a reality. Three longtime observers of the St. Paul scene took the time to review my early drafts. David Beal, John Lindley, and Steve Trimble caught some glaring errors and offered many useful suggestions. Ted Hathaway and his staff at Hennepin County Public Library Special Collections located a number of the archival images included in this book. Rich Arpi from the Ramsey County Historical Society and Eric Mortenson with the Minnesota Historical Society also helped me access the extensive photographic archives maintained by their organizations. Weming Lu and Mary Arvanitis provided photographs from their personal collections. Finally, Angel Hisnanick, my editor at Arcadia Publishing, kept me on track as this project moved from the idea stage to the final product. All images are courtesy of the Minnesota Historical Society unless noted.

INTRODUCTION

In the early 1840s, a tiny frontier settlement took shape along the upper reaches of the Mississippi River. The settlement consisted of a few ramshackle cabins overlooking the riverfront on a site that would later become downtown St. Paul.

In later years, St. Paul would be known as the "Saintly City." But the tiny settlement had a much less lofty name in the beginning. It was called Pig's Eye after a disreputable liquor dealer with a misshapen eye known as Pierre "Pig's Eye" Parrant,- who ran a tavern there. Luckily for future generations, the original name was short-lived. When a French priest, Fr. Lucien Galtier, arrived in 1840 to bring religion to the tiny settlement, he renamed the place for a Christian saint. "The name Saint Paul applied to a town or city seemed appropriate," Father Galtier later recalled. "The monosyllable is short, sounds well and is understood by all denominations of Christians." Later, the Catholic Church, led by Archbishop John Ireland, would play an important role in the social life of St. Paul.

When Father Galtier came to St. Paul, the frontier was moving west into what later became the state of Minnesota. Land had just been opened to white settlement as a result of treaties with the local Indian tribes. With its strategic location at the head of navigation on the Mississippi River, St. Paul soon become the commercial center of a Midwestern region filling in with farms and towns.

In 1849, St. Paul took on a political role when it became the capital of the newly created Minnesota Territory. That led to a real estate boom. When it was designated the territorial capital, St. Paul's population was just under 1,000. Nine years later, when Minnesota was admitted to the union as the 32nd state, that number had ballooned to just under 10,000.

During those boom years, young men on the move were finding their way to St. Paul from all over North America. One of those was an 18-year-old Canadian named James J. Hill. Soon after arriving in town, Hill found a job as a bookkeeper for a steamboat company. Within a few years, he was on his way to becoming St. Paul's wealthiest and most prominent business leader. By the 1890s, as the head of the transcontinental Northern Pacific Railroad, Hill's prominence and wealth had earned him a place on the national stage.

Hill made St. Paul his base of operations, but his reach kept extending farther west as his railroad empire expanded. In Minneapolis, Hill built the landmark Stone Arch Bridge to bring his trains into that city's downtown. The Stone Arch overlooked St. Anthony Falls, the only true falls along with entire length of the Mississippi. With the waterpower it generated, the falls gave Minneapolis, the younger of the Twin Cities, a resource that its older twin, St. Paul, lacked.

St. Anthony Falls powered a series of flourmills that would soon make Minneapolis the flour milling capital of the world. By the turn of the last century, with Minneapolis surpassing St. Paul in terms of population and economic growth, St. Paul civic leaders came to realize that their city would not become the dominant economic center of the Upper Midwest as they had hoped it might one day. Still, they had a thriving downtown serving a community whose population would later exceed 300,000.

During the first half of the 20th century, St. Paul residents flocked to downtown using the network of streetcar lines that converged there. Initially, downtown's retail district was centered on Third Street, at the edge of the bluff overlooking the riverfront. However, by the end of the 19th century, the retail district had moved north and west, away from the riverfront, leaving Third Street to decline into a shabby skid row. It was later replaced by a landscaped roadway known as Kellogg Boulevard.

Beyond Third Street, the blocks between Fifth and Seventh Streets filled in with elegant department stores and elaborate movie palaces. At one point, Seventh Street was home to several dozen movie theaters, making it St. Paul's "Great White Way."

Downtown St. Paul survived the turmoil of the Great Depression and World War II but succumbed to the wave of postwar suburbanization that threatened aging urban centers all across the country. One by one, St. Paul's department stores and movie theaters closed as shoppers abandoned downtown for the new suburban malls.

Downtown was able to offset its decline, at least in part, because of its location as the site of Minnesota's state capitol. State government's expanded role during the post–World War II decades helped fill downtown office buildings with thousands of state employees. But those workers departed at the end of the working day, leaving downtown streets empty and desolate.

During these postwar years, downtown was reshaped by urban renewal and highway projects that cleared away much of its stock of 19th-century commercial buildings. Luckily, a number of downtown's most architecturally significant structures were preserved, even while many of the early commercial blocks were leveled. Starting in the 1970s, the seeds of downtown's revival were planted when local civic leaders came to realize that many of the commercial district's early buildings contained great hidden value behind their shabby facades. The adaptive reuse of St. Paul's turn-of-the-century federal building was the first in a series of important historic preservation efforts that helped rebuild downtown.

During the early years of the 21st century, St. Paul's central business district took advantage of its rich history to become an important cultural and entertainment center. By rediscovering its roots, downtown St. Paul has created a bright future for itself during the new millennium.

One

Early Years

When the early settlers arrived at a wooded site along the Upper Mississippi, they discovered two clefts in the river bluffs about a mile apart. These breaks in the bluffs enabled the settlers to drive their wagons down to the river to meet the boats traveling up and down the Mississippi. The two riverfront sites became St. Paul's Upper and Lower Landings, which served as anchors for the frontier settlement that would later become modern-day downtown St. Paul.

The Lower Landing, at the end of today's Jackson Street, served as the transfer point for goods and supplies arriving in St. Paul, while the Upper Landing, at Chestnut Street, was used more often for passengers coming and going on the Mississippi paddleboats.

St. Paul's era as a river town was short. By the 1870s, the railroads were supplanting the riverboats as the primary mode of transportation serving Minnesota's capital city. The downtown riverfront was soon crisscrossed with rail lines reaching out to both coasts.

At the western end of downtown, the early state capital buildings helped shape the skyline of a growing city. The first capitol, with its modest dome, was completed in 1853 while Minnesota was still a territory. That first building served as the seat of Minnesota's government through the early years of statehood until 1881, when it was destroyed by fire. It was replaced by a new capitol building on the same site.

During the last two decades of the 19th century, as St. Paul was undergoing a population and economic boom, local civic leaders realized that the image of their city needed improvement. That image had suffered a blow when an East Coast reporter described St. Paul as "another Siberia unfit for human habitation in the winter." With their civic pride wounded, community leaders responded by showcasing the glories of winter in their northern city. They organized an elaborate Winter Carnival with its own royalty and a dramatic ice palace built in a large public square. Over the years, the St. Paul Winter Carnival would become a major community event that boosted public spirits during the coldest and darkest time of the year.

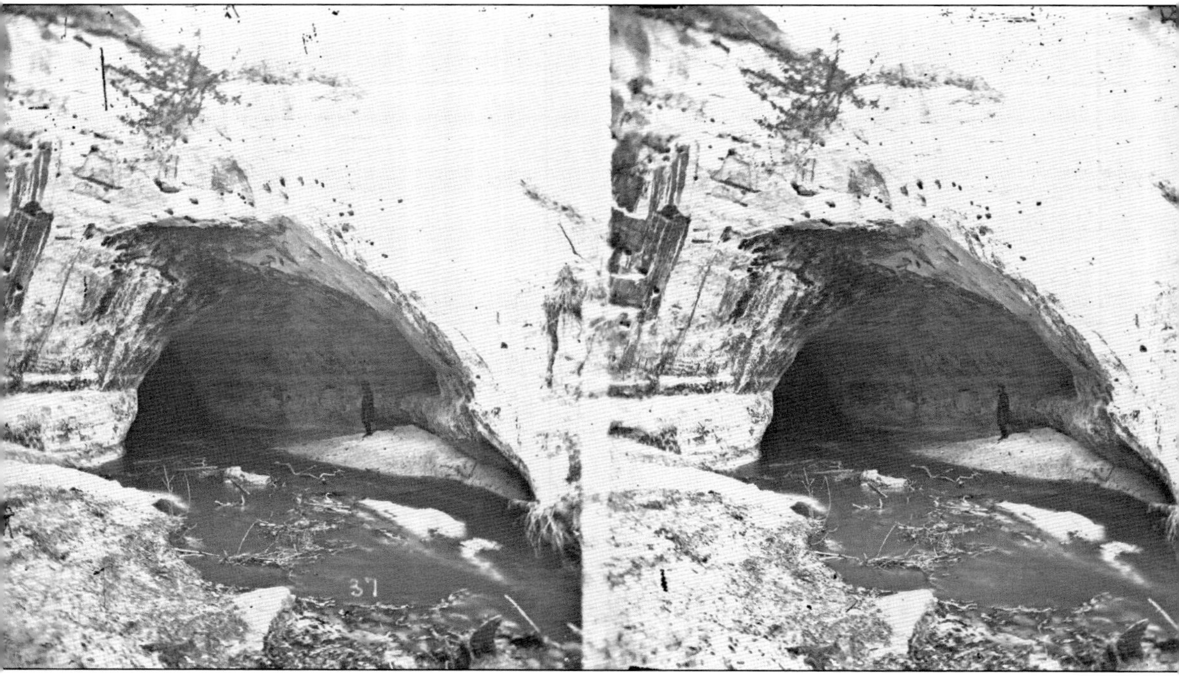

This early photograph shows Fountain Cave, where Pierre Parrant, a French Canadian fur trader, sold liquor to soldiers from Fort Snelling and early settlers along the northern frontier. Known as Pig's Eye because of his misshapen eye, Parrant later moved his ramshackle tavern to a new site farther downstream in what would become downtown St. Paul. Pig's Eye became the name the early settlers used for the tiny settlement that grew up around Parrant's tavern. (Courtesy of Hennepin County Library Special Collections.)

Fr. Lucien Galtier found himself in a bleak, unwelcoming environment when he arrived at a tiny riverfront settlement in 1840. He would later write that the site "was surrounded by a complete wilderness, and without any sign of fields under tillage. I understood that my mission and life must henceforth be a career of privation, hard trials and suffering and will require of me patience, labor and resignation. I had before me a large territory under my charge but few souls to watch over."

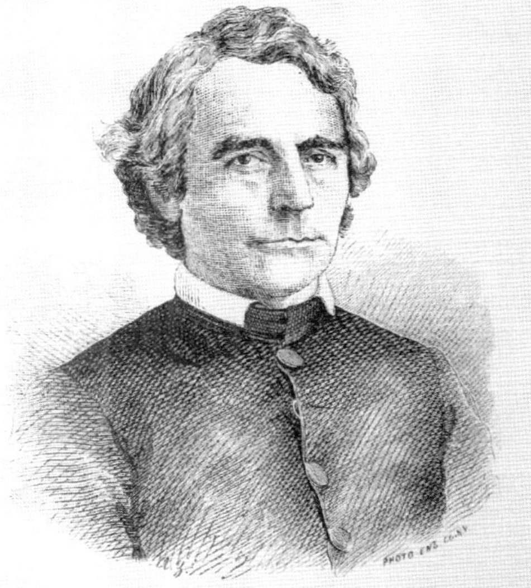

REV. LUCIAN GALTIER.
First Catholic Priest in Saint Paul, and who gave that name to our city.

In October 1841, Father Galtier oversaw the construction of a small log chapel he dedicated to St. Paul. "Logs were prepared and a church erected, so poor that it would remind one of the stable at Bethlehem. It was destined, however, to be the nucleus of a great city," Father Galtier would later note. "I expressed a wish that the settlement would be known by the same name, and my desire was obtained."

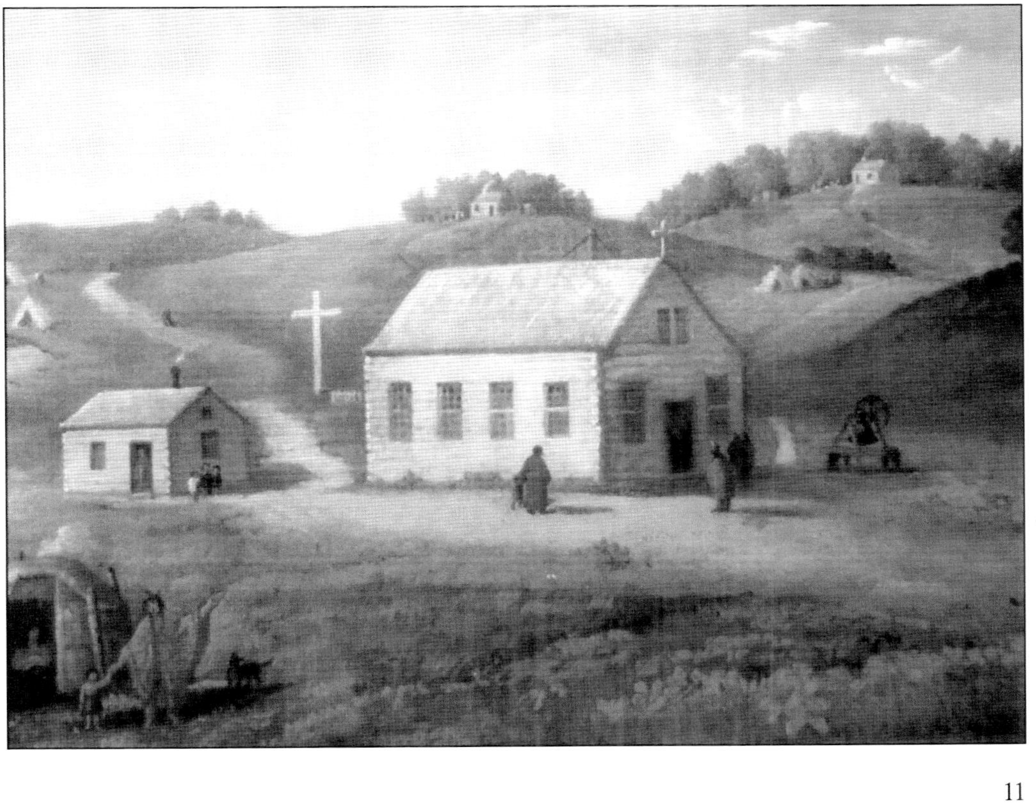

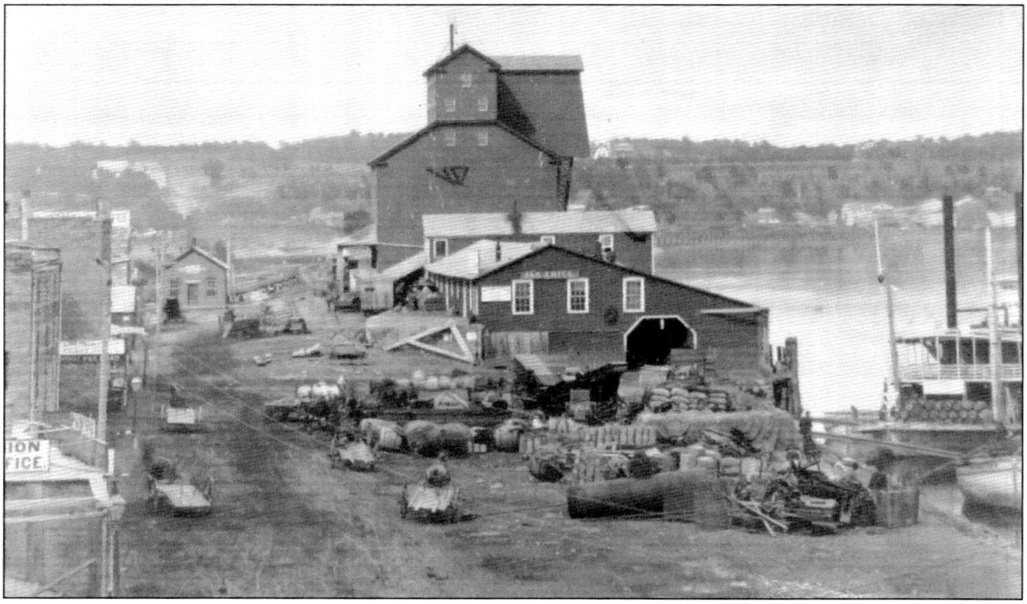

A cleft in the bluffs leading down to the riverfront provided a docking site for riverboats plying the Mississippi. A site at the foot of present-day Jackson Street became known as the Lower Landing. During the town's early years, the Lower Landing became a key transfer point for goods and passengers arriving in St. Paul destined for the frontier settlements in what later became the state of Minnesota.

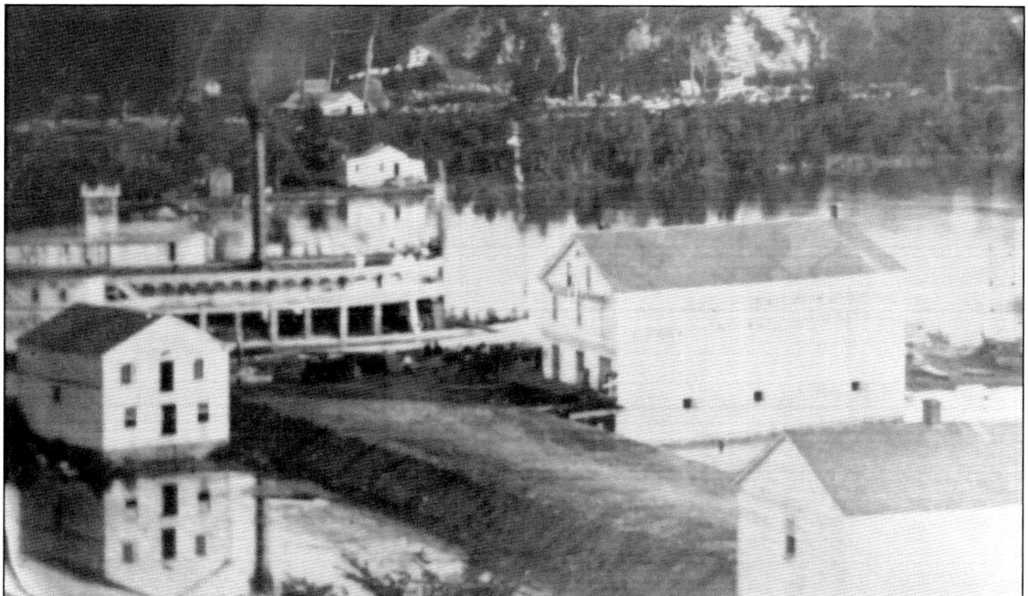

St. Paul's second steamboat docking site, known as the Upper Landing or Levee, was used for passenger traffic. Many Southerners arrived at St. Paul's Upper Landing during the summer months, fleeing their region's oppressive heat. Later, immigrants, many from Italy, settled along the Upper Landing's low-lying riverfront.

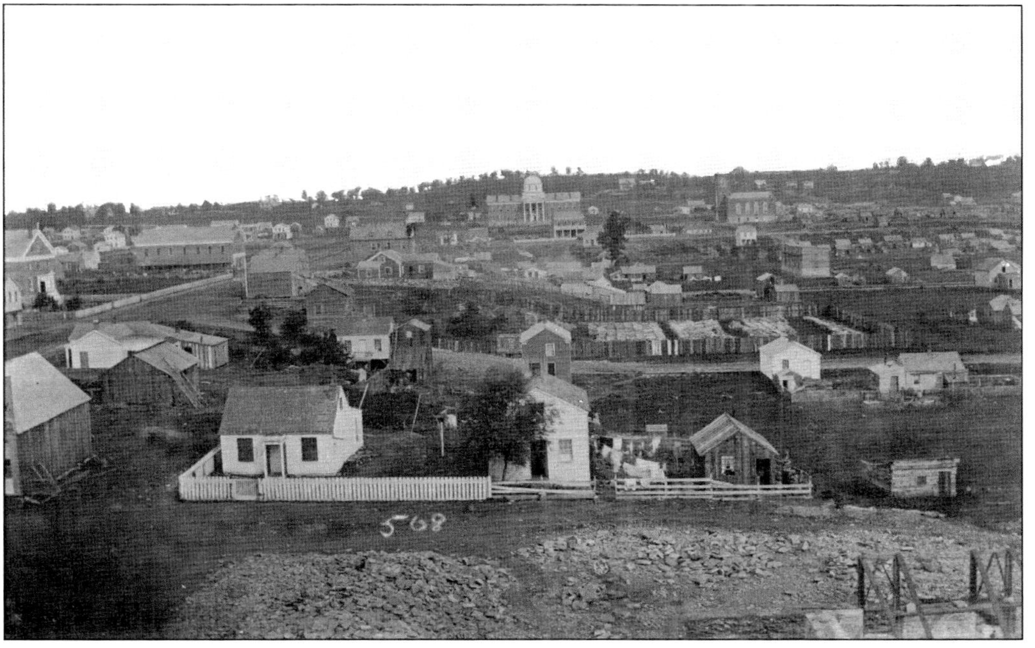

When Minnesota became a territory in 1849, St. Paul became its capital. Then, the town was still a rough frontier settlement with a population of less than 1,000. The building shown in the background of this photograph was built in 1854 to house Minnesota's territorial government. With its distinctive dome, the capitol building dominated St. Paul's early skyline.

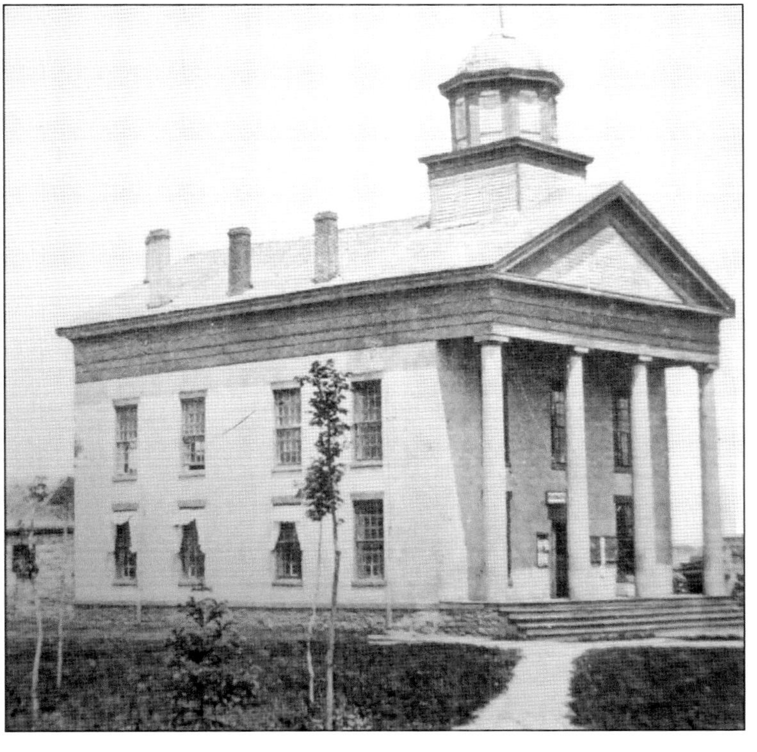

The town's first courthouse, built in 1850, was a modest two-story structure topped with a small dome. In order to give the building some stature and prominence as the seat of government for the small riverfront community, the courthouse was embellished with a portico consisting of four columns topped by a classical pediment.

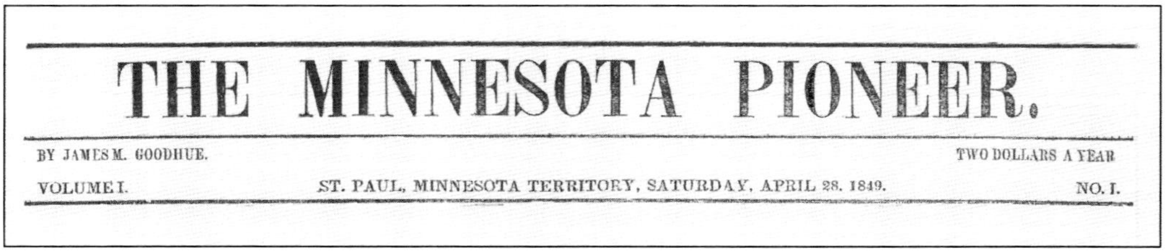

THE MINNESOTA PIONEER.

BY JAMES M. GOODHUE. TWO DOLLARS A YEAR

VOLUME I. ST. PAUL, MINNESOTA TERRITORY, SATURDAY, APRIL 28, 1849. NO. I.

The Minnesota Pioneer, Minnesota's first newspaper, made its appearance in 1849, when the future state had just been declared a US territory. The paper's publisher, James Goodhue, later wrote that he had no subscribers when he published his first issue on April 28. "There were but a handful of people in the whole territory. . . . [They] wanted no politics and we gave them none; they wanted information of all sorts about Minnesota and that is what we furnished them with.'

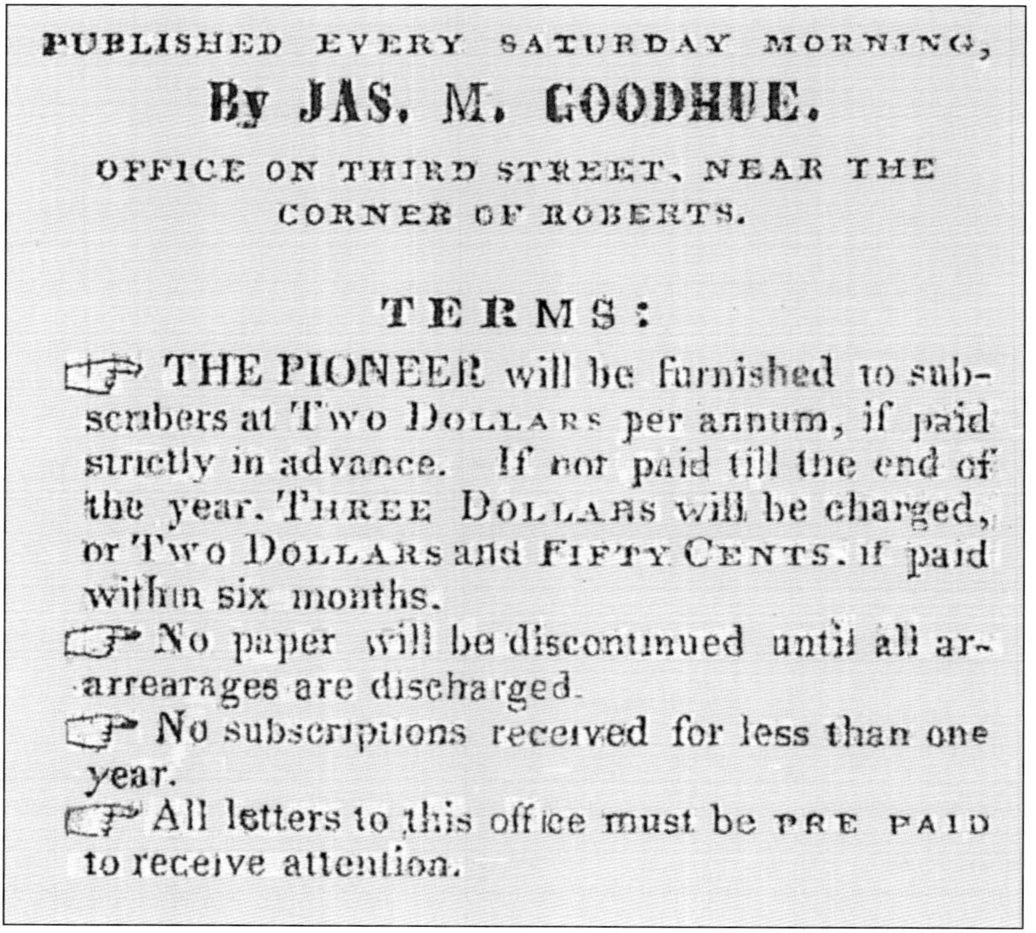

PUBLISHED EVERY SATURDAY MORNING,

By JAS. M. GOODHUE.

OFFICE ON THIRD STREET, NEAR THE CORNER OF ROBERTS.

TERMS:

☞ THE PIONEER will be furnished to subscribers at TWO DOLLARS per annum, if paid strictly in advance. If not paid till the end of the year, THREE DOLLARS will be charged, or TWO DOLLARS and FIFTY CENTS, if paid within six months.

☞ No paper will be discontinued until all ar- arrearages are discharged.

☞ No subscriptions received for less than one year.

☞ All letters to this office must be PRE PAID to receive attention.

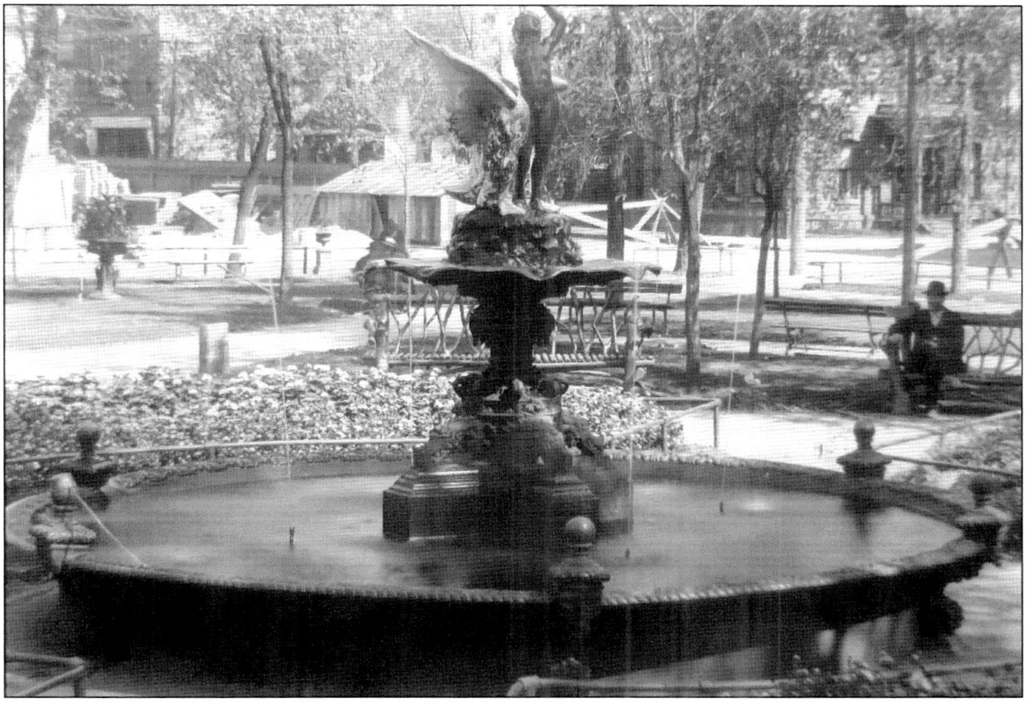

Rice Park was one of three public squares established when St. Paul received its articles of incorporation from the Minnesota Territorial Legislature in 1849. Initially, the public square operated as a commons for local residents, who grazed their animals there. In the 1870s, the park brought a note of Victorian elegance to downtown St. Paul when a decorative fountain was installed in the square. Rice Park was named for US senator Henry M. Rice.

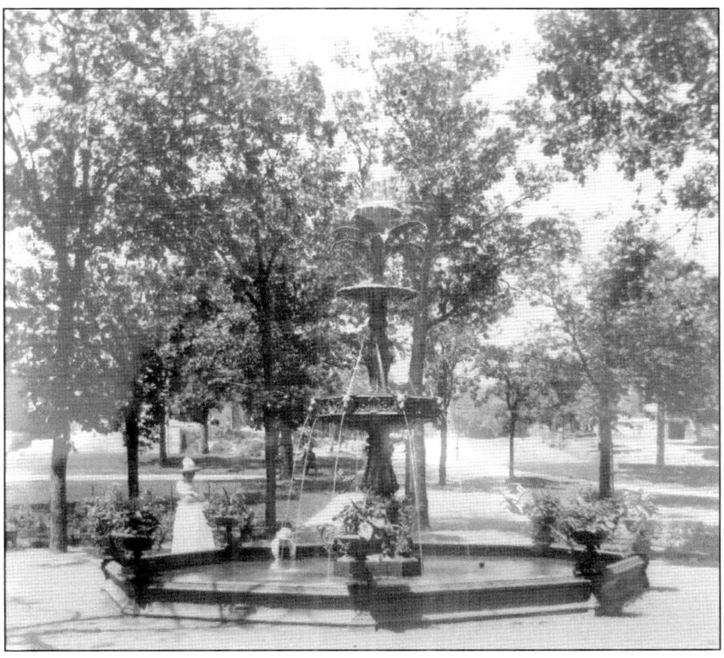

St. Paul pioneer John Irvine donated this site to the village of St. Paul in 1849. Like nearby Rice Park during its early years, this site was initially an open field used as a public square. It did not become a park until 1872, when it was landscaped and named for Irvine. The park's centerpiece was its ornate fountain, installed in 1881. Irvine Park was considered a fashionable address during those years, but the neighborhood fell on hard times after the turn of the 20th century.

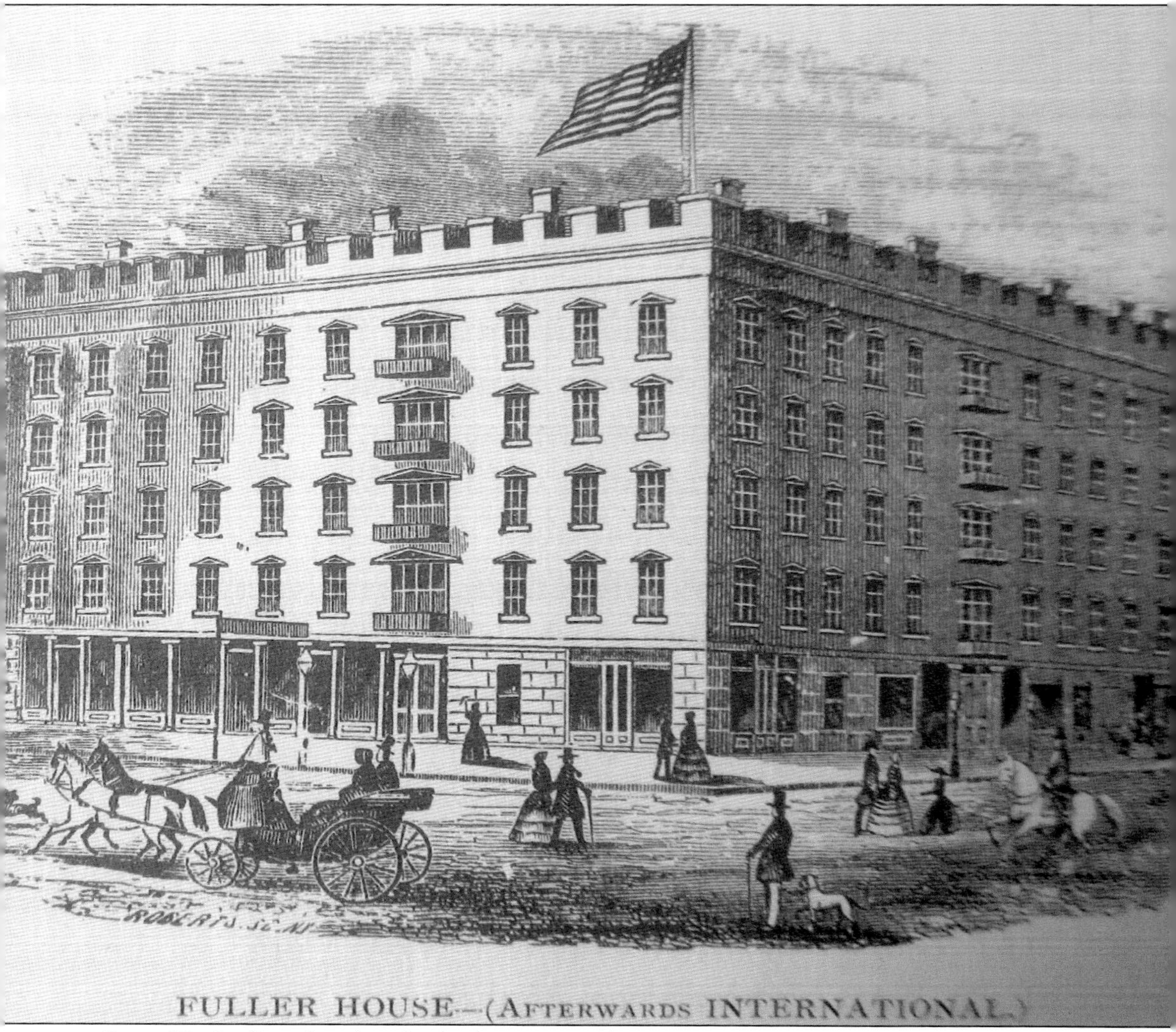

One of St. Paul's earliest hotels, the five-story Fuller House was built by Alpheus G. Fuller in 1856. The hotel was at the center of the local social scene when it opened with a grand ball that year on September 25. "The hotel commenced with a splendid business at once," a local newspaper reported. Later known as the International, the hotel was destroyed in a fire in 1869. (Courtesy of Hennepin County Library Special Collections.)

A Canadian native, James J. Hill was 18 when he arrived in St. Paul in 1856. Soon after arriving, Hill found work as a bookkeeper for a wholesale grocery firm at the Lower Landing. Within a few years, he had gone into business for himself and launched a career that would make him one of St. Paul's most powerful and successful business leaders.

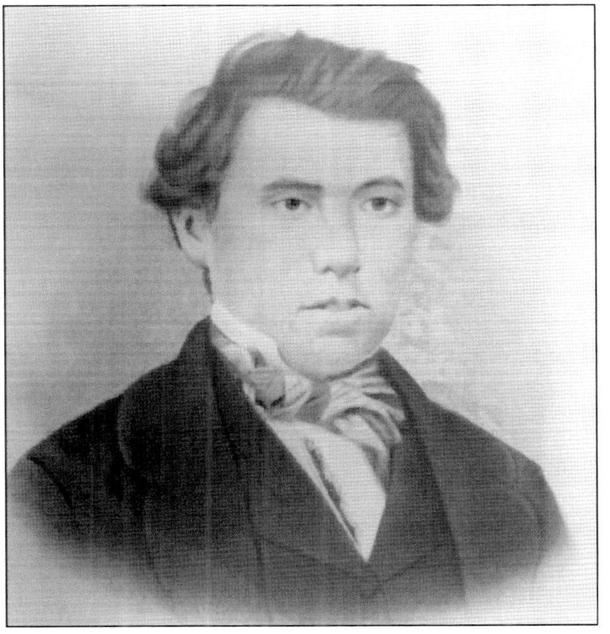

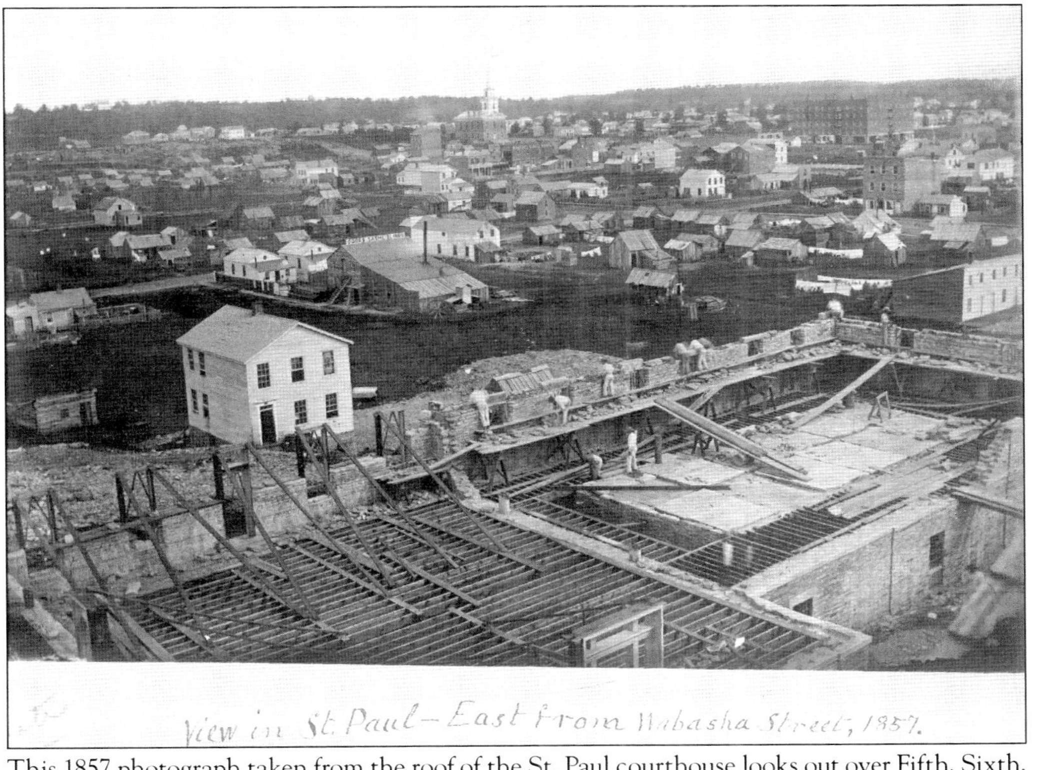

This 1857 photograph taken from the roof of the St. Paul courthouse looks out over Fifth, Sixth, and Seventh Streets. In the foreground, workers are building a new county jail. In the background, the steeple for the Jackson Street Methodist Episcopal Church rises above the line of hills at the town's edge. (Courtesy of Hennepin County Library Special Collections.)

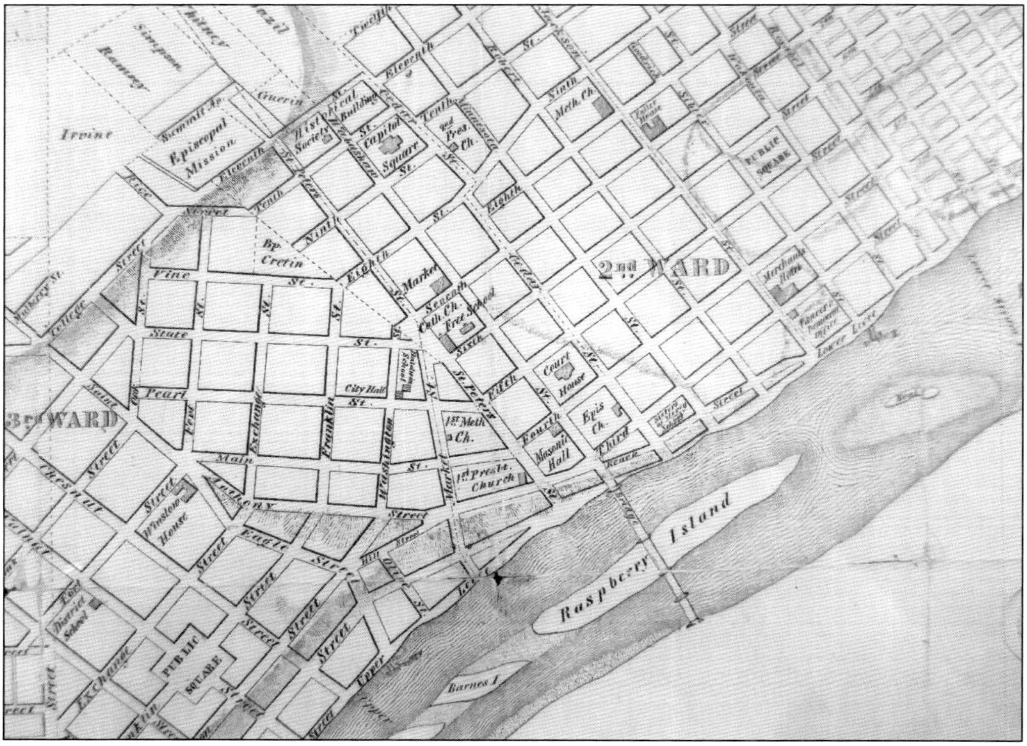

The foundation for downtown's modern-day street pattern was well established by 1860. This street map from the late 1850s shows several current downtown landmarks, including Irvine Park at lower left and the bridge over the Mississippi at Wabasha Street. The map also shows the site of Minnesota's first and second state capitols at Tenth and Cedar Streets. (Courtesy of the St. Paul Public Library.)

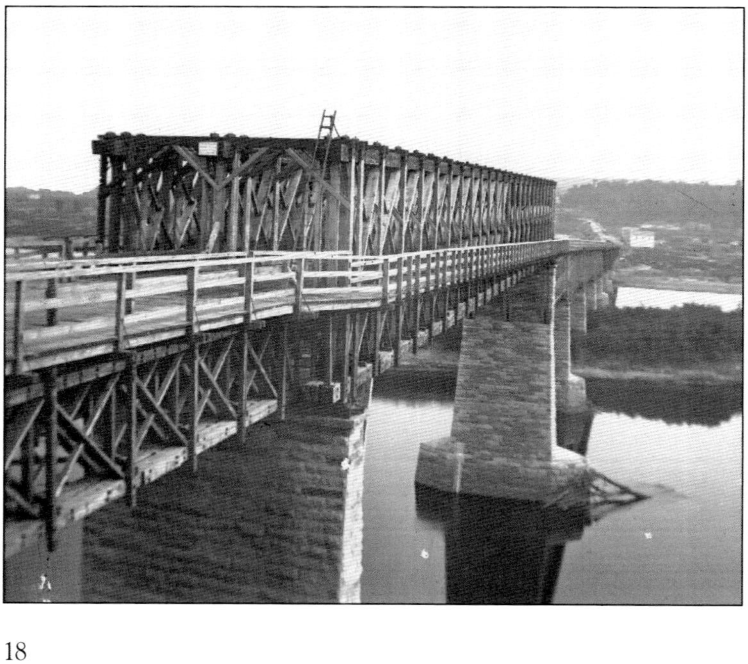

This Mississippi River span was known as the St. Paul Bridge when it opened in 1858. At that time, it connected St. Paul with the community of West St. Paul. Renamed the Wabasha Bridge, it was replaced by an iron cantilevered span in 1889. A third bridge at the same location was built in the 1990s.

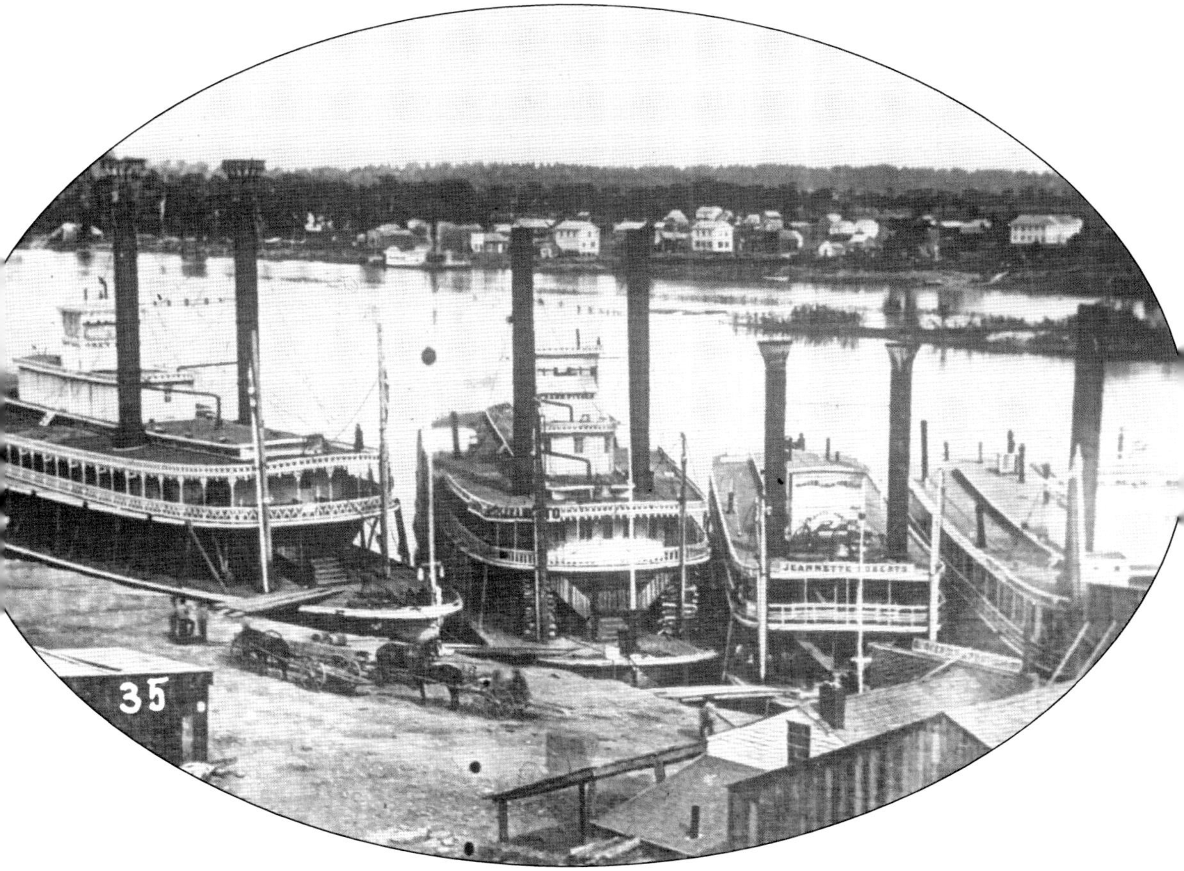

By 1859, St. Paul's Lower Landing, at the foot of Jackson Street, had become an important terminus for steamboats sailing up the Mississippi. More than 40 boats a day were docking at the Lower Landing and a second site a half-mile away known as the Upper Landing. The settlement across the river, then known as West St. Paul, was incorporated into the city of St. Paul in the 1870s. (Courtesy of Hennepin County Library Special Collections.)

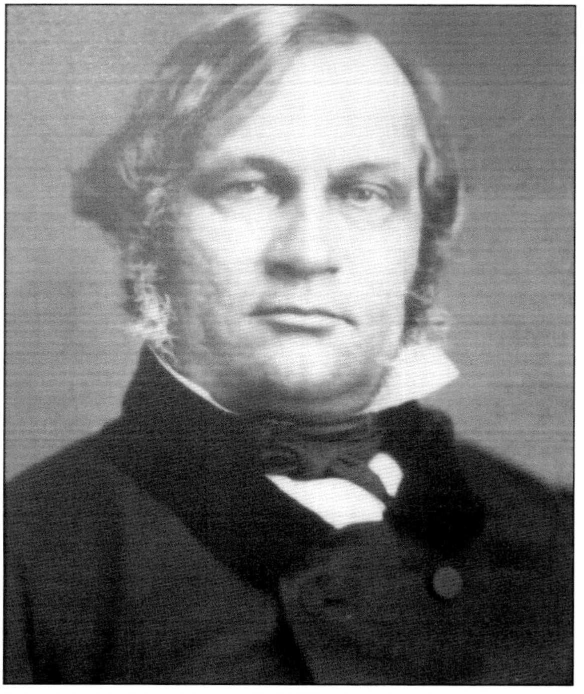

A native of Pennsylvania, Alexander Ramsey was appointed governor of the Minnesota Territory by Pres. Zachary Taylor in 1849. Ramsey and his wife came to St. Paul when it was still a rough frontier town. Back then, the territorial governorship was very much a hardship post. Ramsey had a long career in Minnesota. He served as mayor of St. Paul, Minnesota's second statehood governor, a US congressman, and a Minnesota senator. (Author's collection.)

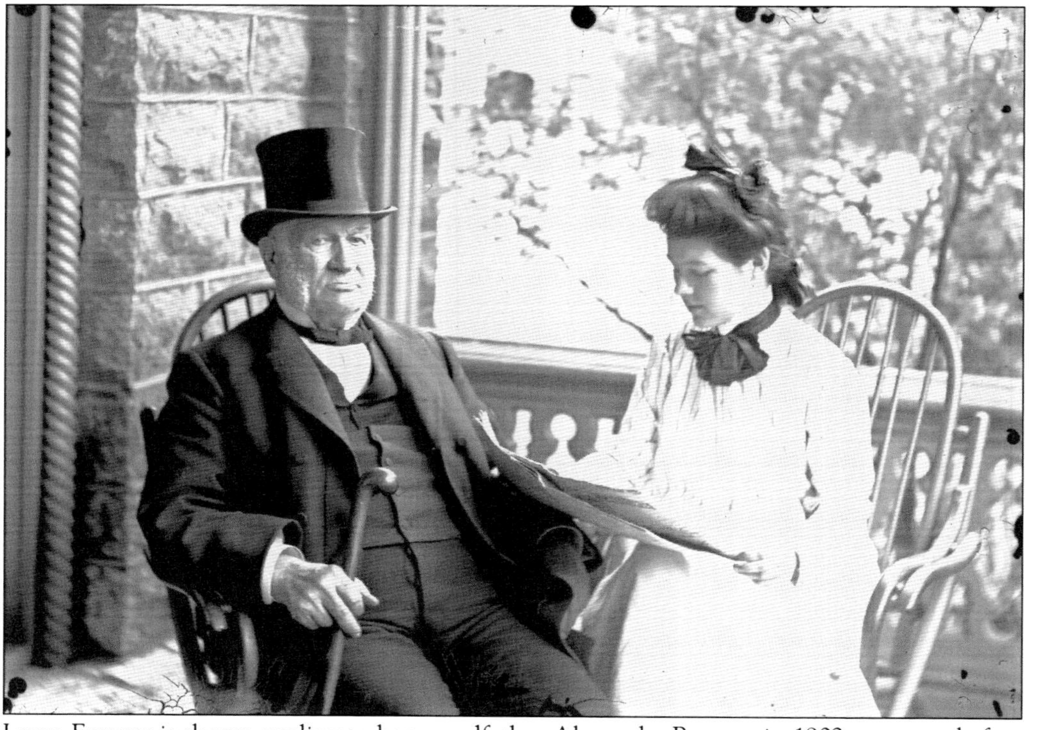

Laura Furness is shown reading to her grandfather Alexander Ramsey in 1902, one year before he died at the age of 87. Ramsey's home on Exchange Street is now a museum operated by the Minnesota Historical Society. (Courtesy of Hennepin County Library Special Collections.)

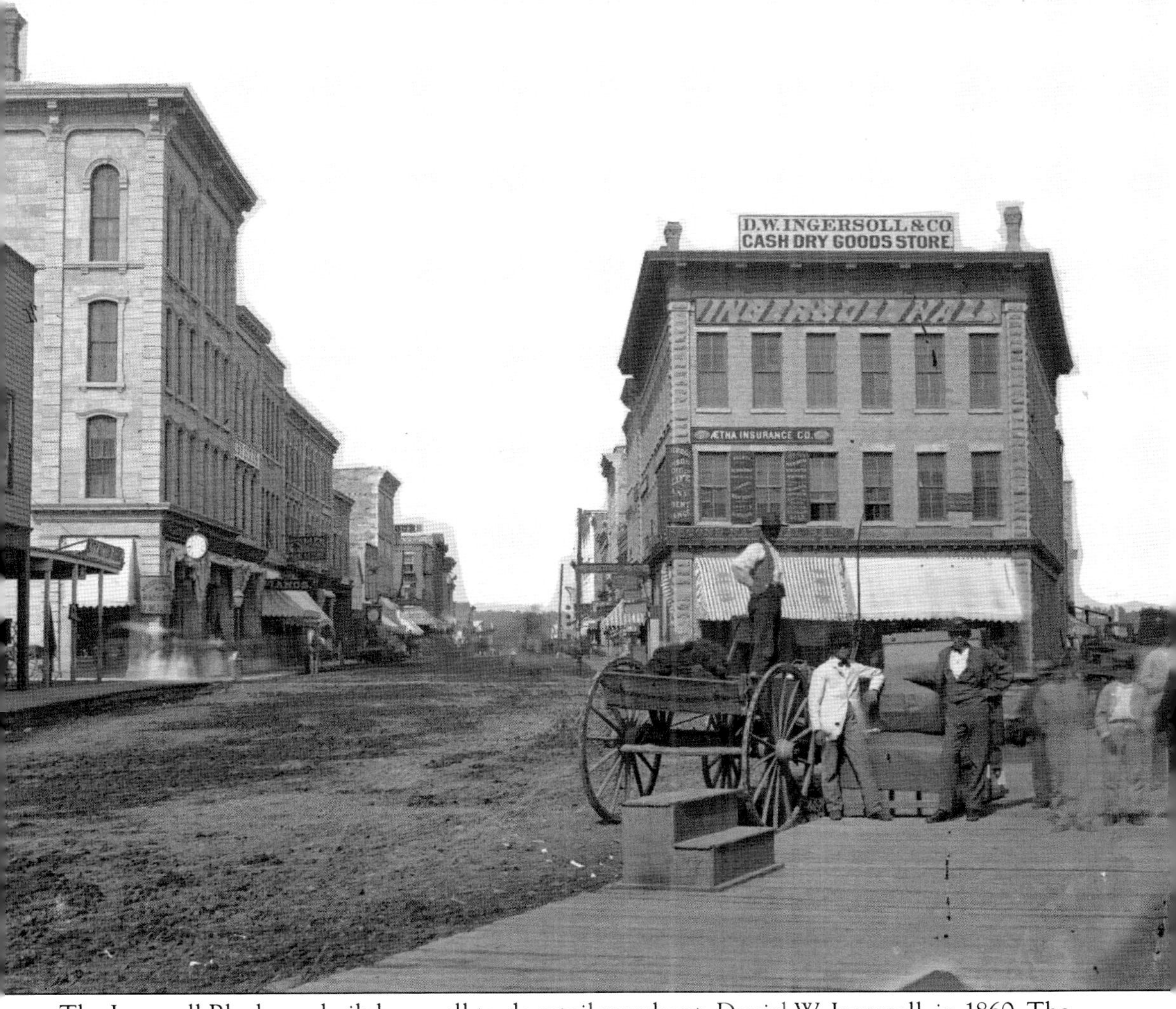

The Ingersoll Block was built by a well-to-do retail merchant, Daniel W. Ingersoll, in 1860. The commercial development overlooked the approach to the St. Paul Bridge at the corner of Third and Wabasha Streets. In 1869, the assembly hall in the Ingersoll Block was the site of a rally by St. Paul's small African American community celebrating an amendment to the Minnesota Constitution that gave them the right to vote. (Courtesy of Hennepin County Library Special Collections.)

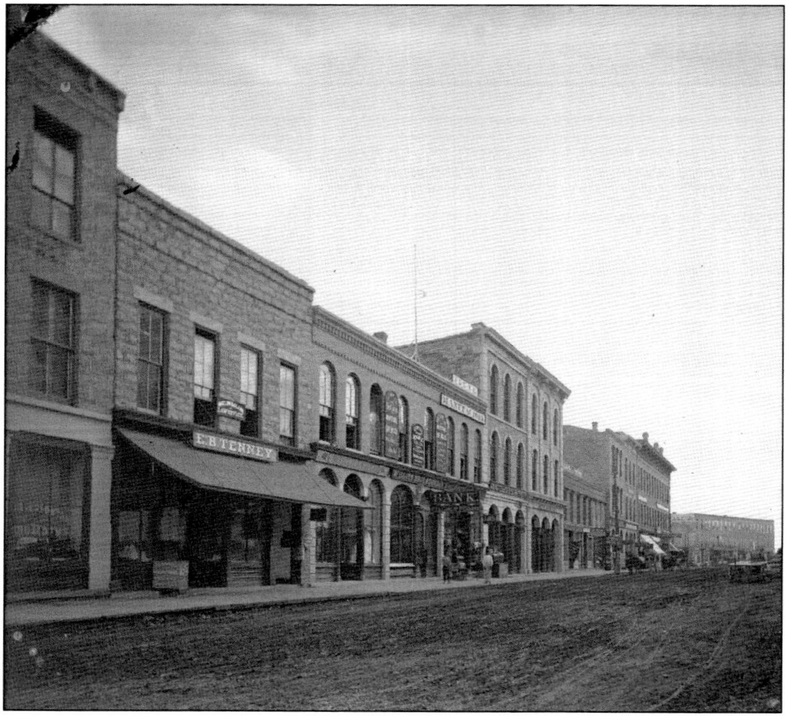

By 1870, Third Street, St. Paul's main commercial thoroughfare, began to take on the feel of a downtown. But St. Paul residents who ventured there still had to contend with wood-planked sidewalks and the dirt streets that were dusty in the summer and muddy in the spring. Downtown did not get its first paved streets until 1873.

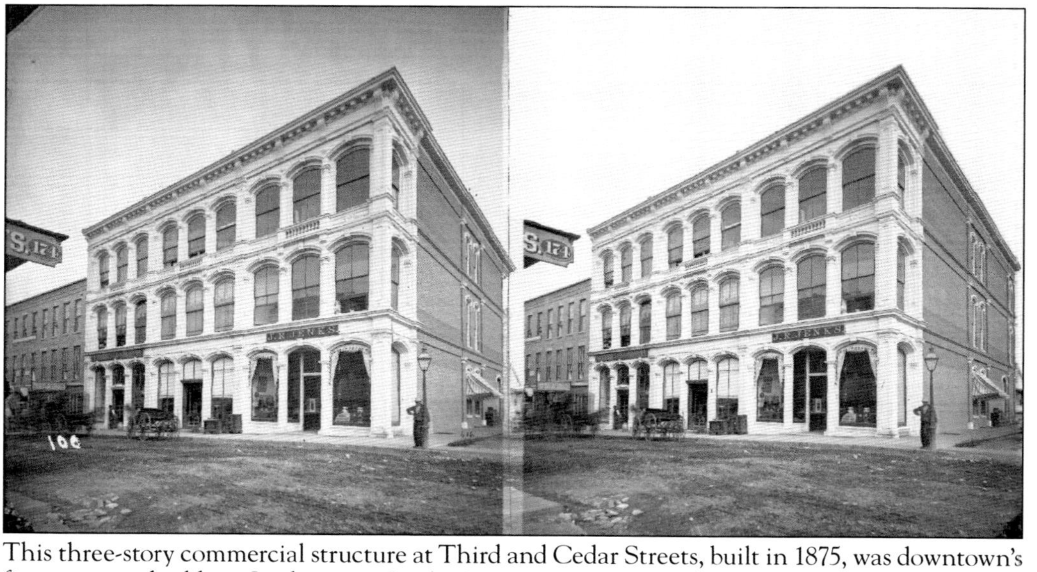

This three-story commercial structure at Third and Cedar Streets, built in 1875, was downtown's first cast-iron building. In the post–Civil War era, commercial developers began to use cast iron because it could be forged cheaply from foundry molds and transported easily to a building site. Here, a cast-iron facade was attached to the front of a brick building. (Courtesy of Hennepin County Library Special Collections.)

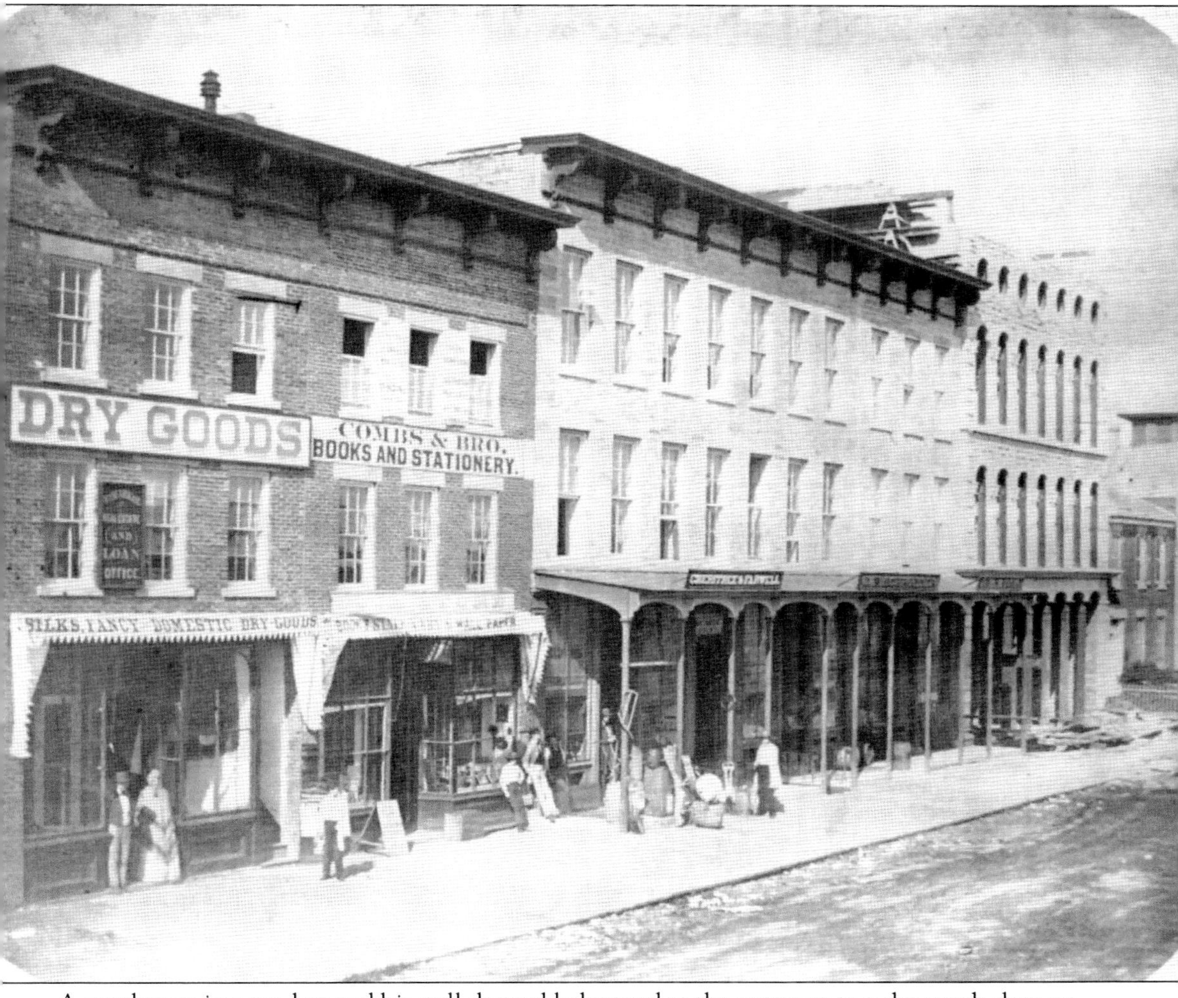

A gentleman in a top hat and his well-dressed lady stand at the entrance to a dry goods shop on Third Street in 1860. She may have been shopping for a new bonnet. Within a few years, St. Paul's dry goods shops would be replaced by the department stores that enhanced the shopping experience for their eager customers. (Courtesy of Hennepin County Library Special Collections.)

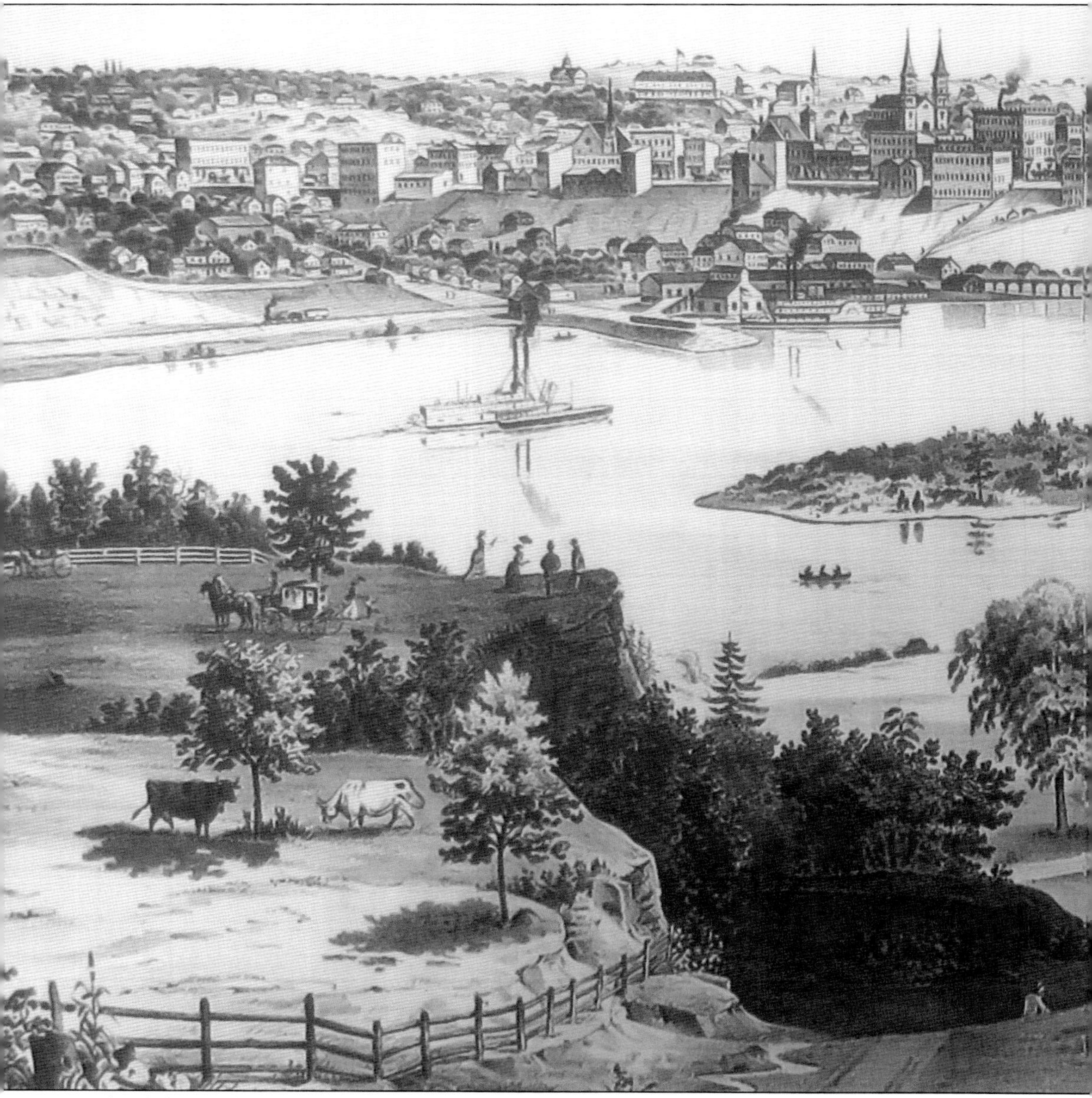

This lithograph from the *Illustrated Atlas of the State of Minnesota* provides a view of downtown St. Paul as it appeared in 1874 from the bluffs on the west side of the Mississippi. Several notable landmarks are depicted in the drawing. They include St. Paul's first bridge across the river and

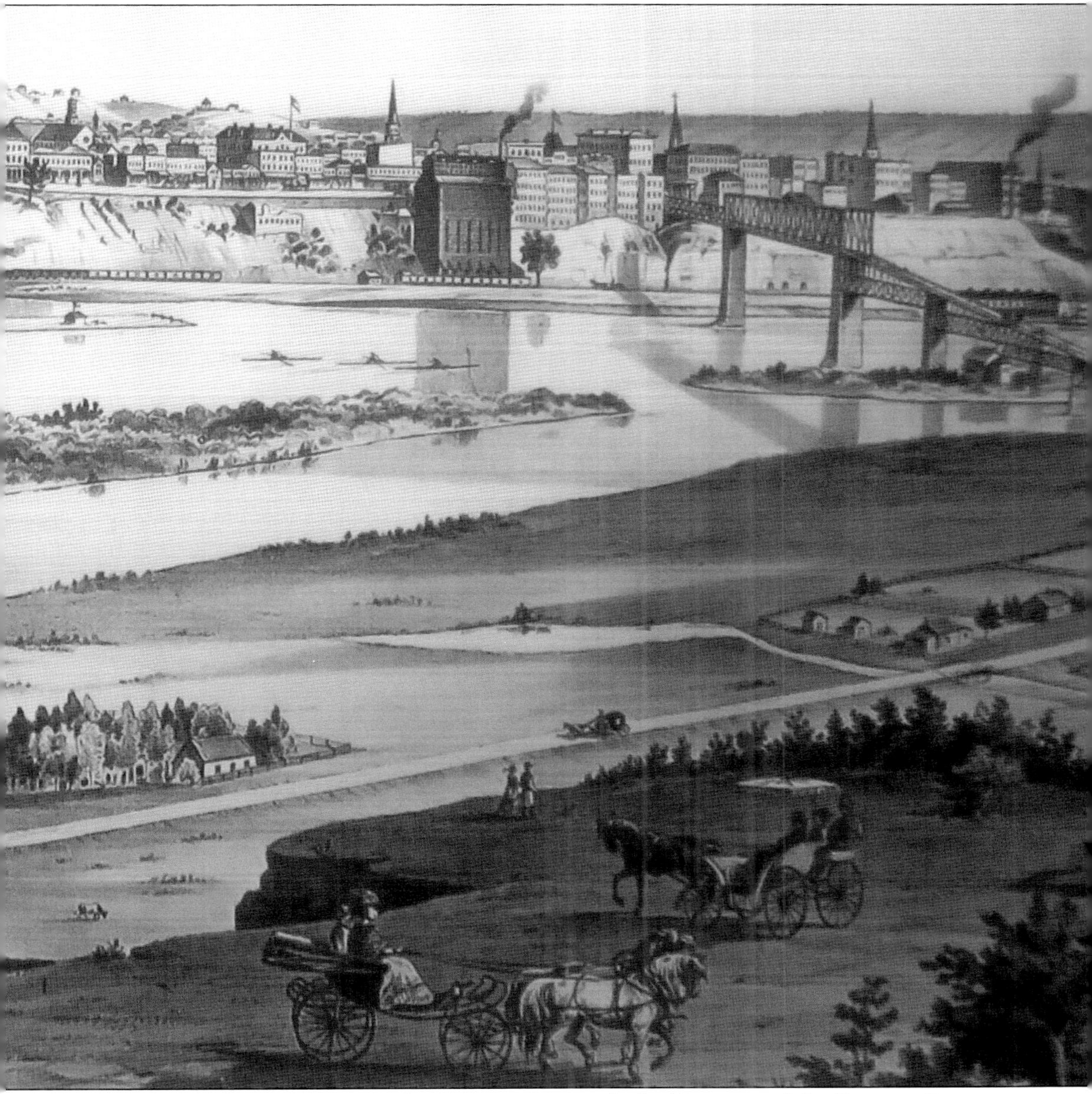

the Upper Landing, where a steamboat is preparing to dock. (Courtesy of the Ramsey County Historical Society.)

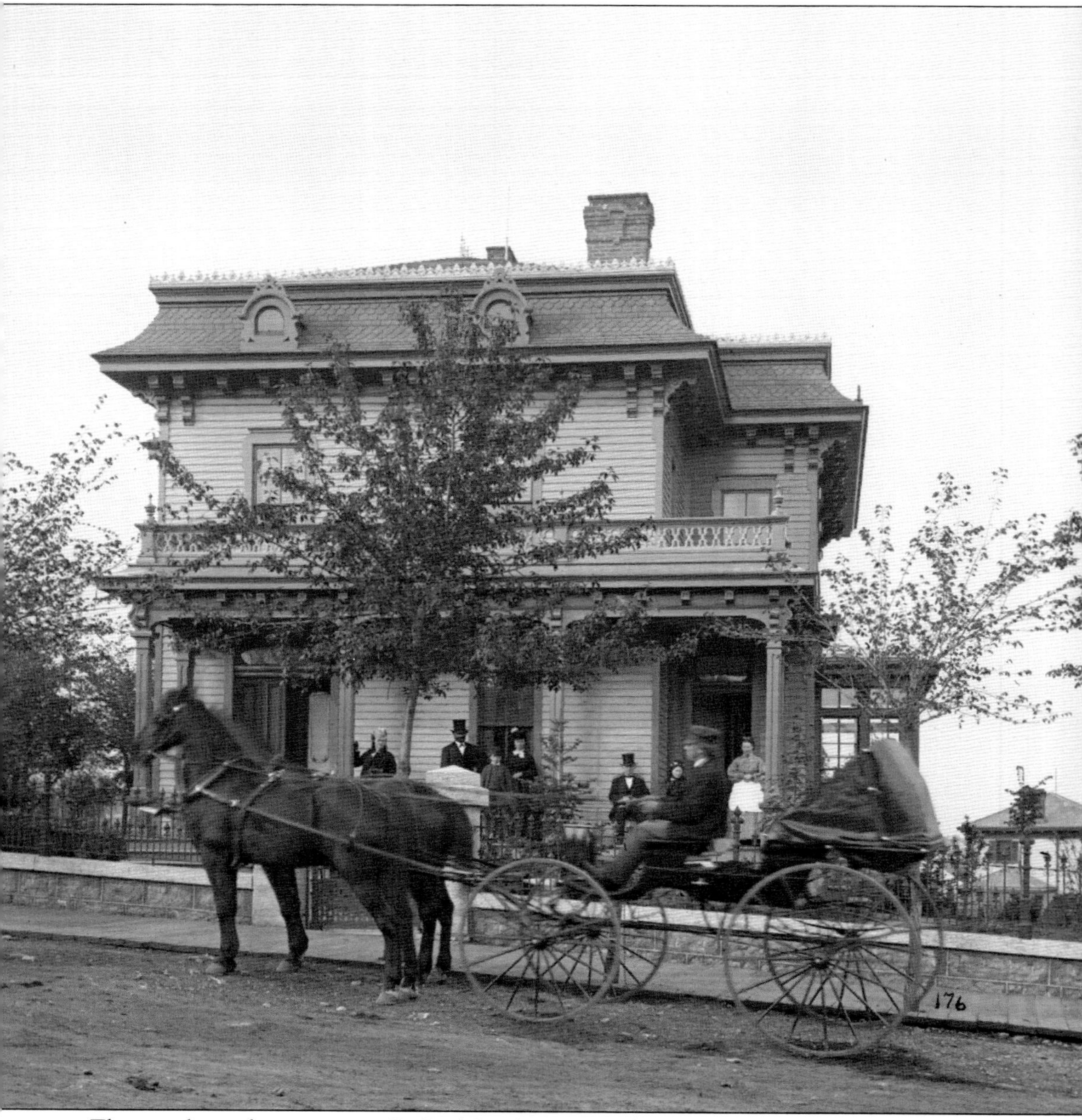

The members of a prosperous St. Paul family pose on the front porch of their substantial home on St. Peter Street. Their French Second Empire home is characterized by its mansard roof with a broad overhang supported by decorative brackets. By the 1880s, homes like these began to disappear from downtown, pushed out by a commercial real estate boom. (Courtesy of Hennepin County Library Special Collections.)

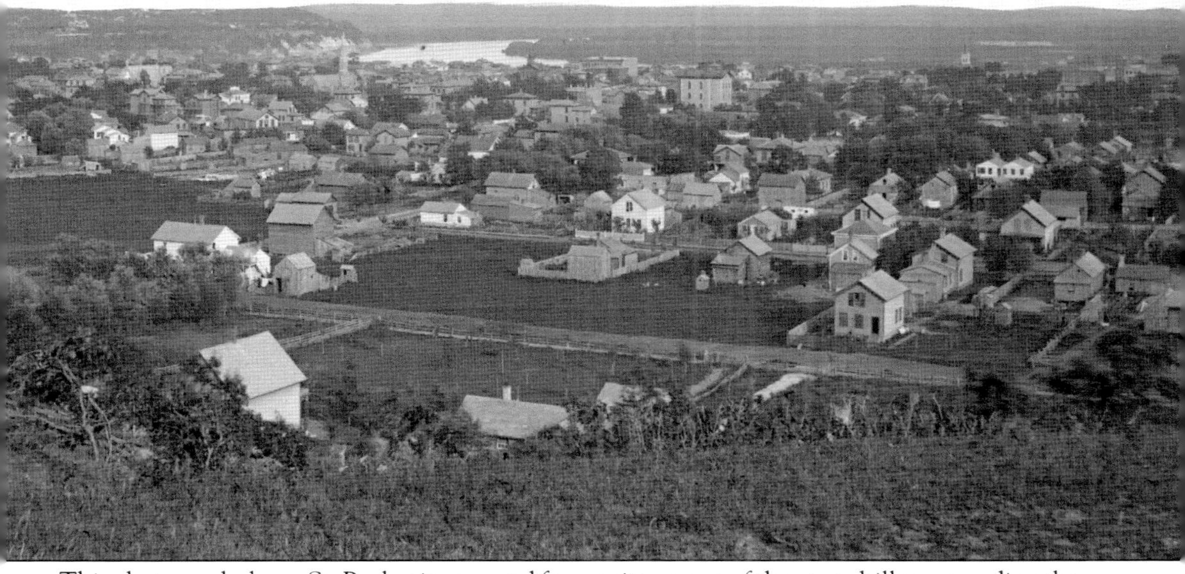

This photograph shows St. Paul as it appeared from a site on one of the seven hills surrounding the town. A loop of the Mississippi appears in the background. Much of modern-day downtown St. Paul was still primarily residential when this photograph was taken in the early 1870s. (Courtesy of Hennepin County Special Collections.)

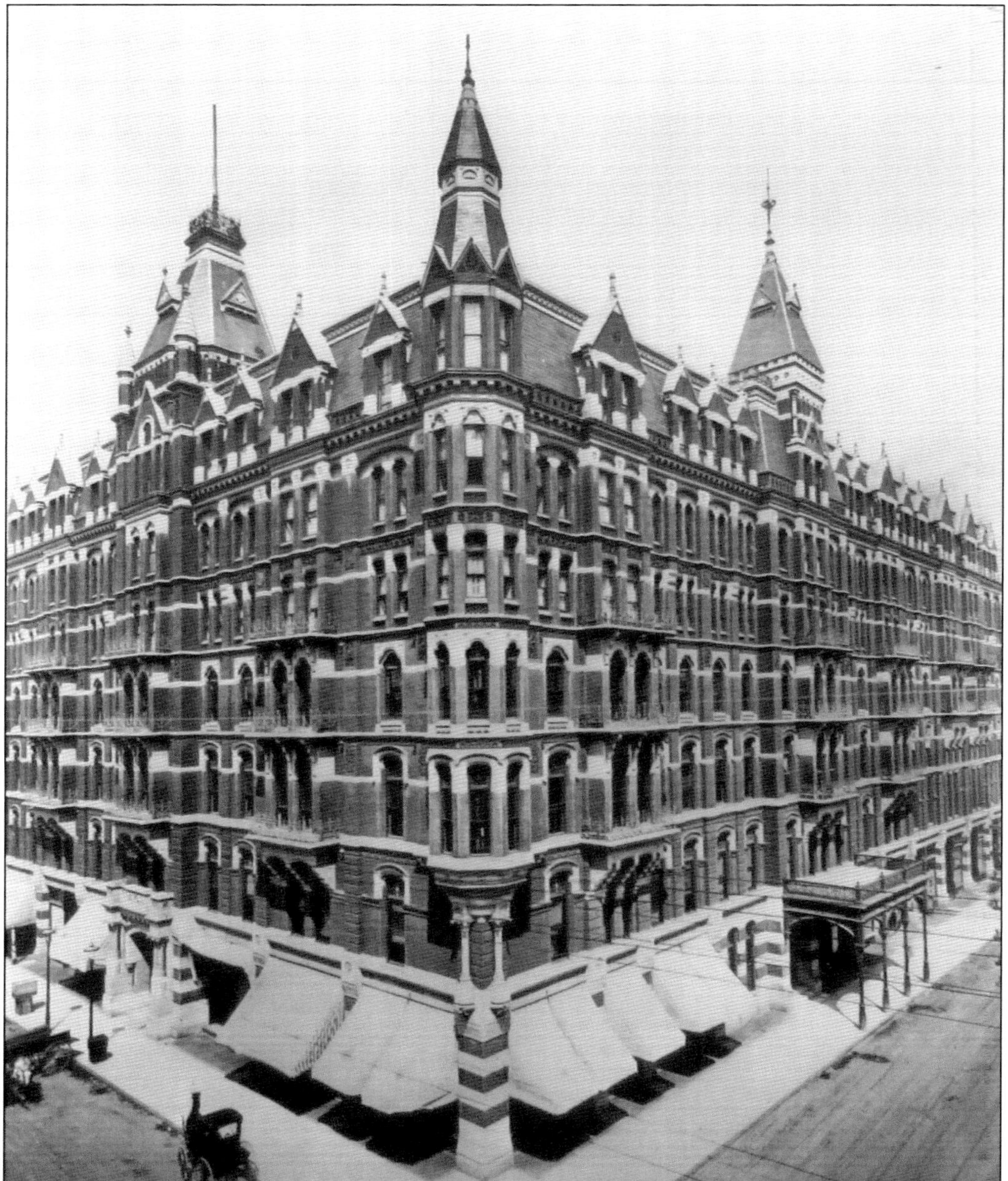

The Ryan Hotel was the place to stay in St. Paul when it opened in 1885. Described by a local historian as a "Victorian Gothic extravaganza," the seven-story brick-and-sandstone building displayed terra cotta ornaments, granite columns, arched windows, and bracketed balconies. The hotel's parlors and ballroom provided an elegant backdrop for St. Paul society's social events. The Ryan Hotel was demolished in 1962 and was later replaced with an office building for a local insurance company.

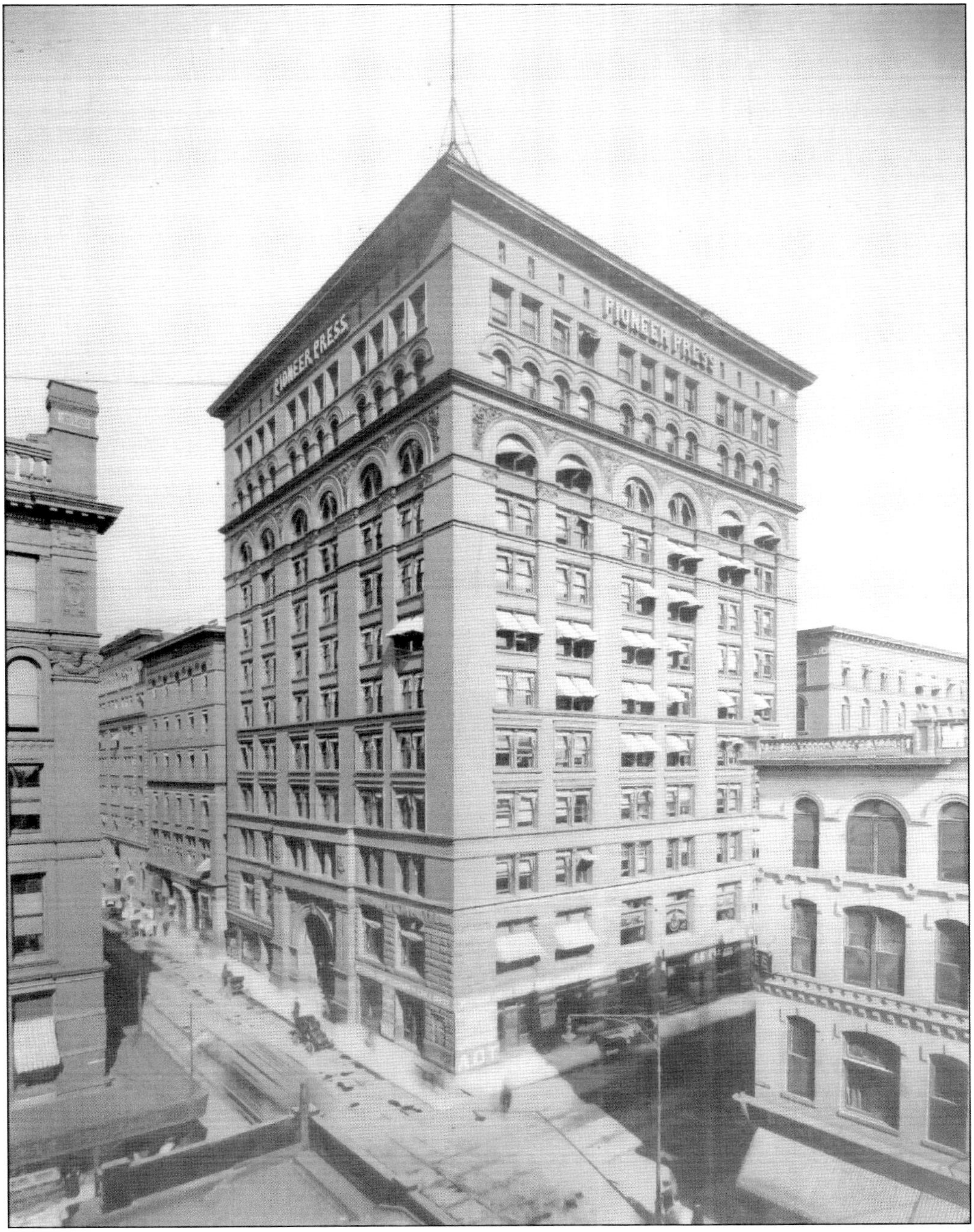

When it was built in 1889, the 12-story Pioneer Building was St. Paul's first skyscraper. It housed the *St. Paul Pioneer Press*, the city's oldest daily newspaper. Later, four additional stories were added to the building, giving it a dramatic 16-story atrium. A spiral staircase led up to the top of the atrium.

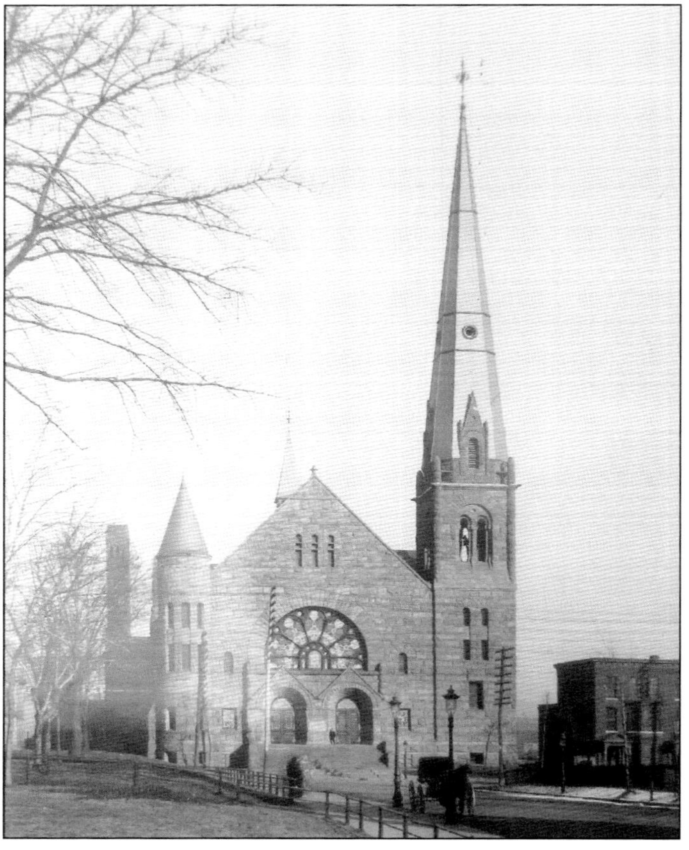

St. Paul's early Presbyterians built their first church at this downtown location in 1852. The current church at 500 Cedar Street dates to 1889. With its arched entrance and heavy brownstone construction, Central Presbyterian is a prime example of Romanesque Revival style. The sanctuary's curved balcony adds a graceful feel to the church's interior space.

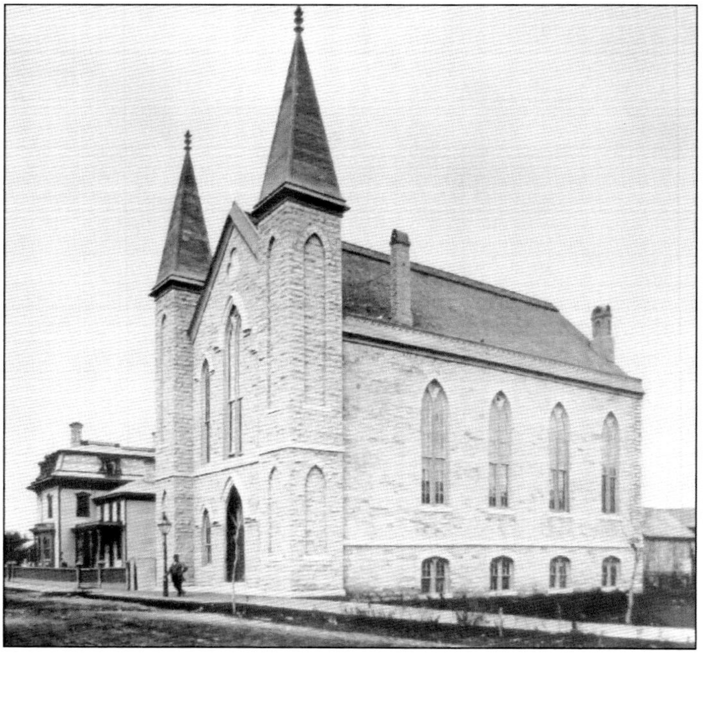

First Baptist Church was established by Minnesota's oldest Baptist congregation in 1849. This church on Wacouta Street was built in 1875, after the congregation outgrew its earlier home four blocks away in what is now Mears Park. First Baptist's substantial corner tower and spire give it a commanding presence at the north end of downtown. (Courtesy of Hennepin County Library Special Collections.)

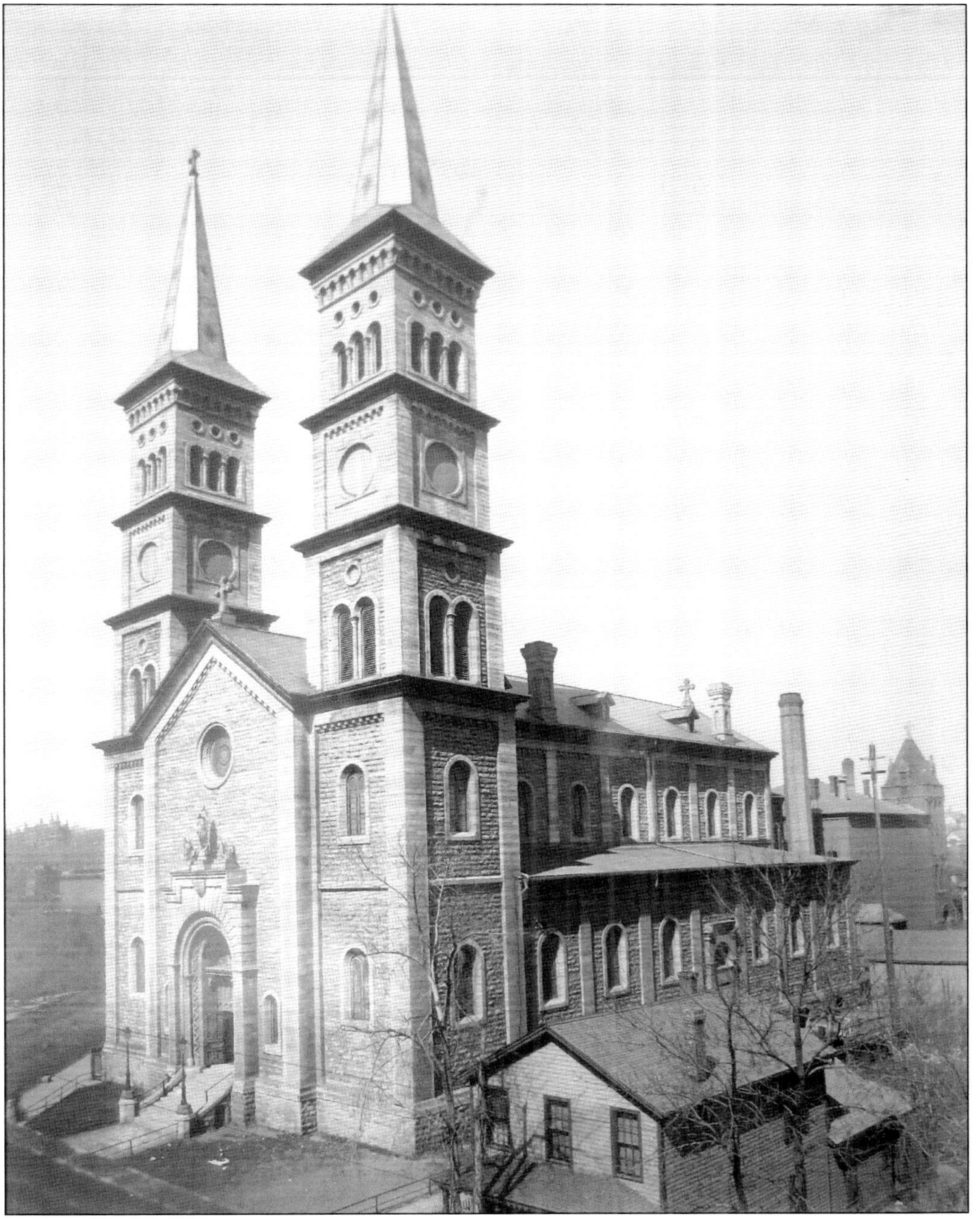

Assumption Catholic Church on West Seventh Street is St. Paul's oldest church structure still in use today. The parish was established in the mid-1850s by a group of German Catholics who wanted their own place of worship. Assumption's twin spires are a familiar downtown landmark.

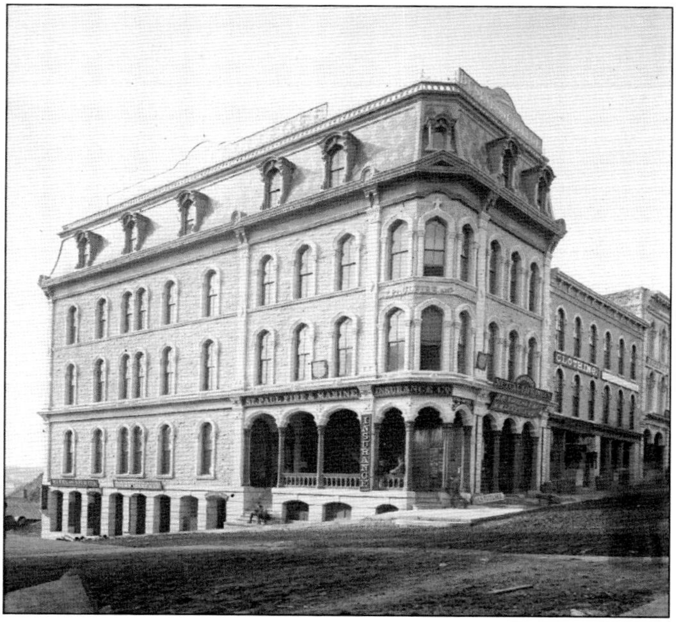

The successor to St. Paul Fire and Marine has maintained a presence in downtown St. Paul up through modern times. The original business was established in 1853 to serve customers who were having difficulty getting claims payments in a timely manner from East Coast insurance companies. Later known as the St. Paul Companies, the business is now a division of the Travelers Companies.

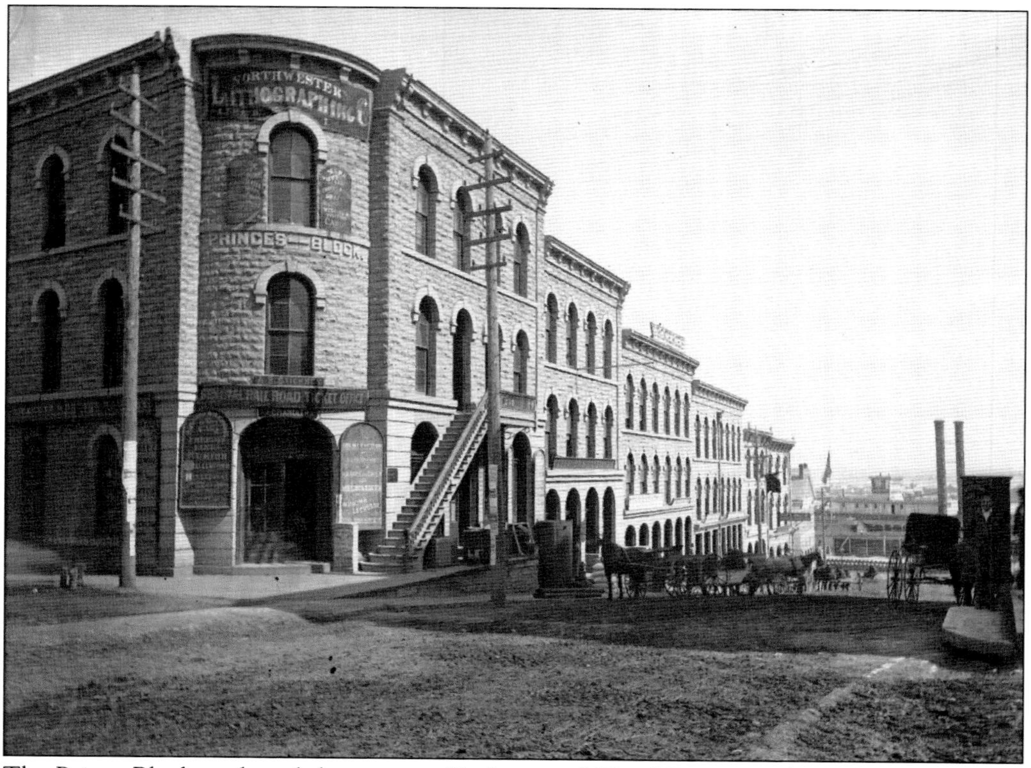

The Prince Block anchored the corner of Jackson and Third Streets in the early 1870s. At the end of Jackson Street, a steamboat can be seen docked at St. Paul's Lower Landing. In the 21st century, the Lower Landing at Jackson Street became an embarkation site for a modern recreation of 19th-century riverboats.

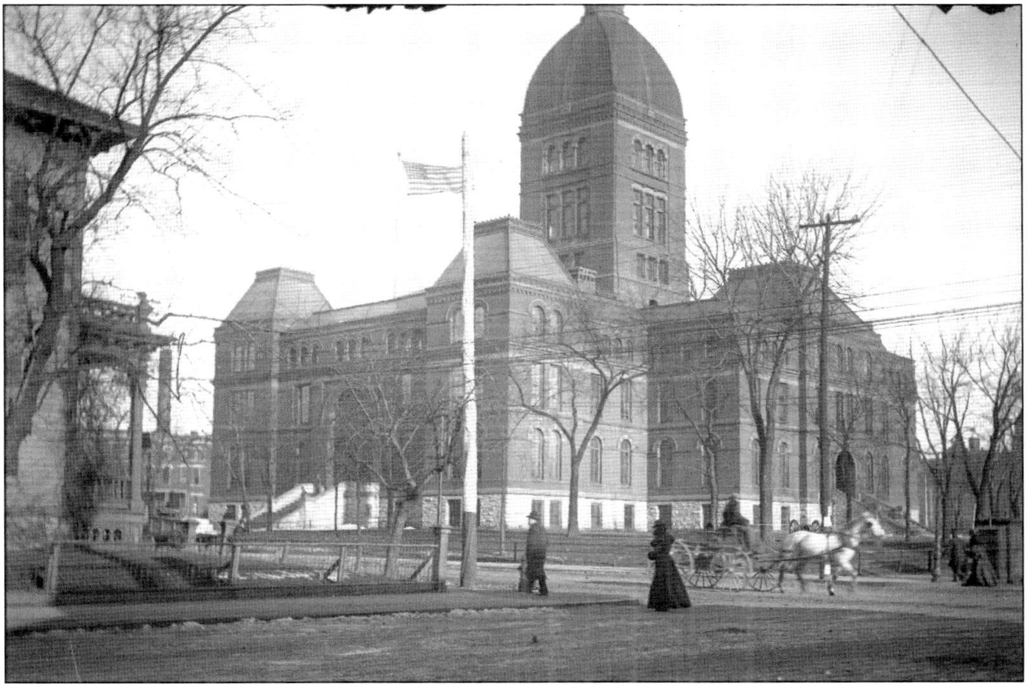

Between 1883 and 1905, this four-story building at the western end of downtown served as Minnesota's second state capitol. As Minnesota underwent an economic and population boom at the turn of the last century, the capitol building soon became outmoded. Plagued by an inadequate heating and ventilating system, the building was replaced by the current state capitol building in 1905. (Above, courtesy of Hennepin County Library Special Collections.)

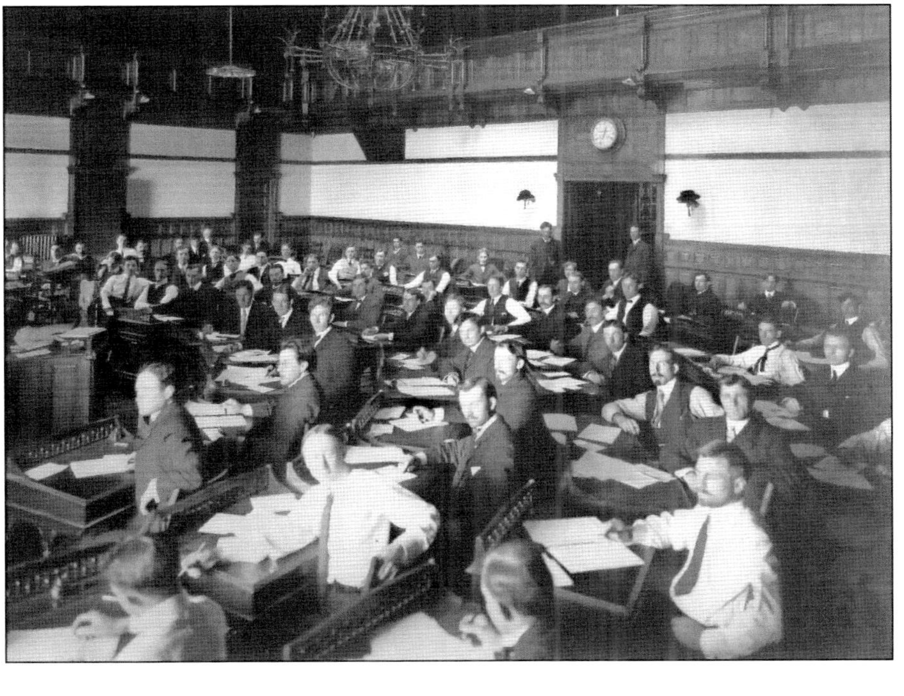

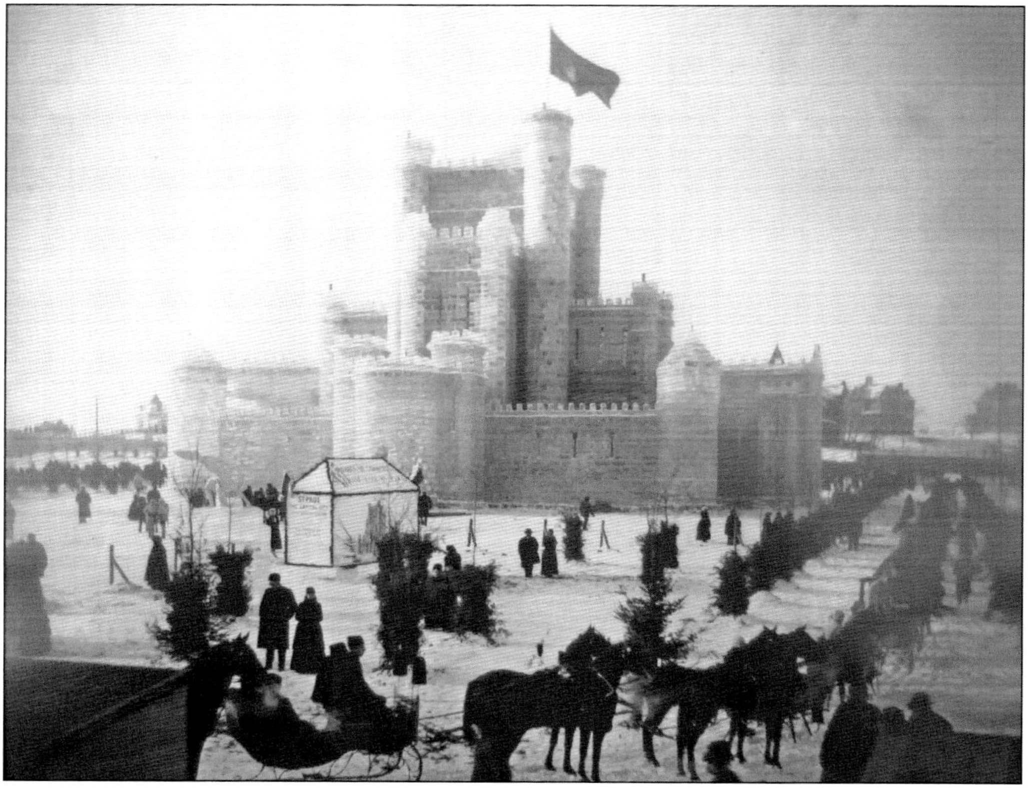

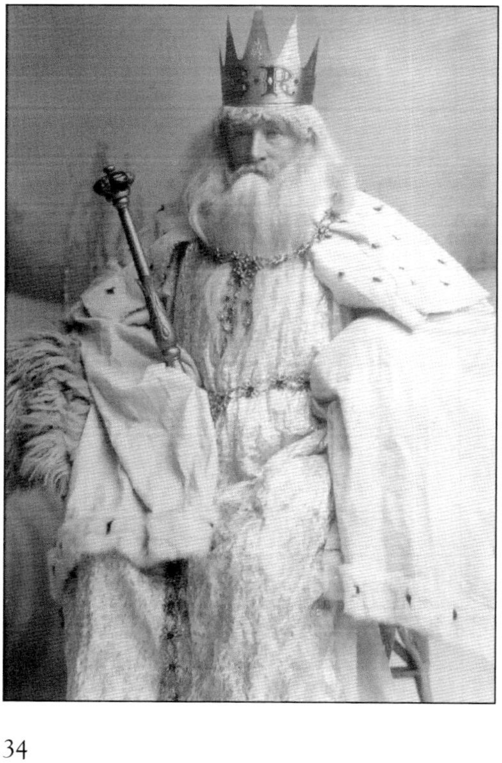

When a New York reporter wrote in 1885 that "St. Paul was another Siberia, unfit for human habitation in the winter," the St. Paul Chamber of Commerce sprang to the defense of its cold-climate city. Chamber leaders organized a carnival to showcase the glories of winter in Minnesota. The Winter Carnival, held for the first time in 1886, featured a palace made of ice harvested from area lakes. St. Paul's very own monarch, King Boreas, presided over carnival festivities.

In the 1880s, prominent St. Paulites organized Winter Carnival clubs, each with their own elaborate rituals and costumes. This elf-like fellow represented the St. George's Snowshoe Club. St. George's was "the principal winter club of St. Paul and [was] destined to become the most popular athletic and social organization in the city," the *St. Paul Globe* reported. "It is contributing largely to the success of the carnival."

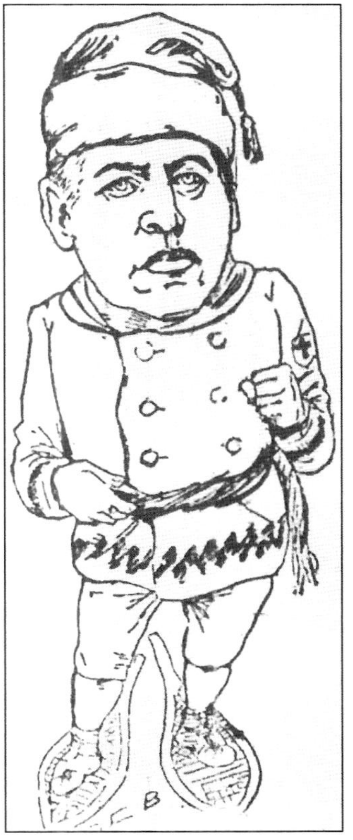

The St. Paul toboggan club posed for this photograph as the club was preparing to participate in St. Paul's first Winter Carnival. One of the club's youngest members is shown riding on top of his father's shoulders. The carnival's first ice palace is in the background.

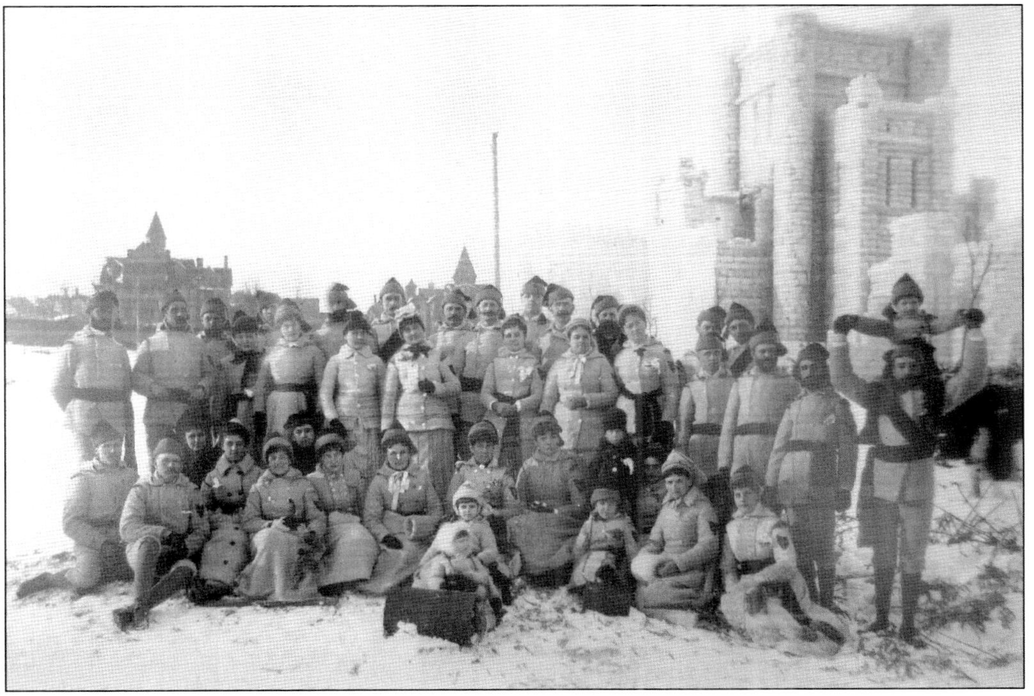

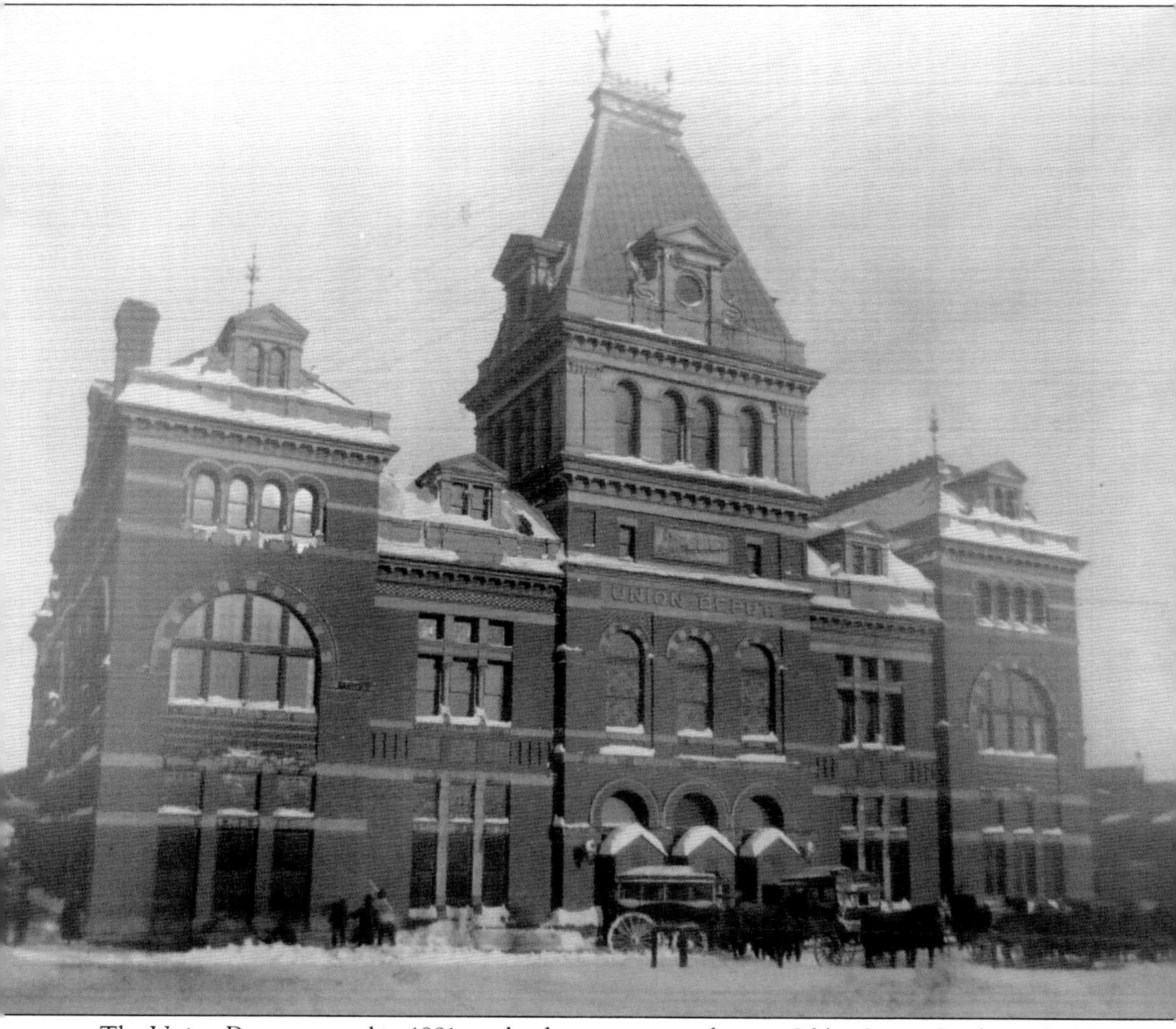

The Union Depot opened in 1881 on the downtown riverfront at Sibley Street. By the end of the 1880s, there were 150 trains a day arriving and departing from the busy railroad station. Those trains brought throngs of new residents to the rapidly growing St. Paul. Between 1880 and 1895, St. Paul's population ballooned from 41,000 to nearly 150,000.

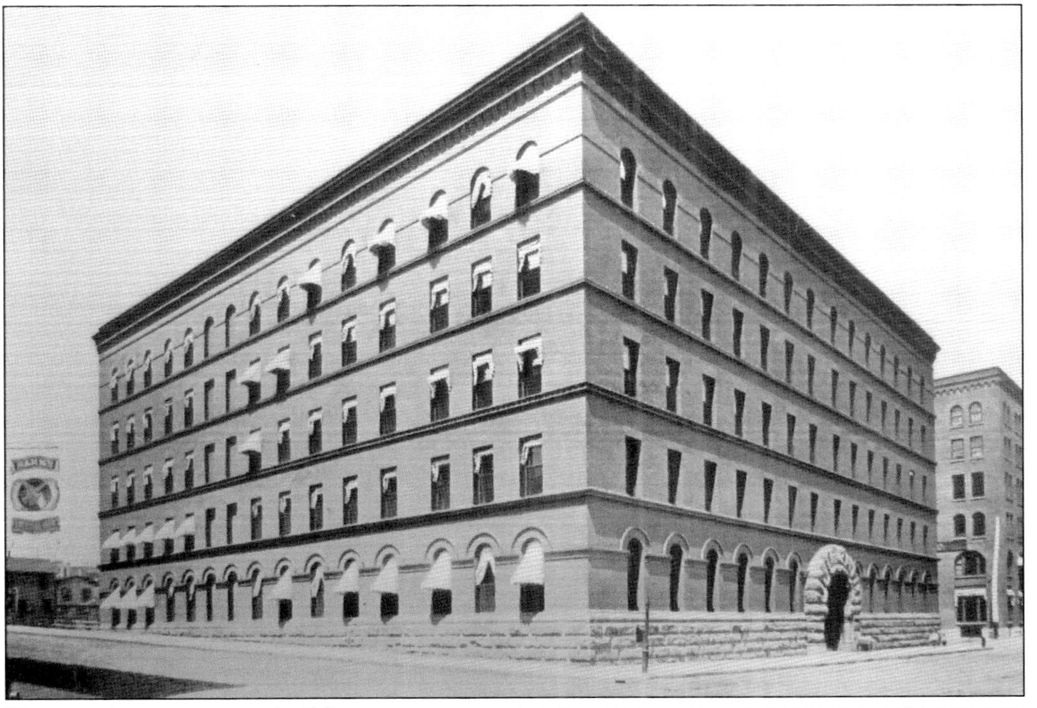

This massive seven-story building, dating to 1888, once served as the headquarters for James J. Hill's Great Northern Railway. Hill amassed his railroad empire in stages, starting in 1878 when his investment group purchased the assets of a failed Minnesota rail line. In 1889, Hill established the Great Northern Railway as the corporate umbrella for his various railroad enterprises. At its height, Great Northern operated 8,000 miles of rail lines extending to the West Coast. (Right, courtesy of Hennepin County Library Special Collections.)

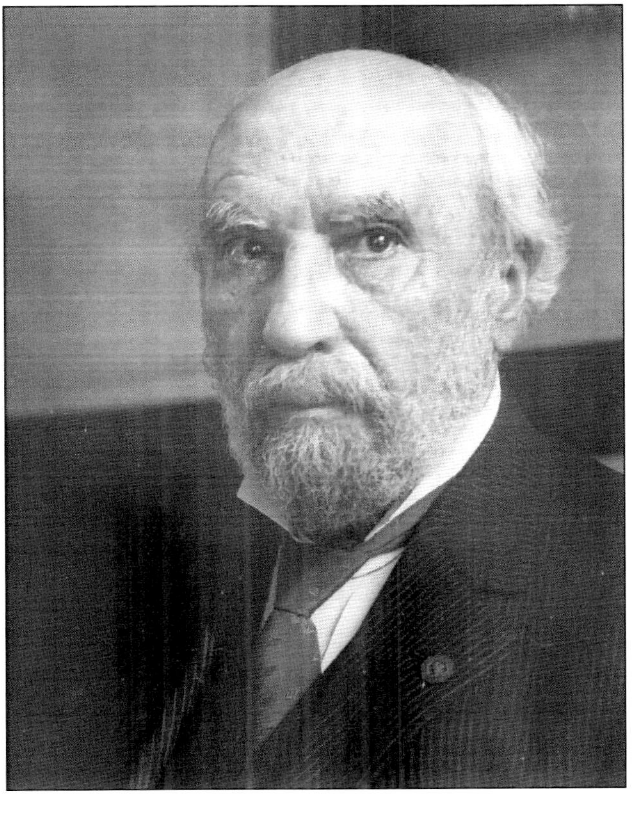

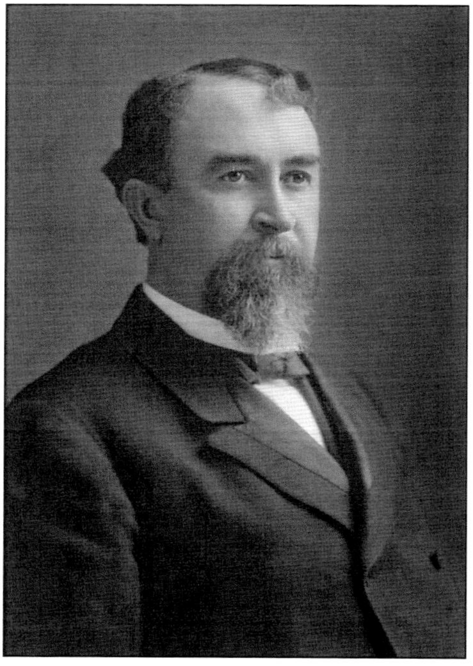

Thomas Lowry, a local entrepreneur and real estate developer, created the Twin Cities Rapid Transit Company (TCRT) in 1891 when he merged the separate street railway companies operating in Minneapolis and St. Paul. The new company began operations just as the streetcars in the two cities, which previously relied on horse power, were being converted to electricity. Lowry's company eventually created a network of streetcar lines stretching from Stillwater to Lake Minnetonka. (Courtesy of Hennepin County Library Special Collections.)

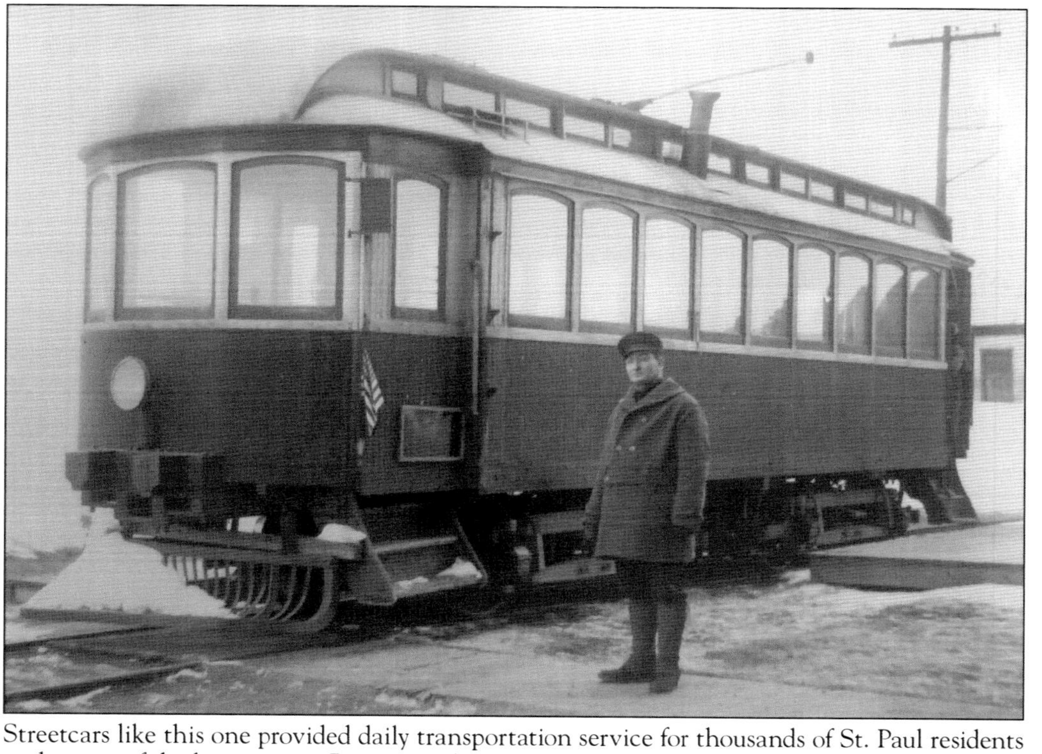

Streetcars like this one provided daily transportation service for thousands of St. Paul residents at the turn of the last century. By 1900, a dozen streetcar lines converged on downtown St. Paul. The TCRT system provided a convenient 11-mile link between the St. Paul and Minneapolis central business districts.

Two

Modern Era

By the turn of the 20th century, downtown St. Paul had expanded to cover a broad plateau extending from the edge of the bluffs overlooking the downtown riverfront north and west to the string of hills that gave St. Paul its unique physical identity.

During those years, downtown emerged as a major retail center. Modest dry goods establishments had evolved into elaborate department stores that drew customers from all over the city and its newly established streetcar suburbs. Downtown's retail core, between Fifth and Seventh Streets, included such landmark establishments as Schuneman's, the Golden Rule, the Emporium, and Field Schlick.

When St. Paulites were done shopping, they could take in a movie at one of the several dozen theaters scattered through downtown. Originally housed in shabby storefronts, the motion picture theaters had become lavish, richly appointed movie palaces by the new century's teen years. One of the most ornate, known as the Palace, operated as a vaudeville house when it opened in 1916 on West Seventh Street. Later it switched to an all-movie format and became the RKO Orpheum and the place to see the latest Hollywood hits.

Along with retail and entertainment, downtown enhanced its role as a government center with the construction of two new public buildings. In 1902, the castle-like federal building was completed in the heart of downtown, across from the city's oldest public square. Three years later, Minnesota's imposing new state capitol was inaugurated at the western end of downtown. Both buildings would become downtown's most identifiable landmarks well into the 21st century.

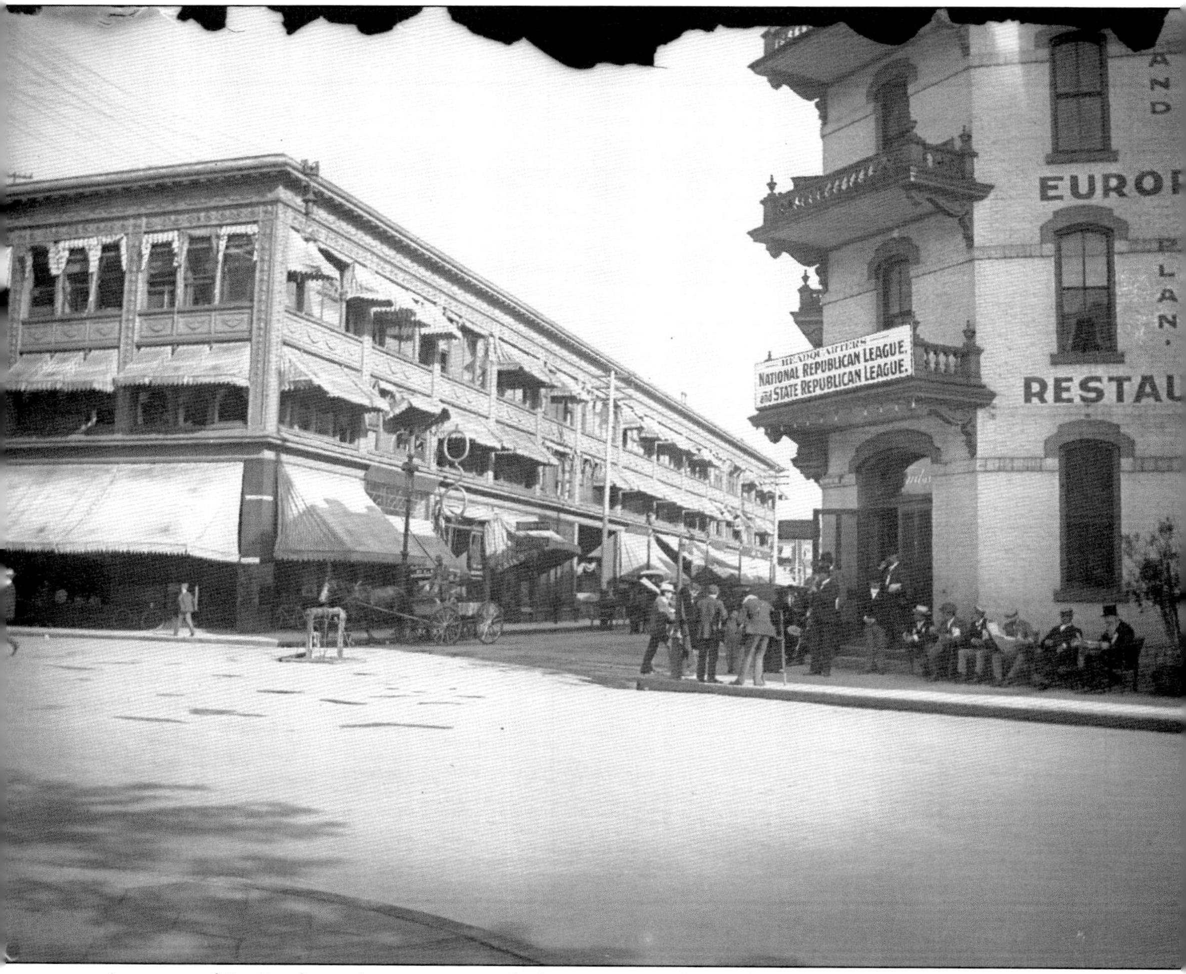

A group of St. Paul gentlemen enjoy a balmy summer day in front of the Windsor Hotel in 1903. The sign above them identifies the headquarters for Minnesota's national and state Republican leagues. Soon after this photograph was taken, the Windsor was demolished to make room for the new St. Paul Hotel. (Courtesy of Hennepin County Library Special Collections.)

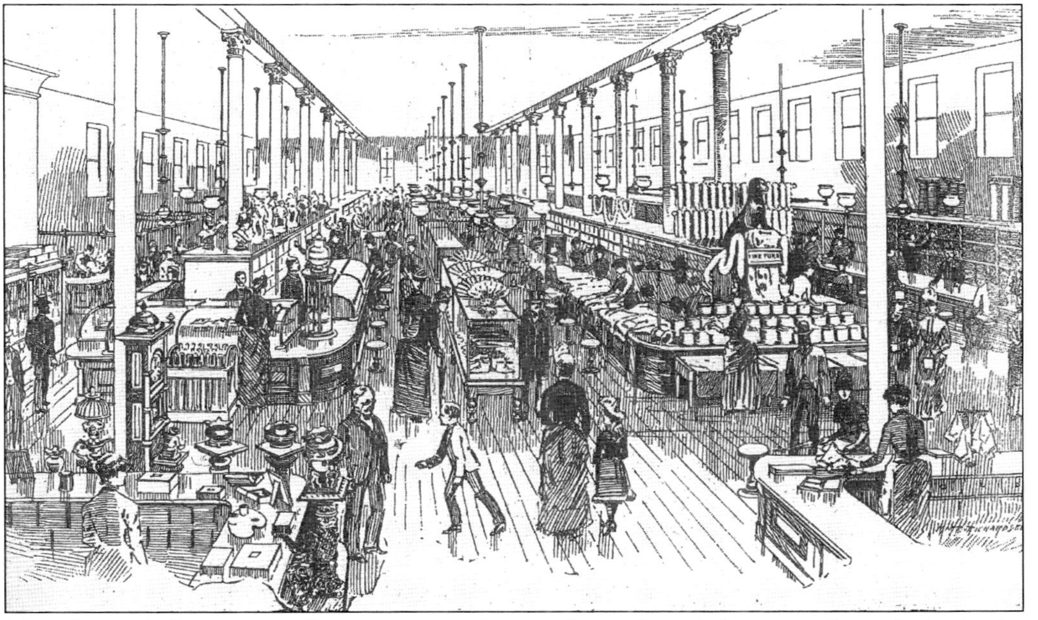

Mannheimer's Department Store represented a new form of retail that gained popularity in the late 19th century. Prior to the advent of department stores like Mannheimer's, women, often with a male companion, visited dry goods shops, where the proprietor would lay out the shop's goods for them to examine. But now, women could shop on their own, wandering past rows of merchandise laid out in an attractive manner.

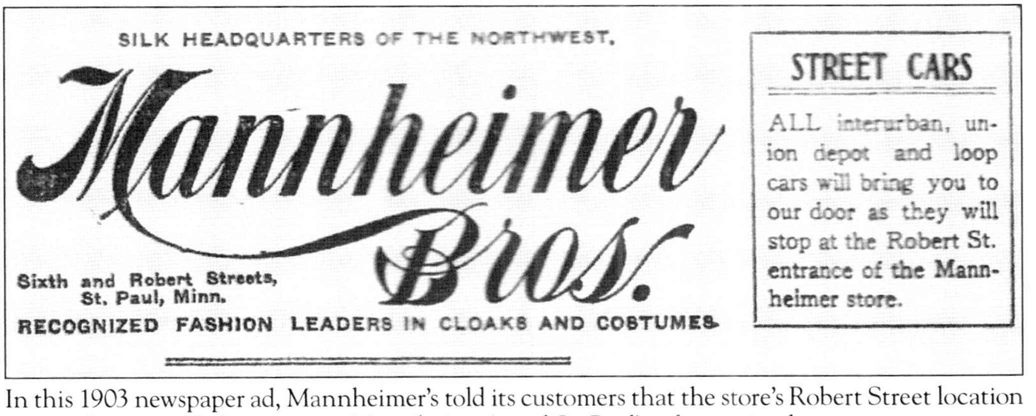

In this 1903 newspaper ad, Mannheimer's told its customers that the store's Robert Street location was easily accessible by streetcar. Mannheimer's and St. Paul's other major department stores were located within a few blocks of each other inside a tight network of converging streetcar lines. Downtown's streetcar network helped make it the city's retail center up through the 1940s.

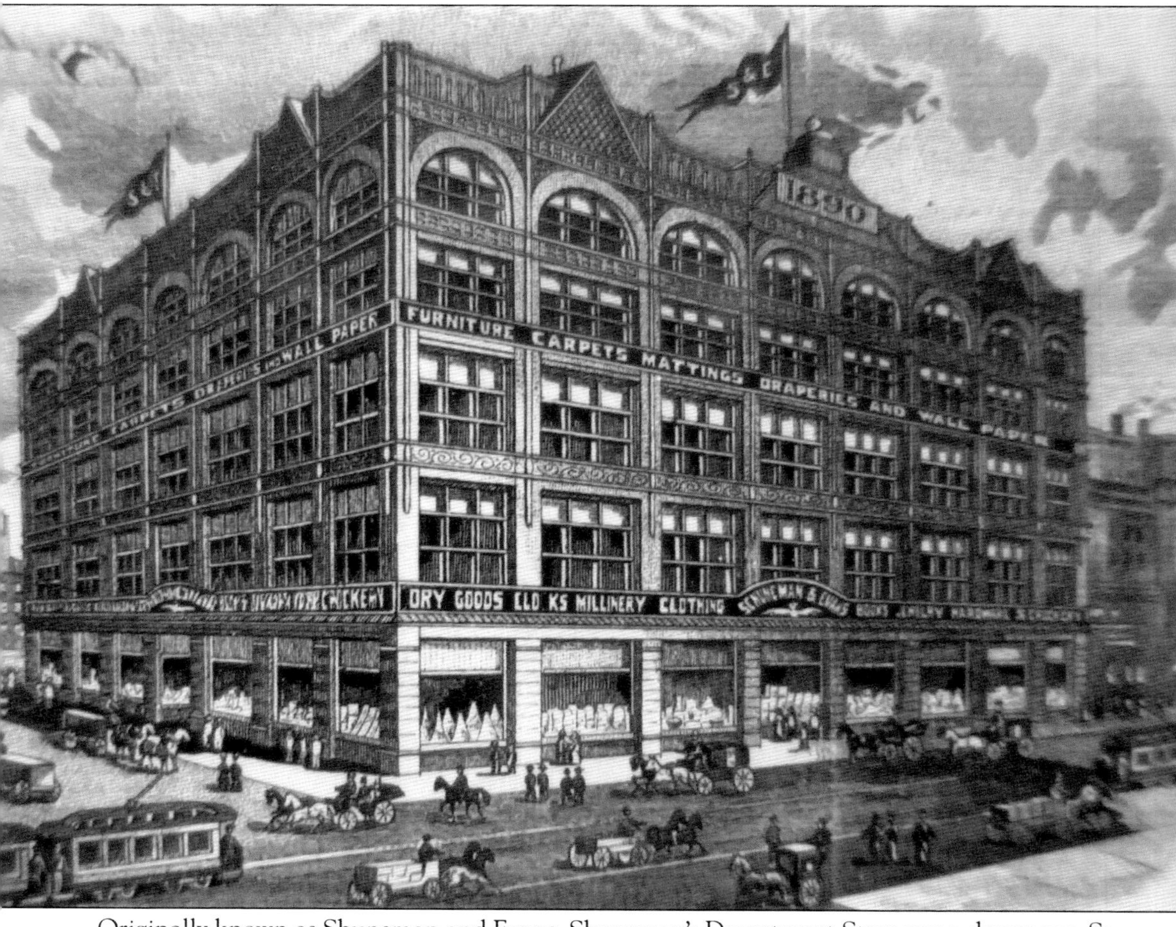

Originally known as Shuneman and Evans, Shuneman's Department Store was a downtown St. Paul fixture for more than 70 years. The store was established by Charles Shuneman, an emigrant from Hamburg, Germany, in 1888. In 1890, Shuneman built this impressive five-story department store at Sixth and Wabasha Streets. In 1959, Minneapolis-based Dayton's purchased Schuneman's, and Dayton's later tore down the 1890 building.

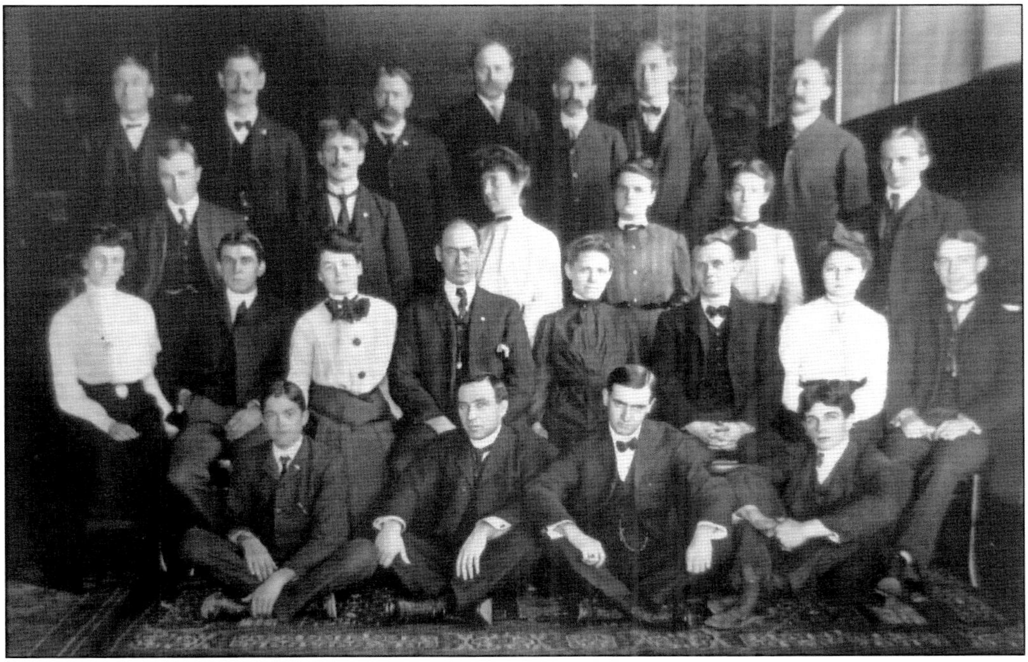

This group of well-dressed young men and women represented the sales force for the Shuneman and Evans department store in 1901. These sales clerks made use of their polished manners to provide service and build sales for the store. Working as a clerk could provide a ladder into the middle class for an eager and hardworking department store employee.

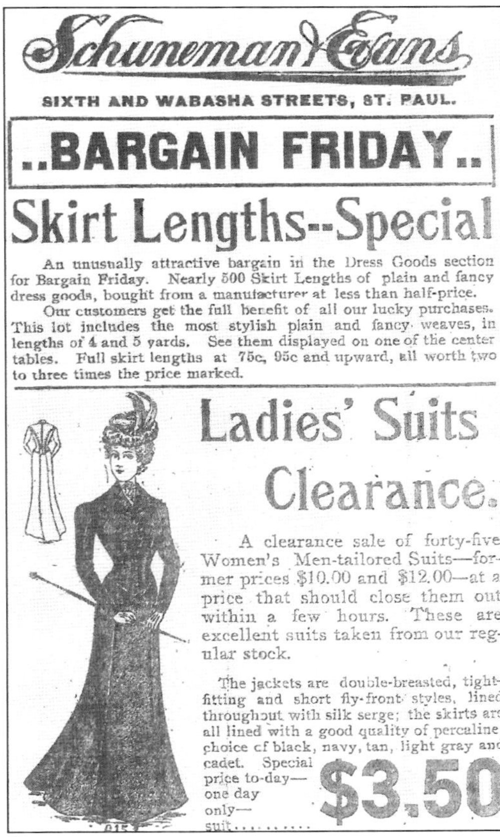

Schuneman's sales clerks were kept busy during a sale on May 3, 1901. That day, a stock of 45 women's suits regularly selling for $10–$12 were marked down to $3.50. At that price, the suits would sell out in a few hours, the store told its customers in a local newspaper advertisement.

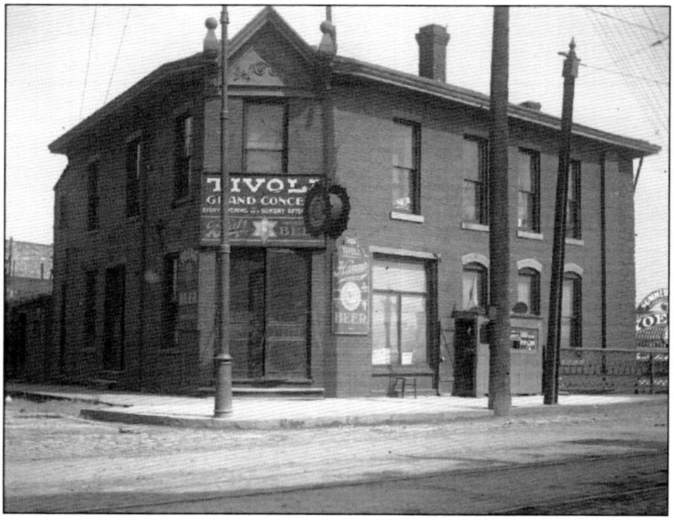

The Tivoli was a popular concert hall and entertainment center at Bridge Square. The concert hall advertised St. Paul's hometown beer, Hamm's, along with Blatz and Pabst from Milwaukee. The rear of the building housed a popular outdoor beer garden overlooking the Mississippi. The Tivoli was destroyed by a tornado that blew through downtown St. Paul in 1904. (Courtesy of Hennepin County Library Special Collections.)

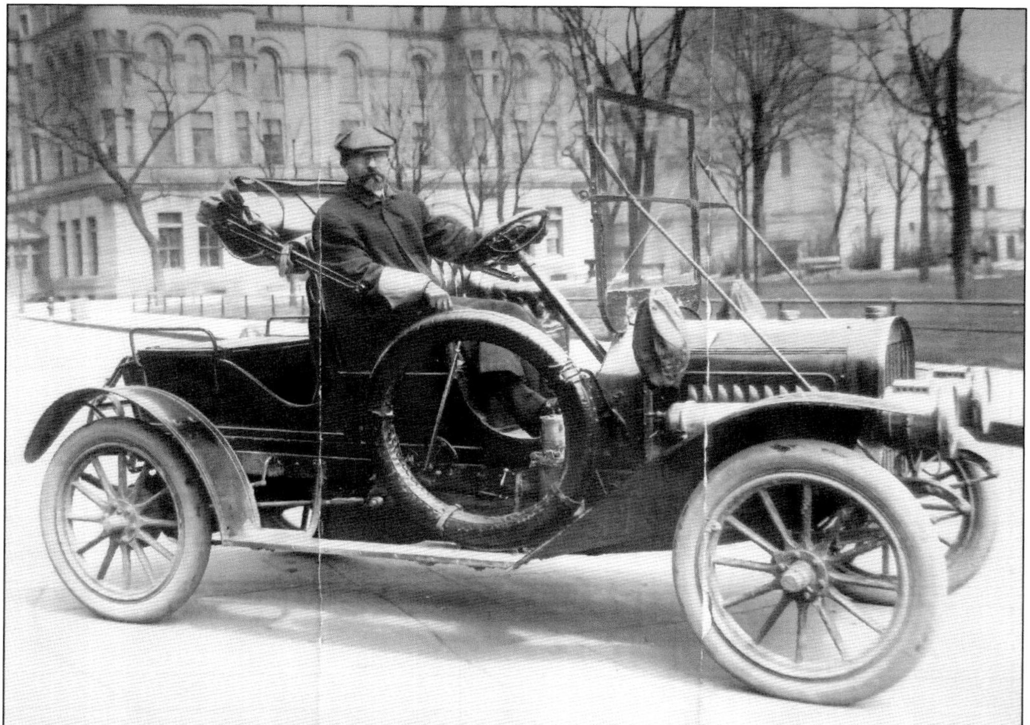

Automobiles were still a rarity on the streets of downtown St. Paul in 1905 when T.W. Ingersoll drove his open-air roadster along Rice Park. But downtown would soon be clogged with traffic when Henry Ford began producing his popular Model T in 1908. In the mid-1920s, St. Paul became a major auto assembly center when Ford established his Highland Park plant.

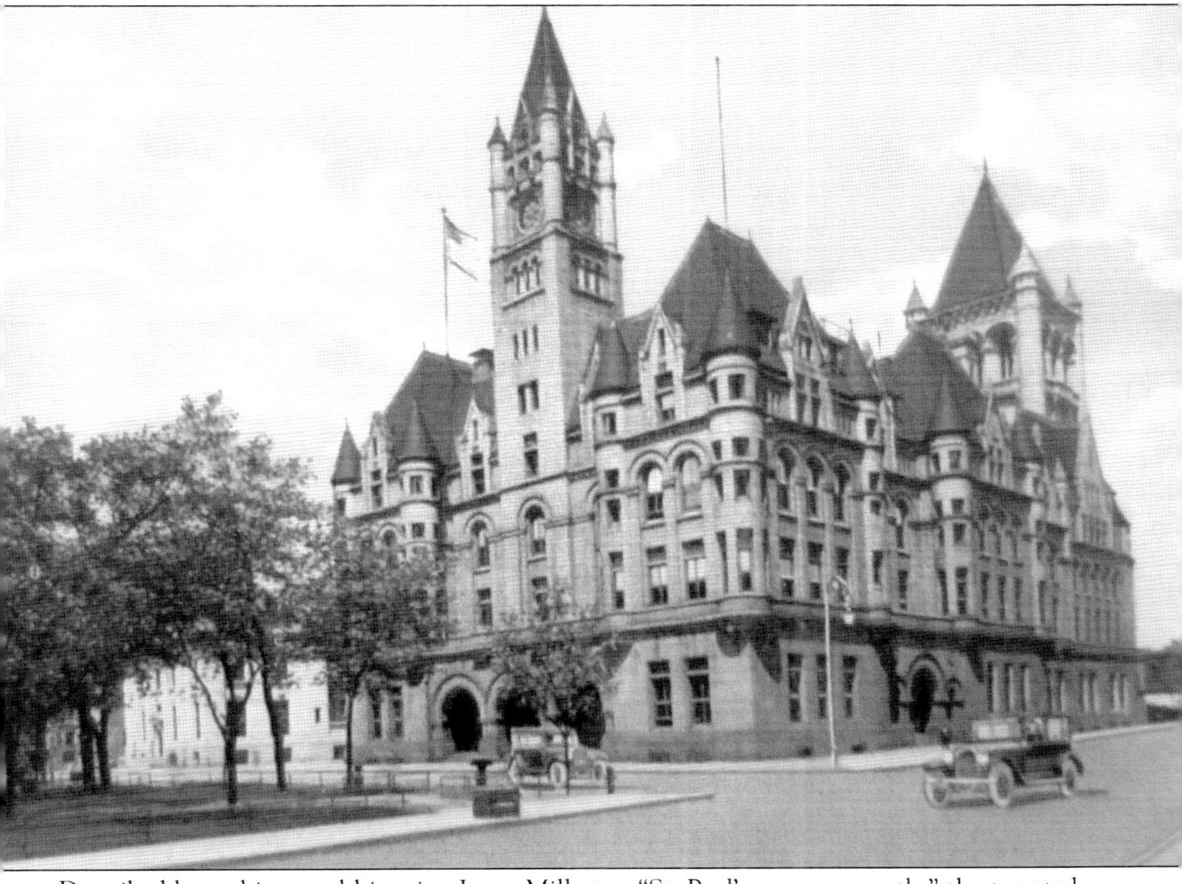

Described by architectural historian Larry Millett as "St. Paul's very own castle," the turreted structure facing Rice Park was known as the Federal Courts Building and Post Office when it opened in 1902. Millett has said that the building, later renamed the Landmark Center, offers "a cheery array of tourelles, arcades and gables, all rendered in smooth blocks of St. Cloud granite. The result is pure architectural romance."

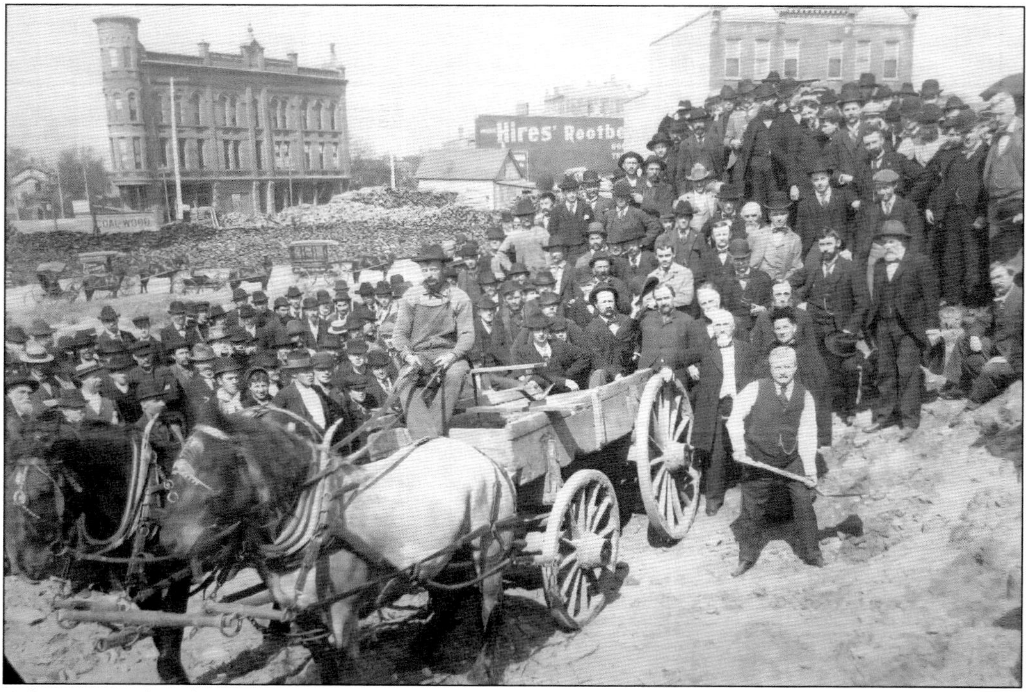

A large crowd gathers to watch the ground breaking for Minnesota's new state capitol on May 6, 1886. Channing Seabury is shown turning the first shovelful of dirt at the ceremony. As chairman of the Minnesota Capitol Commission, Seabury spent the previous three years shepherding the project through an often contentious public approval process.

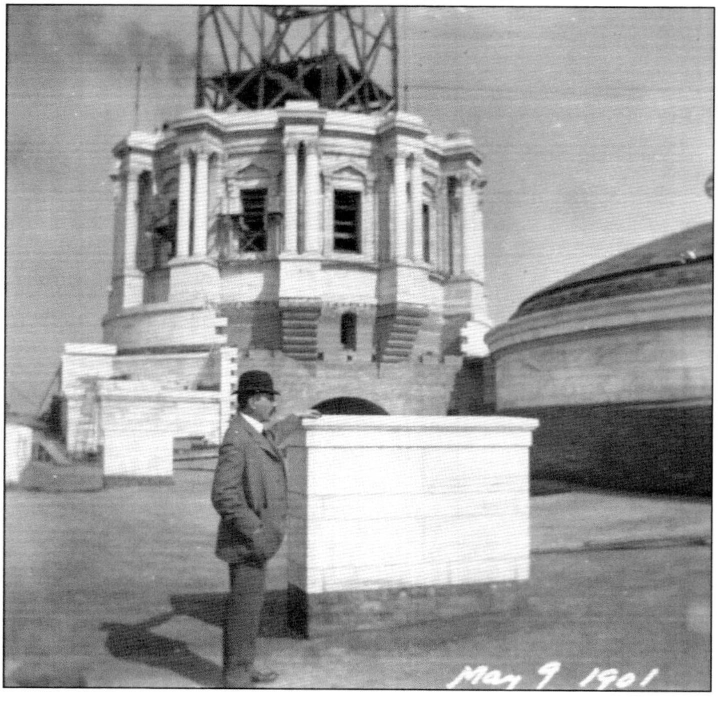

One of America's most prominent early-20th-century architects, Cass Gilbert, began his career at the age of 17 when he went to work for a St. Paul architectural firm. In 1895, he won a national commission to design Minnesota's new state capitol. Gilbert is shown inspecting the still-uncompleted building.

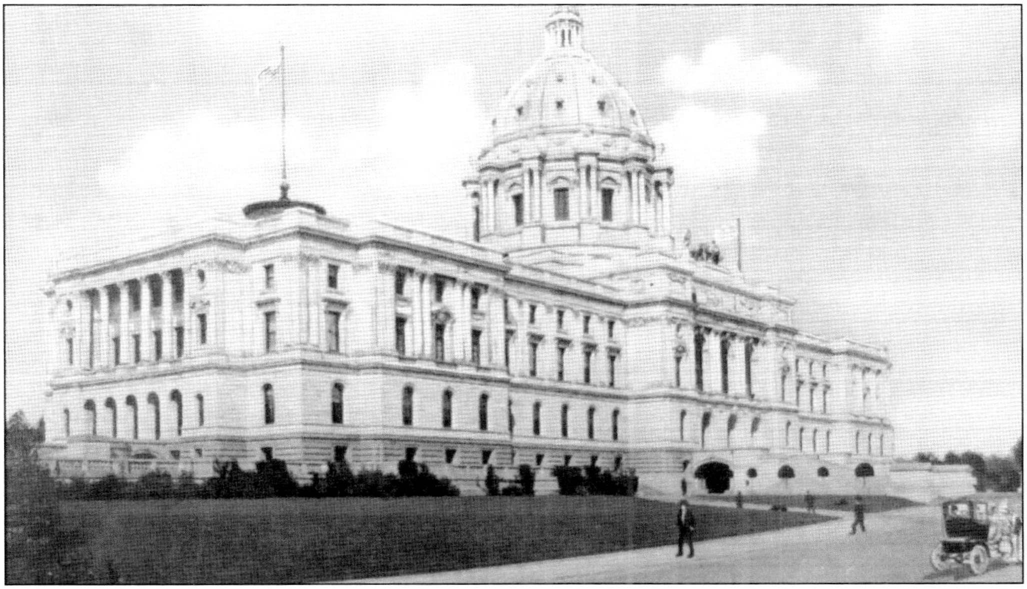

The Minnesota State Capitol was built over a nine-year period at the turn of the last century. The facade is built of Georgia white marble on a base of sandstone quarried in southern Minnesota. The capitol's unsupported marble dome is the second largest in the world after St. Peter's Basilica in Rome.

Civil War veterans are shown carrying battle flags from the old capitol building on Tenth Street to the new Minnesota State Capitol on June 14, 1905. Civil War commemorations were an important part of the decor for the new capitol. Two paintings in the governor's reception room depicted Civil War battles in which Minnesota soldiers, fighting for the Union, played a key role. (Courtesy of the Hennepin County Library Special Collections.)

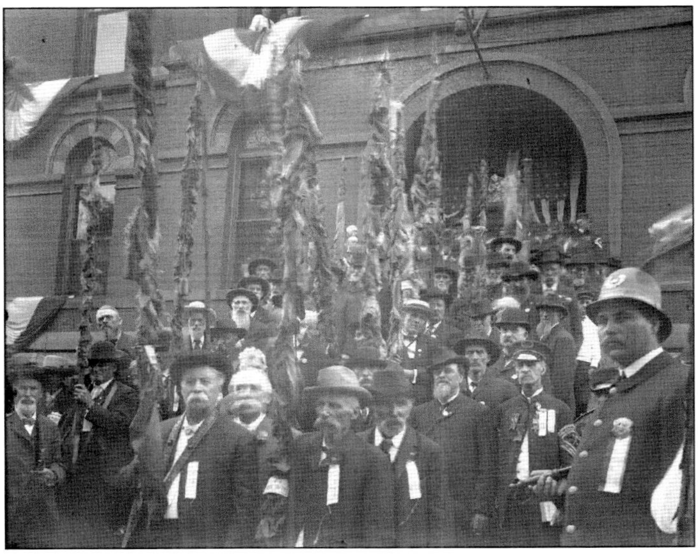

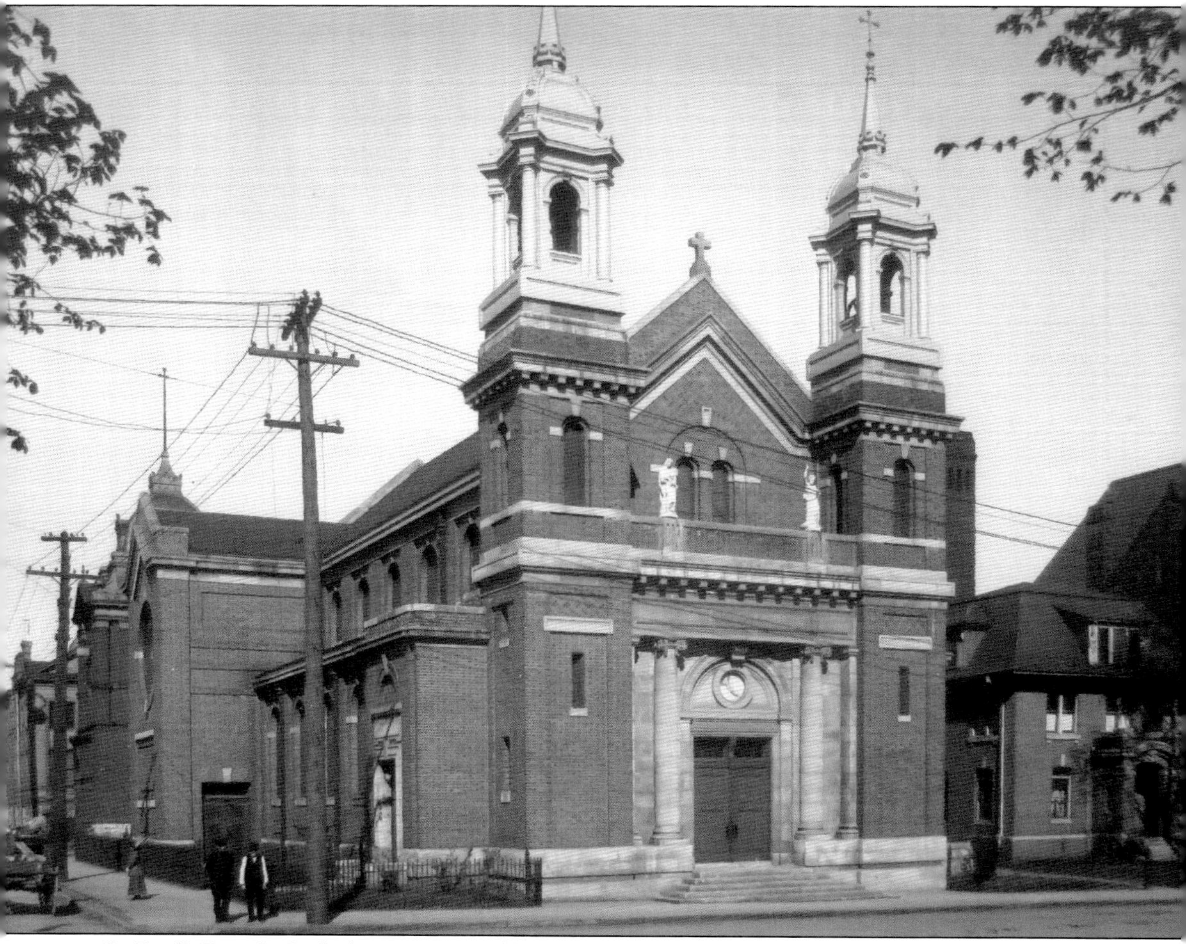

St. Paul's French Catholic roots extend back to the city's earliest years; most of the original settlers had French Canadian origins. In 1868, the city's French Catholics established their own parish and built their own church. This French Revival church, built in 1910, is the parish's third home. Known as Church of St. Louis King of France, it was designed by Emmanuel Masqueray, who also built the Catholic Cathedral of St. Paul.

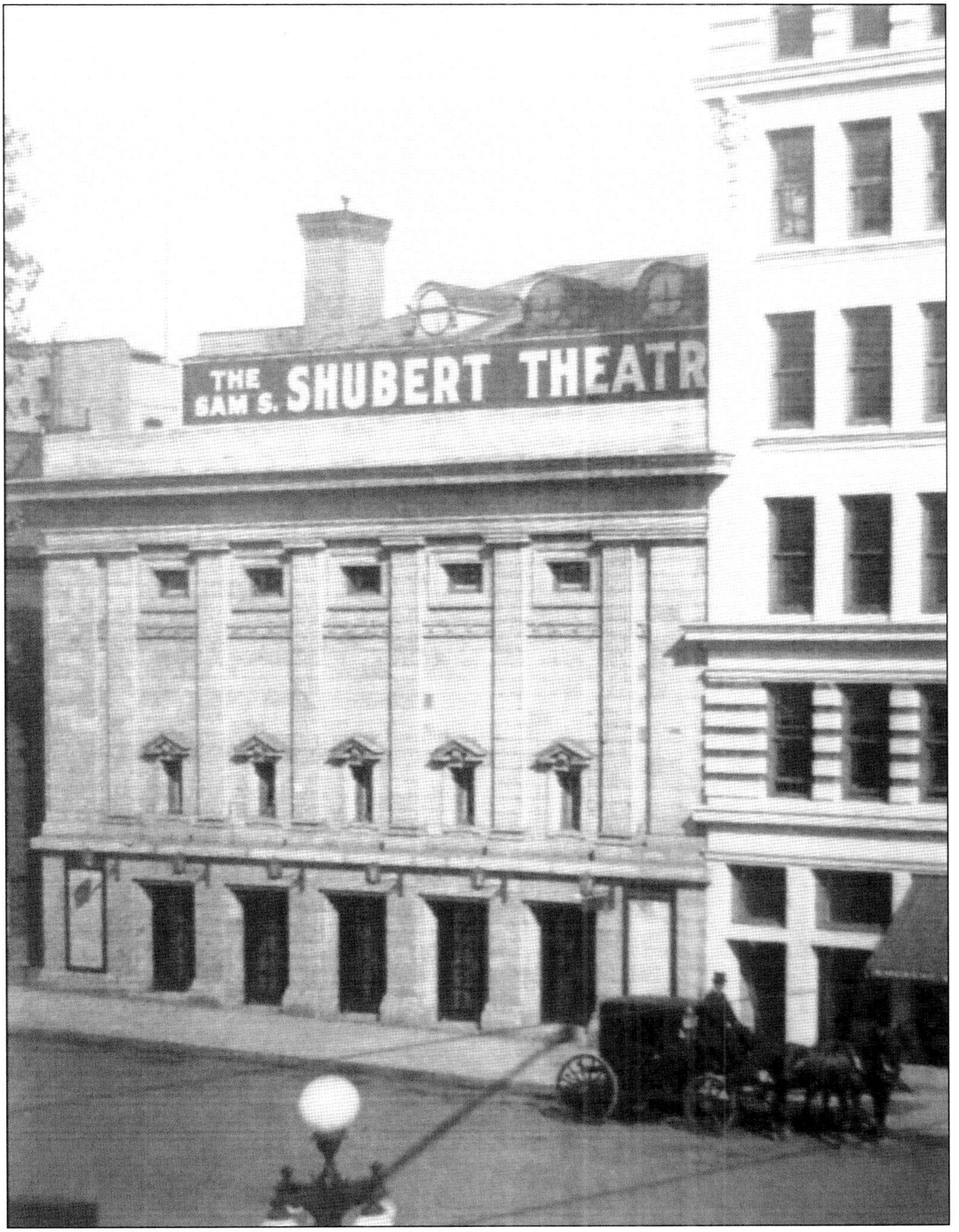

The Shubert Theater was one of St. Paul's most impressive entertainment venues when it opened in 1910. At a time when many movie theaters were little more than shabby firetraps, the Shubert was called "a model of sanitary perfection" by the *St. Paul Pioneer Press*. In 1933, the Shubert was renamed the World, and it continued to show movies until 1977. Later, the theater became the home of the popular radio show *A Prairie Home Companion*. (Author's collection.)

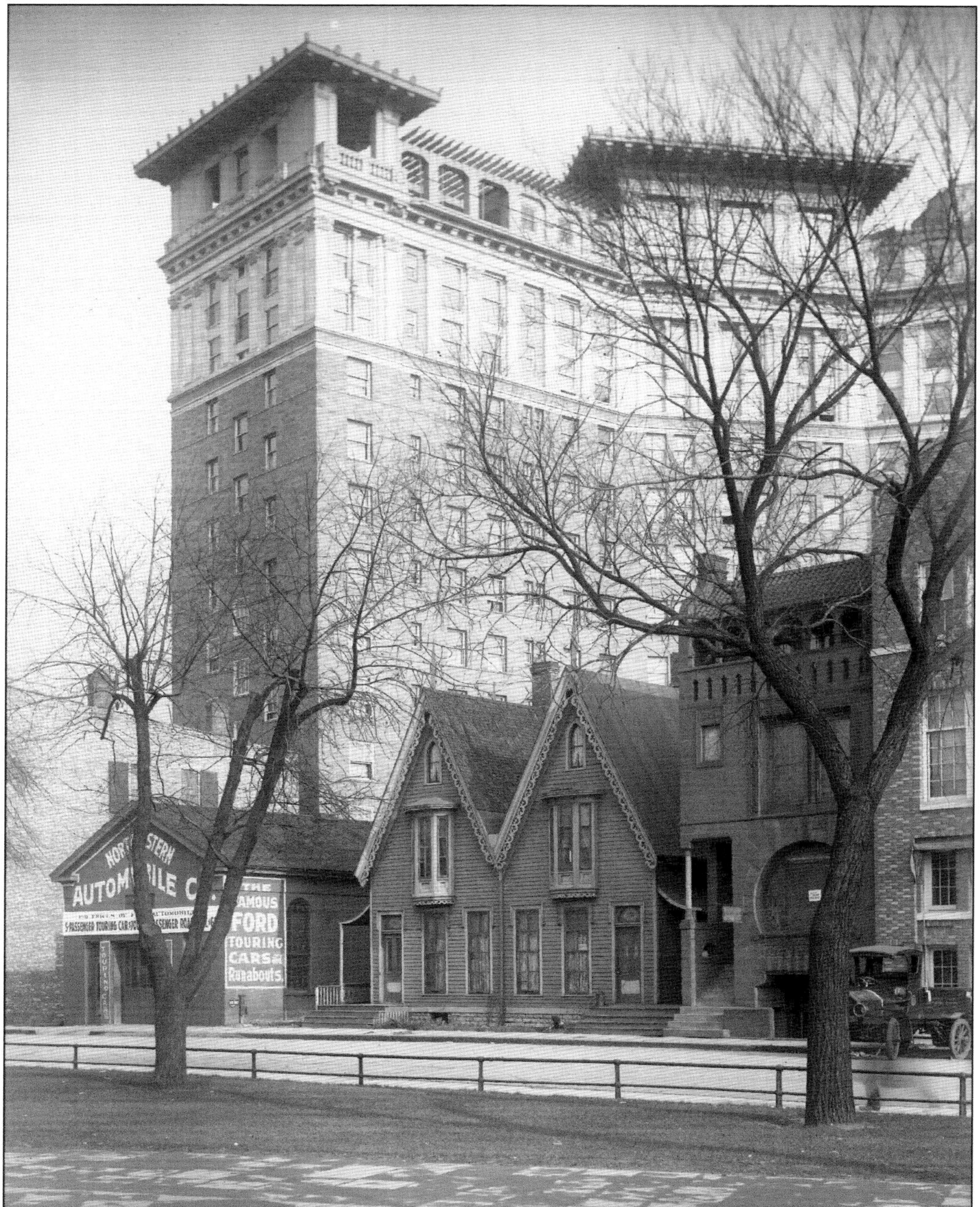

The St. Paul Hotel dates to 1910. It is the last of the Twin Cites' grand hotels still in use in the 21st century. The hotel closed in 1979 and was reopened and renovated in the 1980s. The Northwestern Automotive Company, shown at left, was an early Ford dealership. (Courtesy of Hennepin County Library Special Collections.)

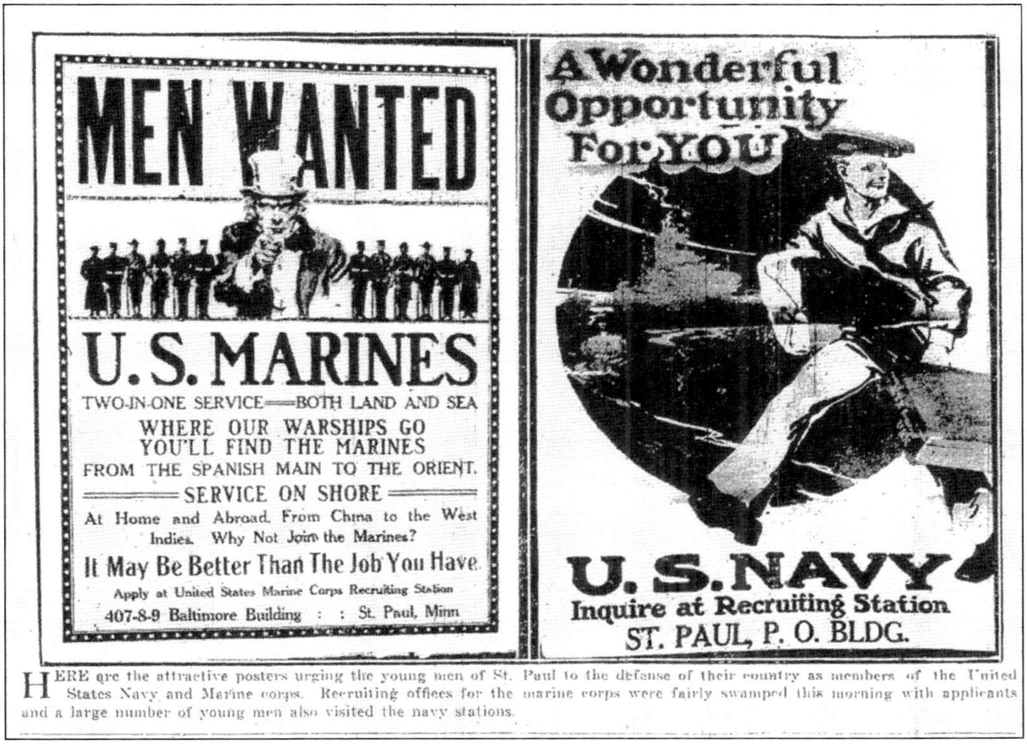

MEN WANTED

U.S. MARINES

TWO-IN-ONE SERVICE—BOTH LAND AND SEA

WHERE OUR WARSHIPS GO YOU'LL FIND THE MARINES

FROM THE SPANISH MAIN TO THE ORIENT.

SERVICE ON SHORE

At Home and Abroad. From China to the West Indies. Why Not Join the Marines?

It May Be Better Than The Job You Have.

Apply at United States Marine Corps Recruiting Station

407-8-9 Baltimore Building : : St. Paul, Minn

A Wonderful Opportunity For YOU

U.S. NAVY

Inquire at Recruiting Station

ST. PAUL, P. O. BLDG.

HERE are the attractive posters urging the young men of St. Paul to the defense of their country as members of the United States Navy and Marine corps. Recruiting offices for the marine corps were fairly swamped this morning with applicants and a large number of young men also visited the navy stations.

These posters appeared on the front page of the *St. Paul Dispatch* soon after the United States entered World War I in April 1917. With rapidly increasing manpower needs, the US armed services employed the country's most talented graphic artist to promote military recruitment. The Marine poster made use of the image created by James Montgomery Flagg, "Uncle Sam Wants You."

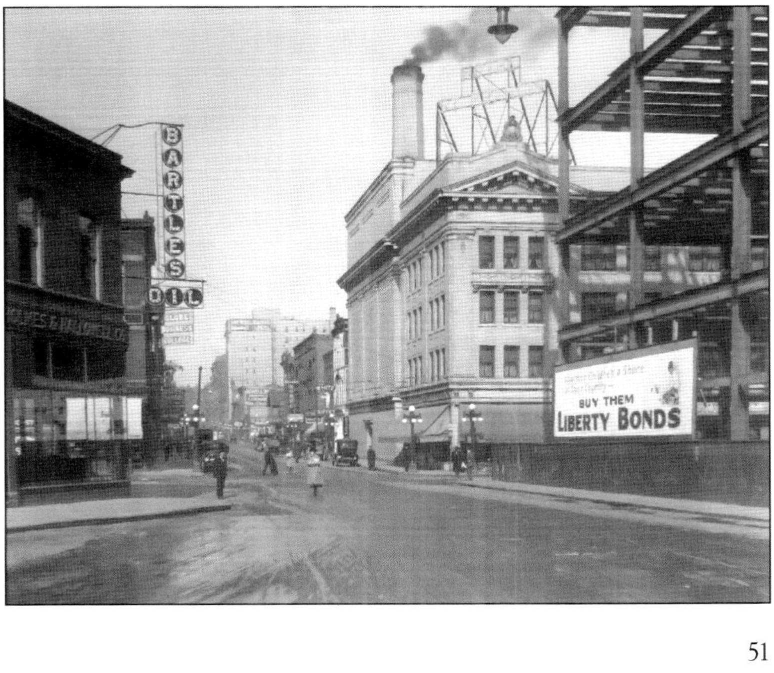

The US Treasury Department used modern advertising techniques to promote the sale of Liberty Bonds during World War I. This billboard was posted on the framework for the Hamm Building, which opened in 1920 at Fourth and St. Peter Streets.

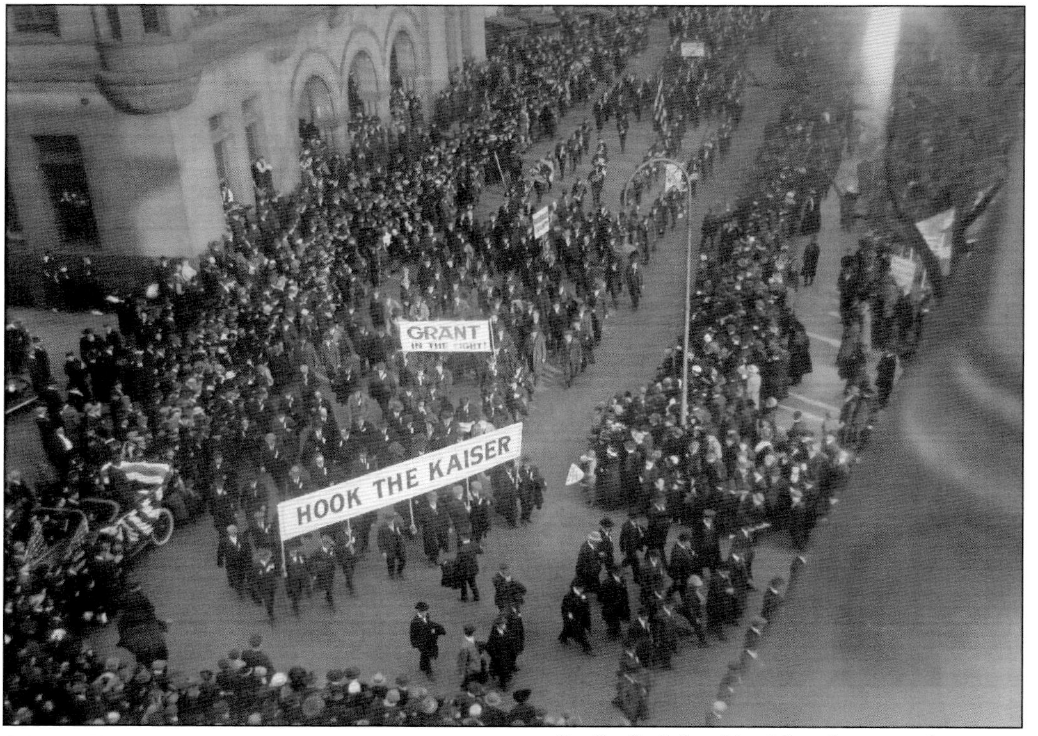

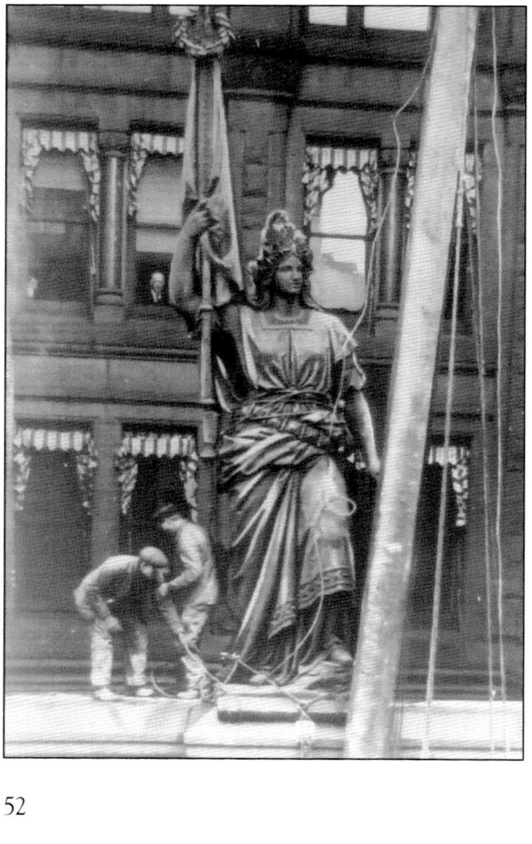

St. Paul's federal building became the focal point for loyalty parades during the war years. In 1917 and 1918, the parades were intended to generate support for the war effort on the home front. The loyalty crusades used Germany's Kaiser Wilhelm as a symbol of America's military enemy.

As war fervor intensified in 1917, St. Paul's German American community found that it was being viewed with suspicion by some loyalists who considered themselves superpatriots. The open expression of German culture was frowned upon during the war years. The statue *Germania* was removed from the front of the Germania Life Insurance Building in response to this view. The structure itself was renamed the Guardian Building to erase its German connections.

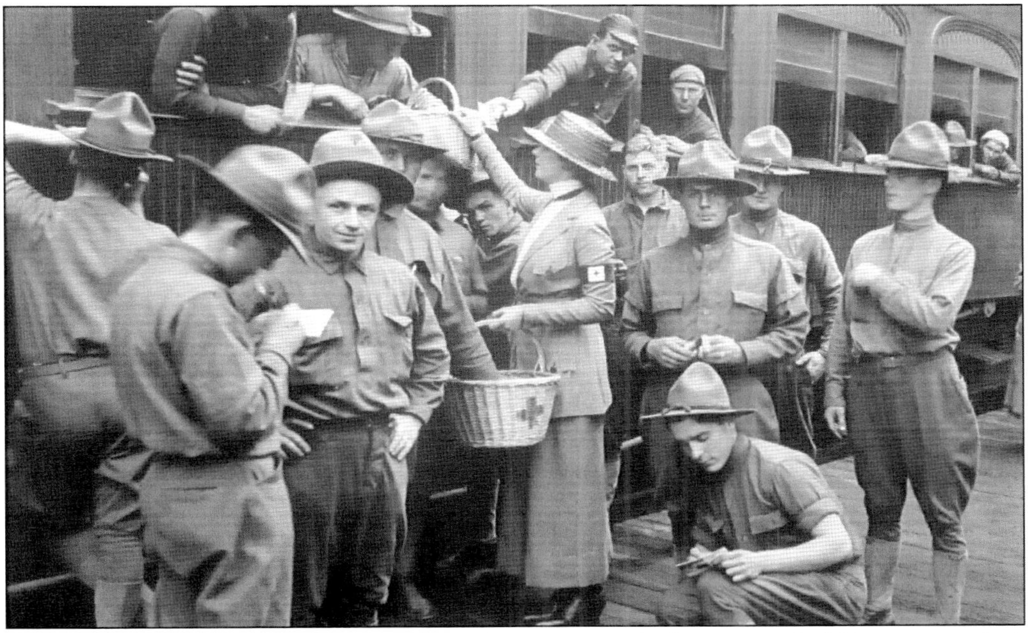

During World War I, St. Paul's Union Depot became an embarkation site for US troops on their way to France to join the American Expeditionary Forces. These young soldiers wearing their distinctive broad-brimmed Army hats are about to leave on a Great Northern Railway train that will take them on the first leg of their journey to the western front. A young Red Cross volunteer is collecting messages that the soldiers are writing to friends and loved ones.

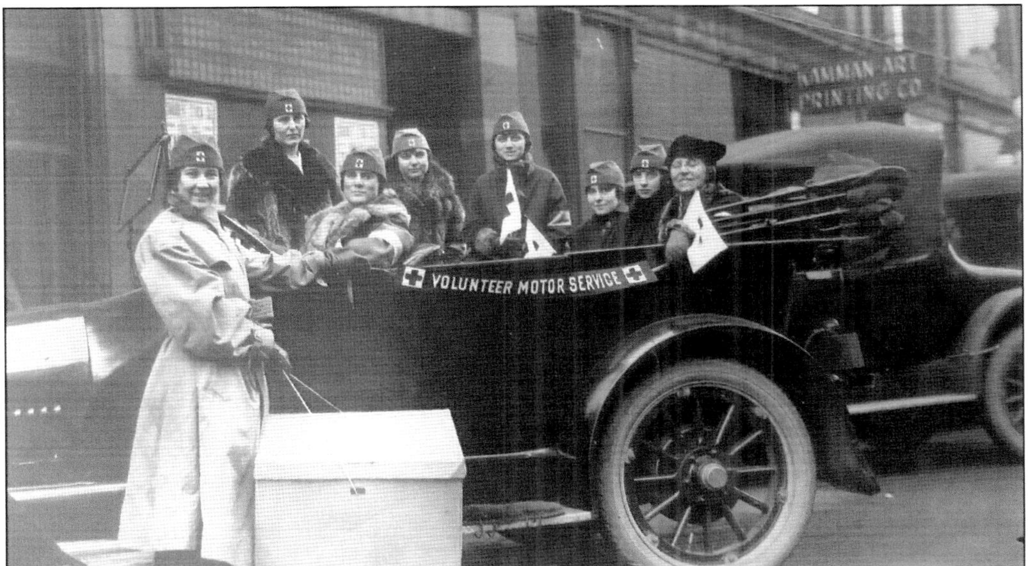

These smiling young women are members of the Red Cross Motor Corps. In cities all across the country, the corps provided transportation services during World War I. Red Cross volunteers transported sick and wounded soldiers from troop trains to local hospitals. They delivered supplies to military installations and took nurses and canteen workers to their posts. By the end of World War I, women of the Red Cross Motor Corps had driven over 35 million miles.

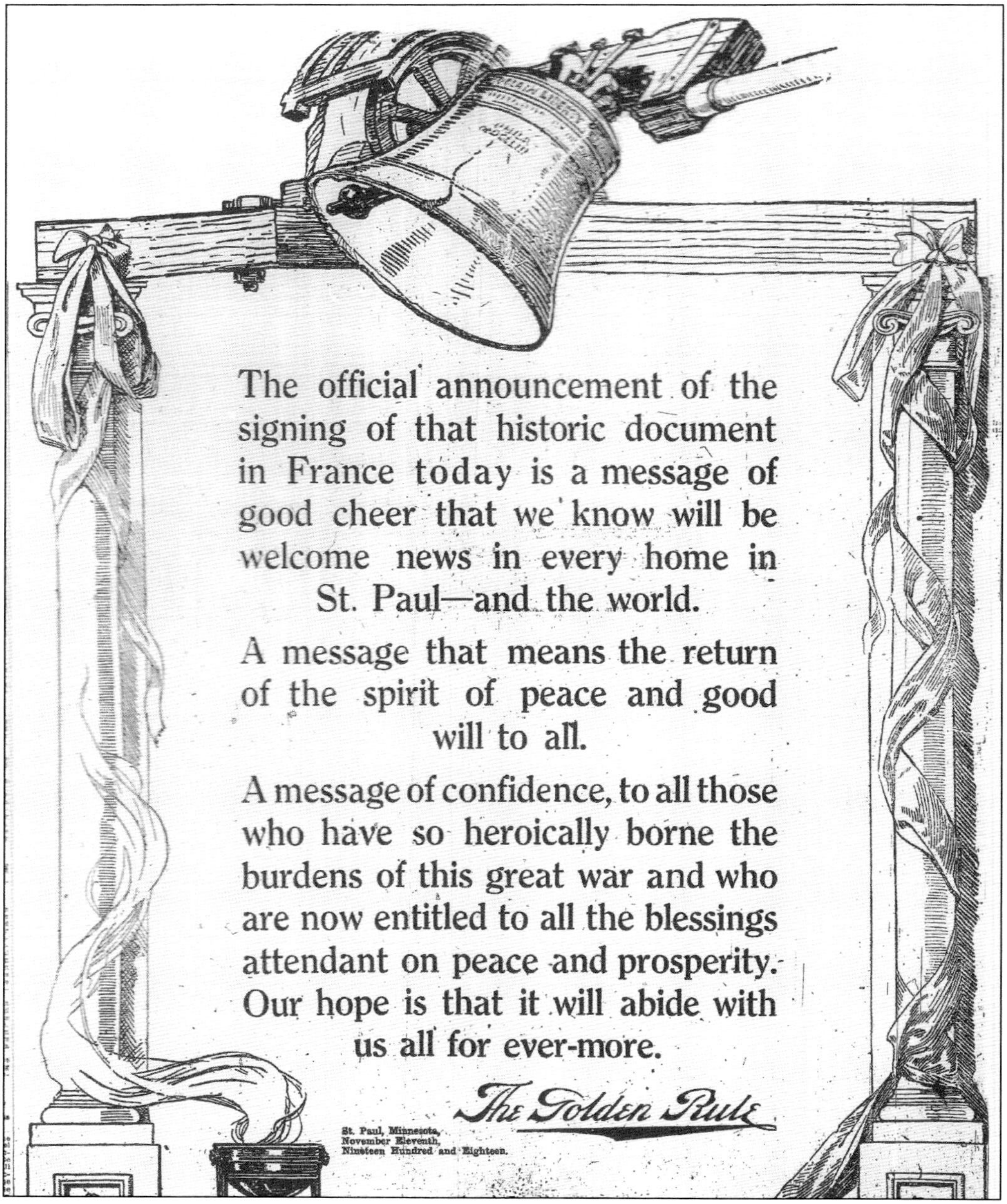

The Golden Rule department store placed this ad in the *Pioneer Press* to celebrate the World War I armistice on November 11, 1918. When word reached St. Paul that the war was over, the *Pioneer Press* reported that "riotous hilarity" converted downtown's streets into a "bedlam of peace enthusiasts while a blizzard of fine cut paper and confetti shrouded the heads and shoulders of the shouting, tooting, clanging crowd of noisemakers." (Author's collection.)

Horace Lowry, the son of TCRT's founder, Thomas Lowry, headed the transit company during the World War I years. Lowry resisted the demands of many of his workers for union recognition and pay increases. His hardline stance escalated tensions with the TCRT workforce just as the war was getting underway. (Courtesy of Hennepin County Library Special Collections.)

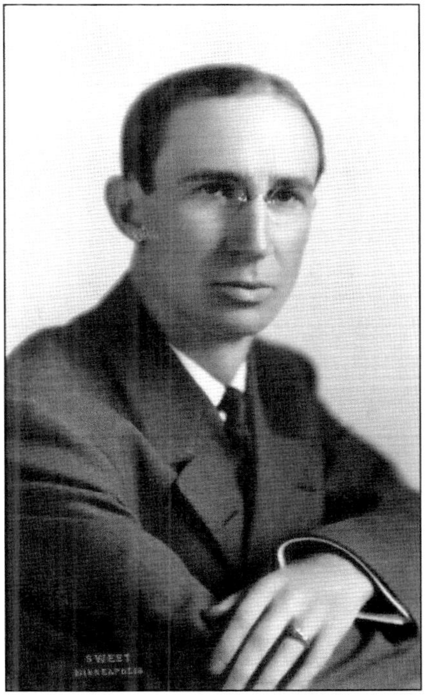

In 1917, TCRT workers went out on strike. Soon, their anger mounted when Lowry refused to negotiate with their union. Following a December rally in Rice Park, a group of disgruntled workers took matters into their own hands and began halting trolley service in downtown St. Paul. Lowry provided a small increase in wages to his workers, but the strikers did not achieve their ultimate goal—recognition of their union by the TCRT.

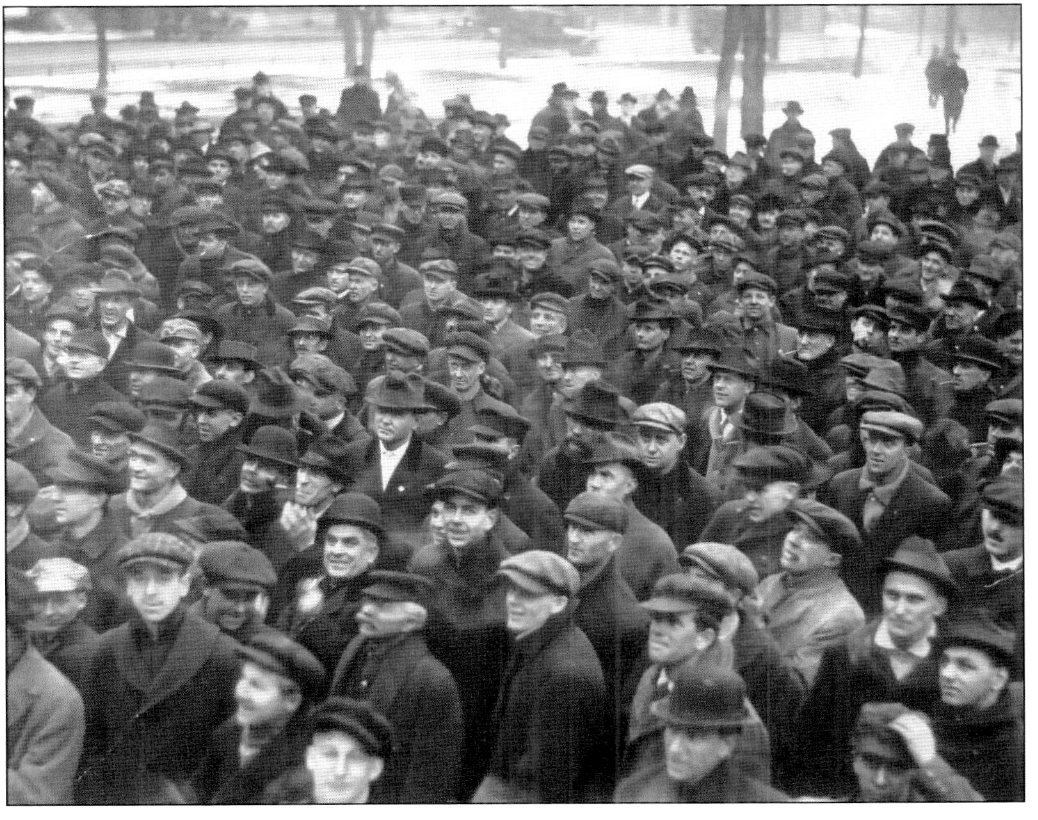

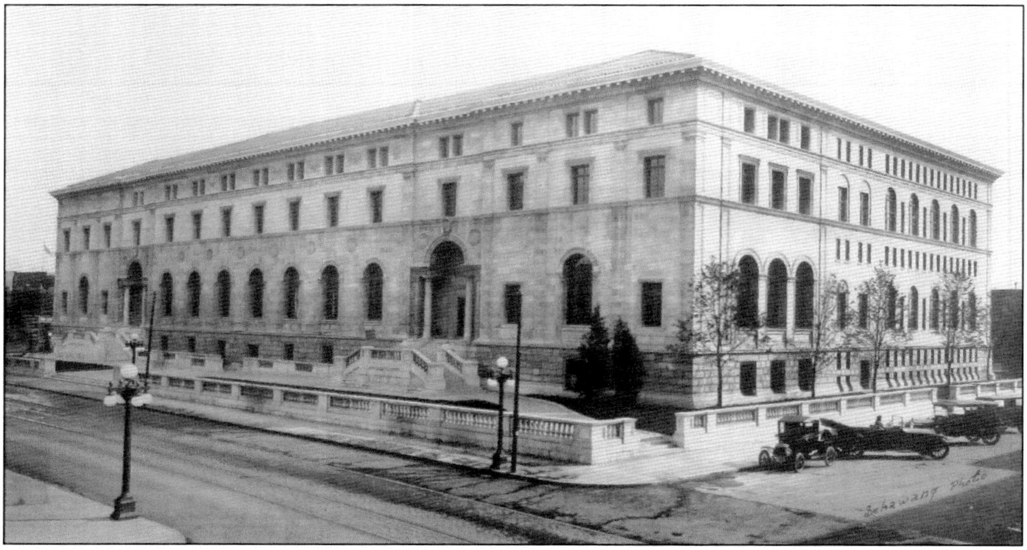

This Beaux Arts–style building was constructed in 1917 to house St. Paul's central public library and the adjoining privately operated James J. Hill Reference Library. The library fronted Rice Park, facing the federal courthouse and post office, now renamed Landmark Center. In 2014, the St. Paul central library was renamed for former St. Paul mayor George Latimer.

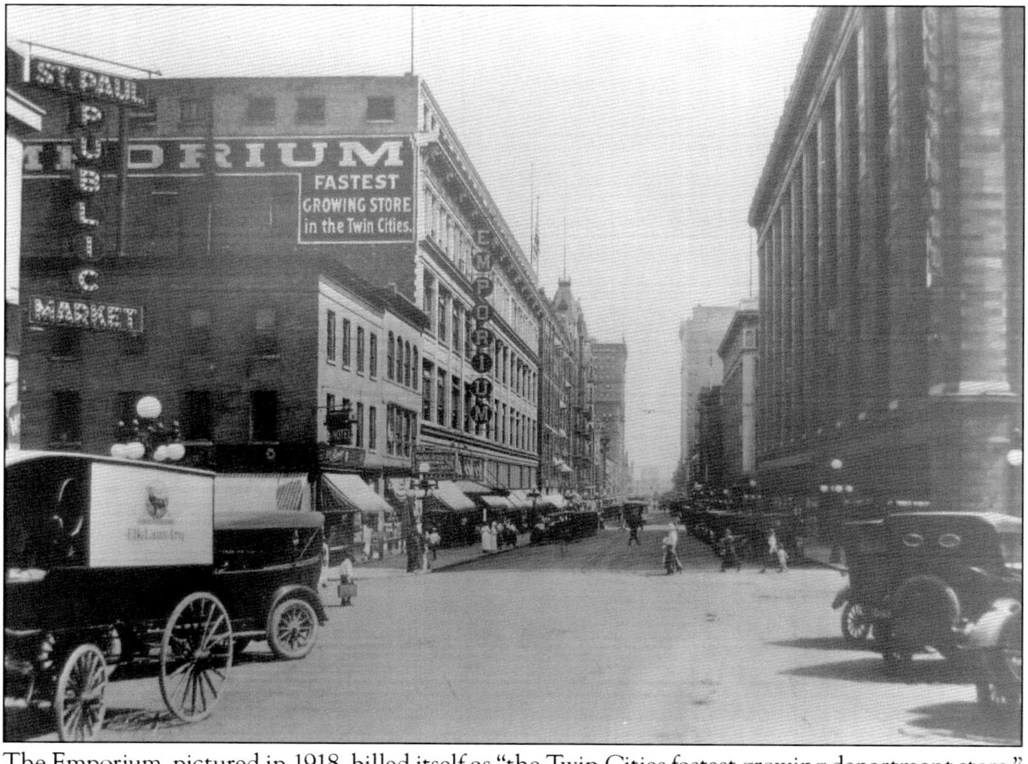

The Emporium, pictured in 1918, billed itself as "the Twin Cities fastest growing department store." The St. Paul–based store was located across from its archrival, the Golden Rule. The Emporium survived until 1968, when it was finally forced to close.

Three

Tumultuous Decades

St. Paul experienced the jazz age of the 1920s, exemplified by its best known literary figure, F. Scott Fitzgerald. Then, in the 1930s, St. Paul, like most American cities, was buffeted by the Great Depression. On New Years Day 1933, at the height of the Depression, St. Paul mayor William Mahoney declared that his city had to contend with economic and political difficulties "more severe than anything it had faced in the past."

Despite the hardships caused by the Depression, the economic downturn had one positive result for St. Paul. Because material and labor costs were so low, the city was able to use its available funds to build an architecturally impressive government center. The Art Deco city hall and courthouse opened in 1932 just as nationwide unemployment was peaking. "The City Hall project provided a much needed economic infusion but it also was designed to symbolize the capital city's progressivism and civic pride," historian Mary Lethert Wingerd later observed.

In the 1930s, the Depression overlapped with the gangster era, which brought many of the country's most notorious criminals to St. Paul seeking a temporary haven provided by the local authorities. One of those was FBI "public enemy" Alvin Karpis, whose gang had kidnapped two of St. Paul's most prominent business leaders and held them for ransom. Karpis was eventually tried and convicted of his crimes at a sensational trial in St. Paul's federal courthouse.

During World War II, St. Paul's Union Depot served as an embarkation point for US troops heading off to the battlefields. Nearly 30 years earlier, the station had served the same role during World War I. On VJ Day, August 14, 1945, St. Paulites came downtown to celebrate the end of the war just as they had on Armistice Day in 1918.

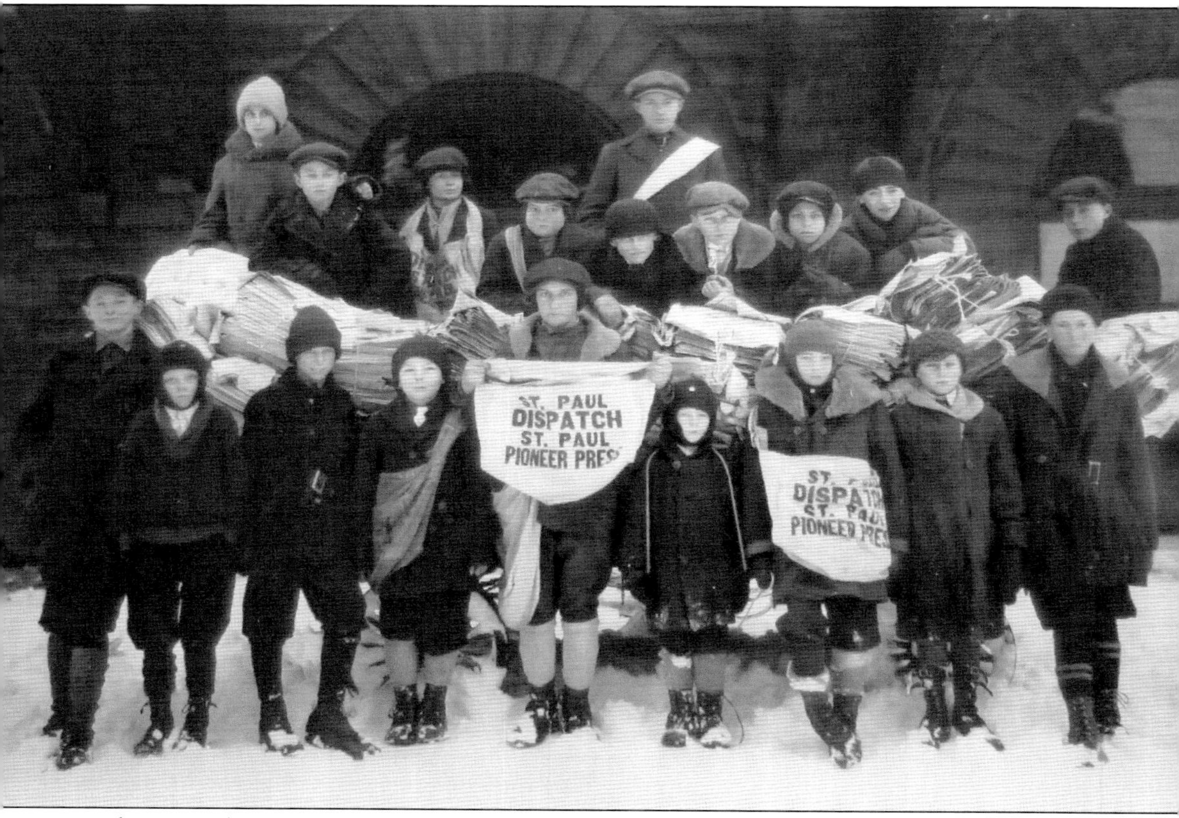

These newsboys are bundled up, ready to peddle their papers on a cold winter day in the early 1920s. In an era before home delivery, the "newsies," as they were known, jostled with each other to stake the best corners to ply their trade. These boys are selling the morning *Pioneer Press* and the afternoon *Dispatch*.

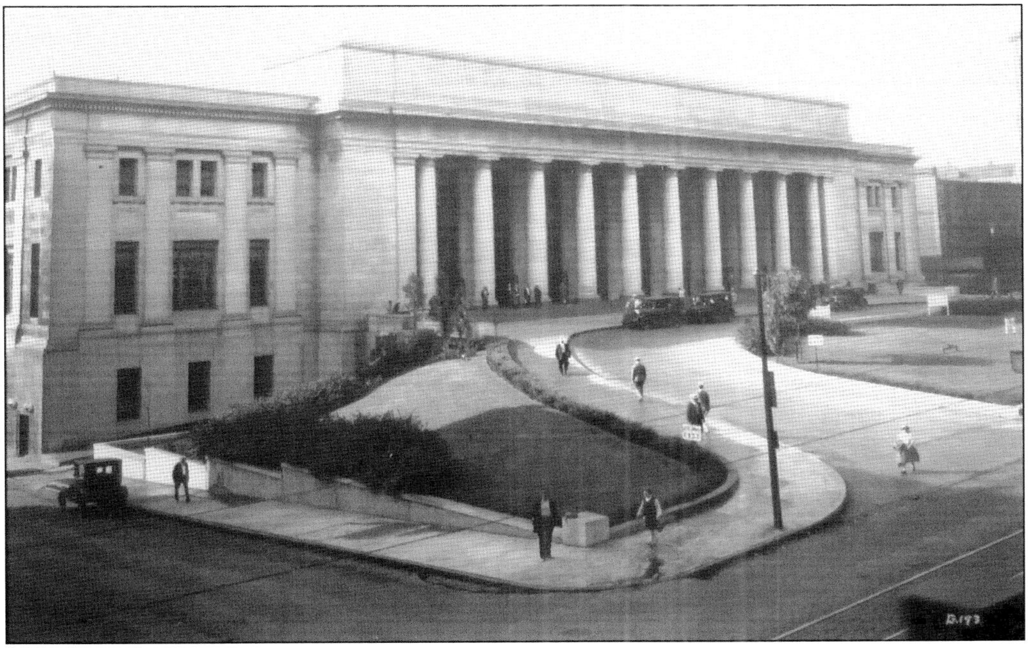

This classically styled train station, with its row of columns lining the front entrance, opened in 1923. It replaced St. Paul's first Union Depot, which burned down in 1913. The earlier passenger station, dating to the early 1880s, was located on the downtown riverfront. The new Union Depot was situated on higher ground, which required a reconfiguration of St. Paul's historic riverfront railyard.

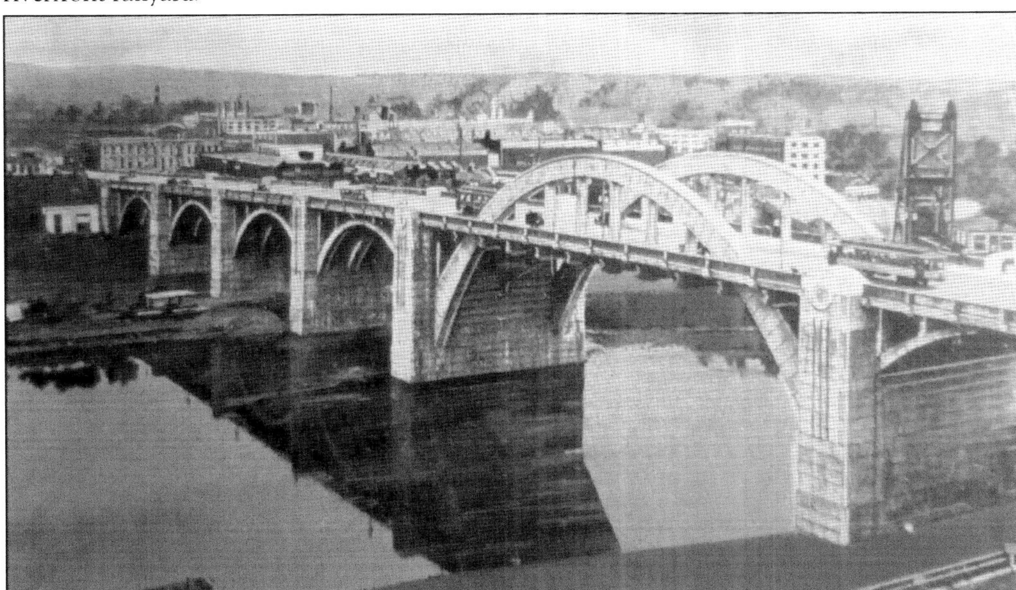

The Robert Street bridge, built in 1926, replaced an earlier river span that connected downtown St. Paul to the city's west side. The bridge consists of a series of arches, one of which rises above the roadway. The Robert Street bridge was designed by the St. Paul–based firm of Tolz, King, and Day. In 1989, it was rebuilt by the same firm, then known as TKDA.

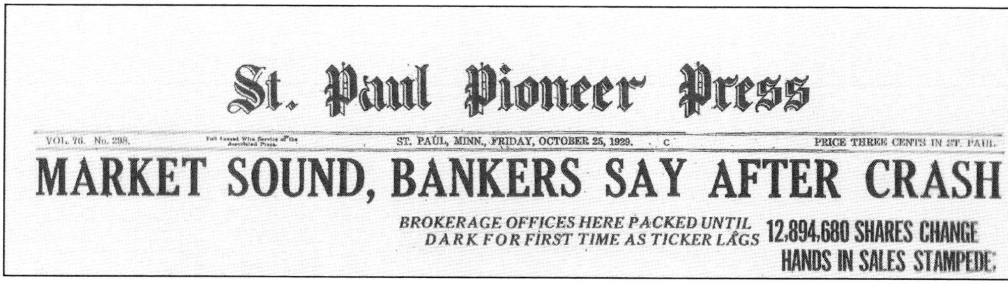

St. Paul Pioneer Press

VOL. 76. No. 298. ST. PAUL, MINN., FRIDAY, OCTOBER 25, 1929. PRICE THREE CENTS IN ST. PAUL.

MARKET SOUND, BANKERS SAY AFTER CRASH

BROKERAGE OFFICES HERE PACKED UNTIL DARK FOR FIRST TIME AS TICKER LAGS

12,894,680 SHARES CHANGE HANDS IN SALES STAMPEDE

This newspaper headline tried to convey a note of optimism following the stock market crash of October 24, 1929, known as "Black Thursday." But any optimism was tempered by uneasiness in the downtown brokerage offices, where the ticker tape was more than four hours late in recording stock sales. The next week, on "Black Tuesday," October 29, the market suffered an even greater plunge, setting the stage for the Great Depression. (Author's collection.)

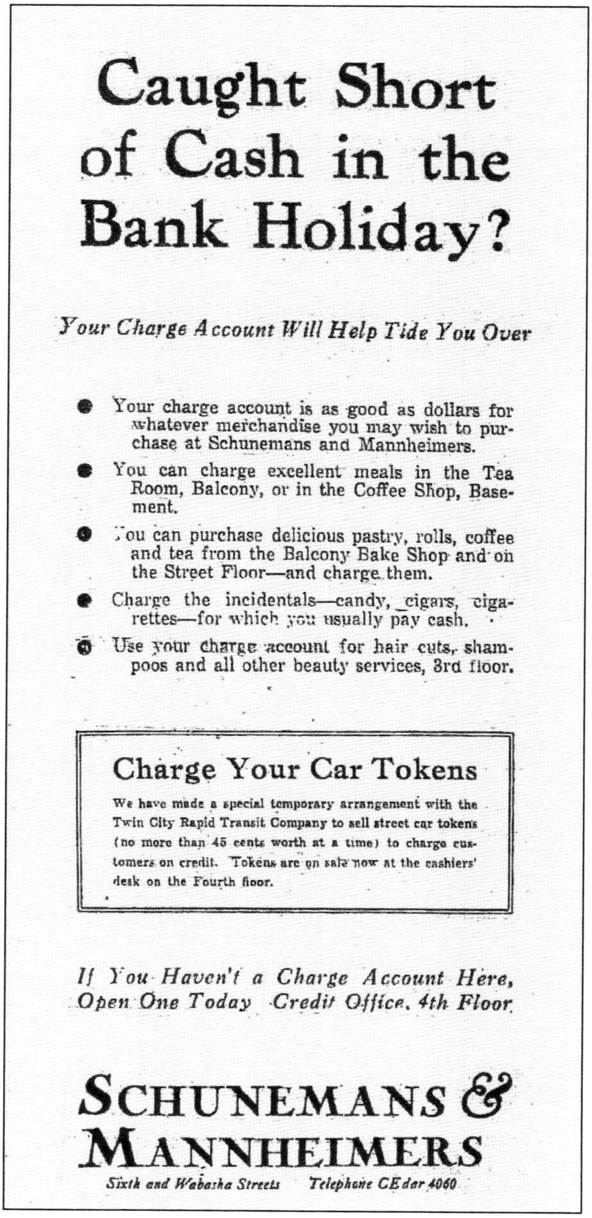

As the Depression deepened in 1933, states began closing their banks in an effort to prevent a financial panic. On March 4, Minnesota became the 37th state to close its banks. The next day, the newly inaugurated president, Franklin Roosevelt, extended the bank holiday to the entire country. Schunemans & Mannheimers Department Store told its customers they could use their charge cards for purchases if they ran out of cash during the bank holiday. (Author's collection.)

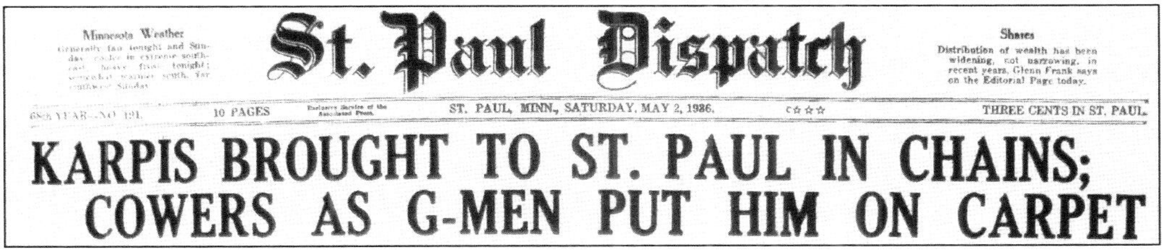

Minnesota Weather

St. Paul Dispatch

Shares

Distribution of wealth has been widening, not narrowing, in recent years, Glenn Frank says on the Editorial Page today.

10 PAGES | ST. PAUL, MINN., SATURDAY, MAY 2, 1936. | THREE CENTS IN ST. PAUL.

KARPIS BROUGHT TO ST. PAUL IN CHAINS; COWERS AS G-MEN PUT HIM ON CARPET

Alvin Karpis gained notoriety during the Depression years as one of the FBI's most wanted public enemies. In the early 1930s, Karpis and his gang kidnapped two prominent St. Paul businessmen and held them for ransom. After evading law enforcement officials for several years, he was finally captured by the FBI in 1936. Karpis is shown being brought into the St. Paul federal court building after his capture. The FBI's J. Edgar Hoover came to St. Paul so he could personally escort Karpis into the courtroom where he was tried and convicted of kidnapping and extortion.

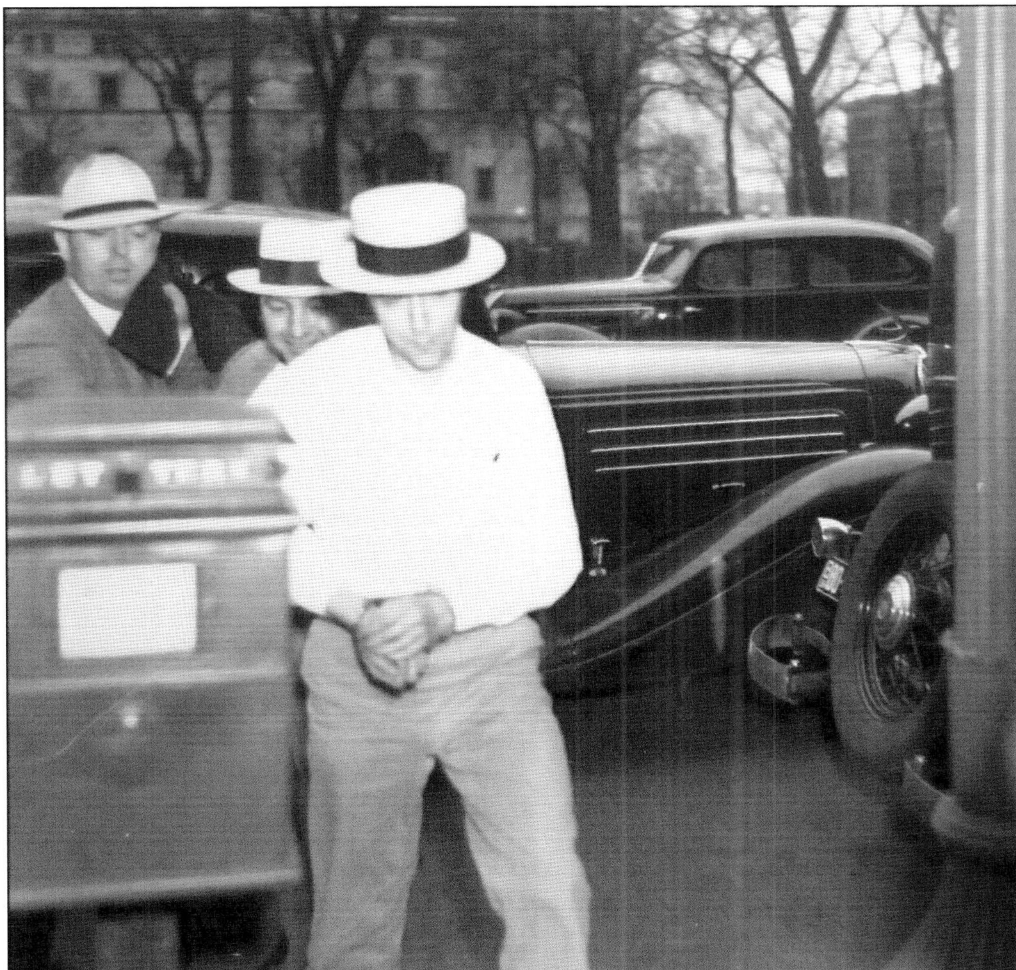

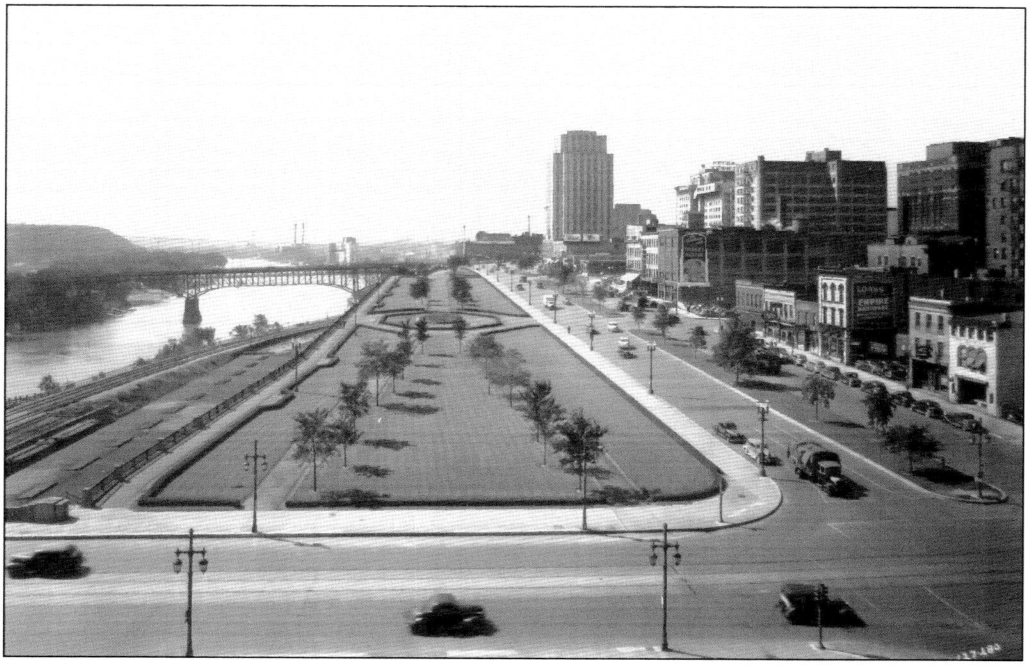

The Kellogg Mall represented an early effort to beautify downtown St. Paul. The landscaped mall and boulevard, built in 1932, replaced aging Third Street. The mall's broad expanse of lawns between Robert and Wabasha Streets provided a view of the river that had been obscured by the line of storefronts along Third Street. The mall was named for Frank Kellogg, a US senator from Minnesota. Kellogg later served as US secretary of state and won the Nobel Peace Prize.

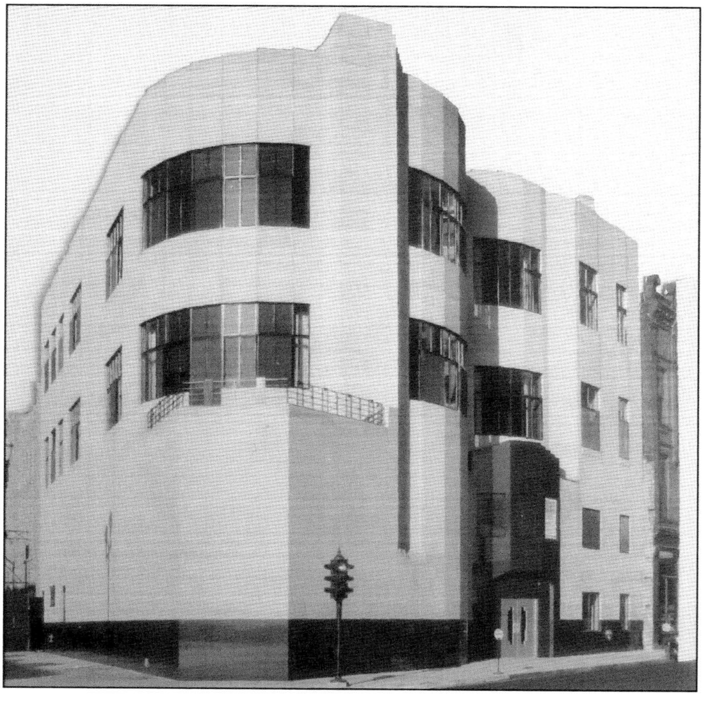

Architectural historian Larry Millett has described this building at the corner of Kellogg Boulevard and St. Peter Street as an architectural "jewel." Millett says the building is "a sophisticated work that skillfully mixes zigzag and streamlined phases of art deco. [It] has a delicacy rarely seen in institutional architecture yet also holds down its corner site with convincing authority." The building was constructed for the Women's City Club in 1931.

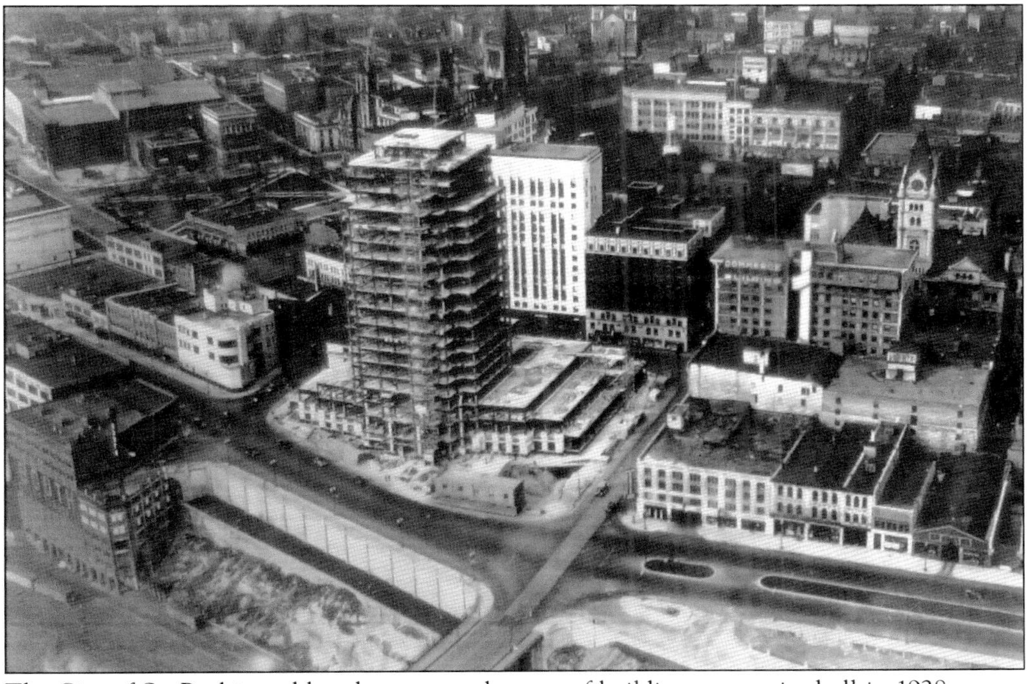

The City of St. Paul issued bonds to cover the cost of building a new city hall in 1928, a year before the stock market crash and the onset of the Great Depression. By the time construction began in 1931, building costs had dropped substantially. The funds available for the project—$4 million—enabled the city to substantially upgrade building materials and furnishings for the new civic building.

The Chicago architectural firm Holabard and Root was able to use the finest materials and the most skilled artisans to build the Art Deco–style building. The political leaders of the time deserved some credit for this fortuitous development. They could have cut back the project substantially to save money, but they chose not to and gave the architects full reign to deliver a building of the very highest quality.

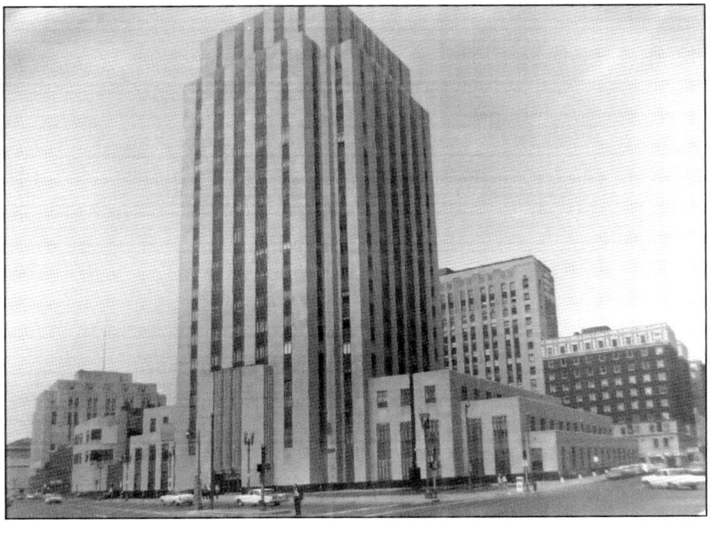

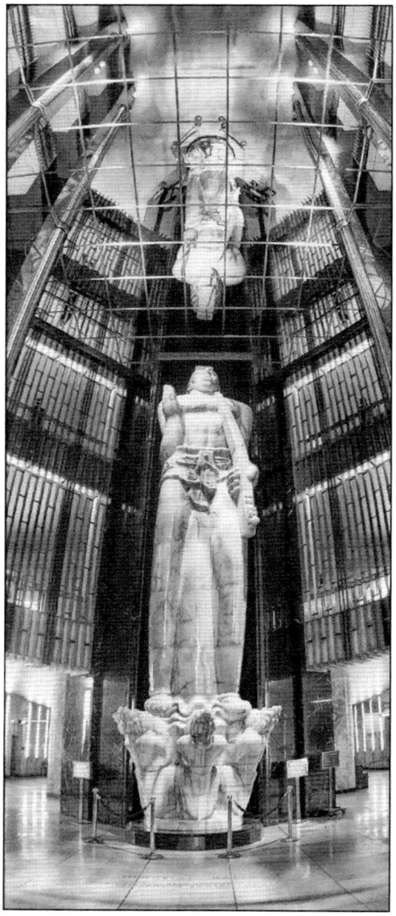

The centerpiece of city hall's atrium is a 36-foot-tall statue carved in Mexican onyx originally known as the *Indian God of Peace*. In the 1990s, his name was changed to *Visions of Peace*. To longtime city hall denizens, he is known affectionately as "Onyx John." (Courtesy of Visit St. Paul.)

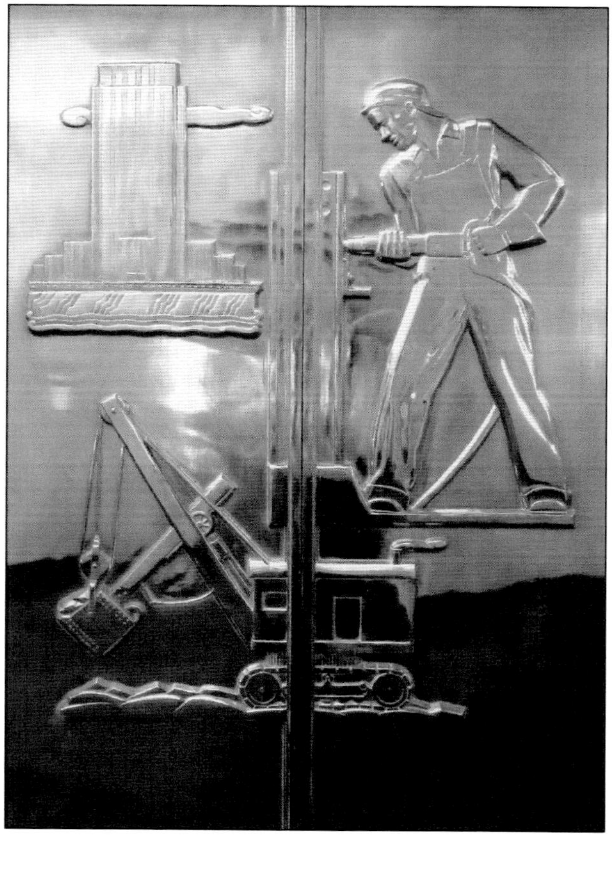

Each of city hall's six bronze elevator doors illustrates a theme from St. Paul history. This door depicts a construction worker with an image of city hall in the background. The bronze doors were designed by New York artist Albert Stewart.

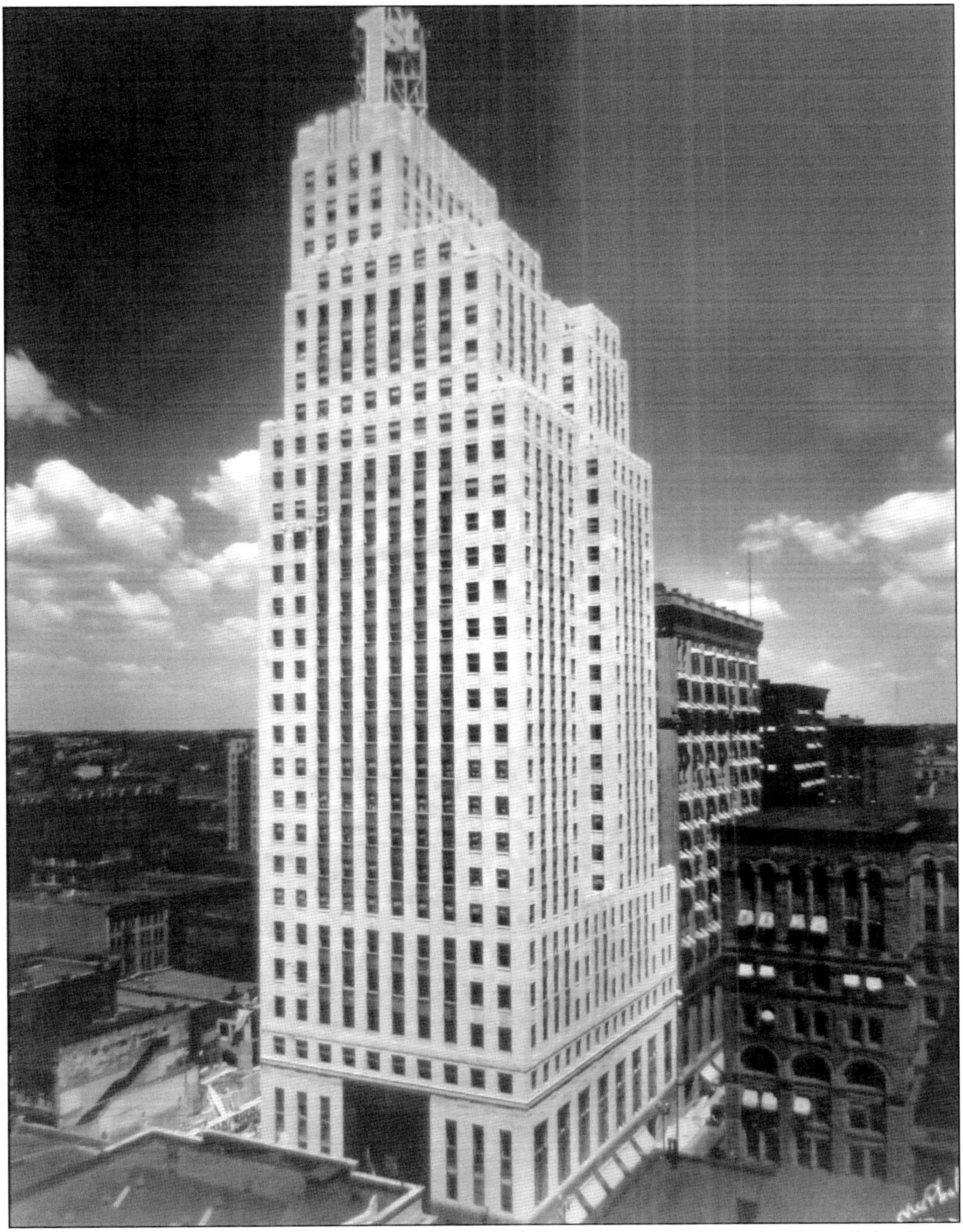

Like St. Paul City Hall, the First National Bank Building was completed at the start of the Great Depression. With its series of setbacks, the Art Deco bank building resembles the Manhattan skyscrapers that were being built at the same time. First National Bank has evolved into a new financial entity known as US Bank, but the huge "1st" sign on top of the building remains a major St. Paul landmark.

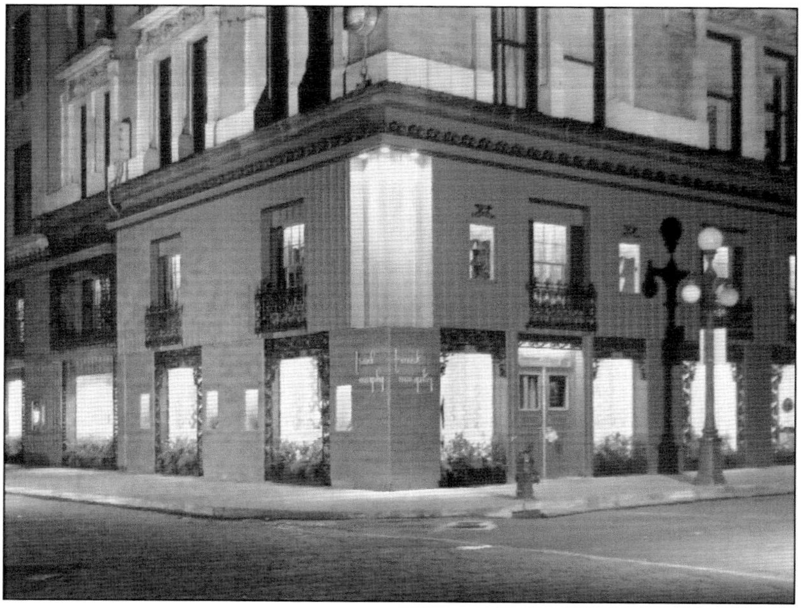

Frank Murphy was downtown St. Paul's home of high fashion from 1931 to 1997. The store, at Fifth and St. Peter Streets, was known for its designer clothing, sold at marked-down prices during the annual "Give Away" sale. An Italian restaurant now occupies the former Frank Murphy site.

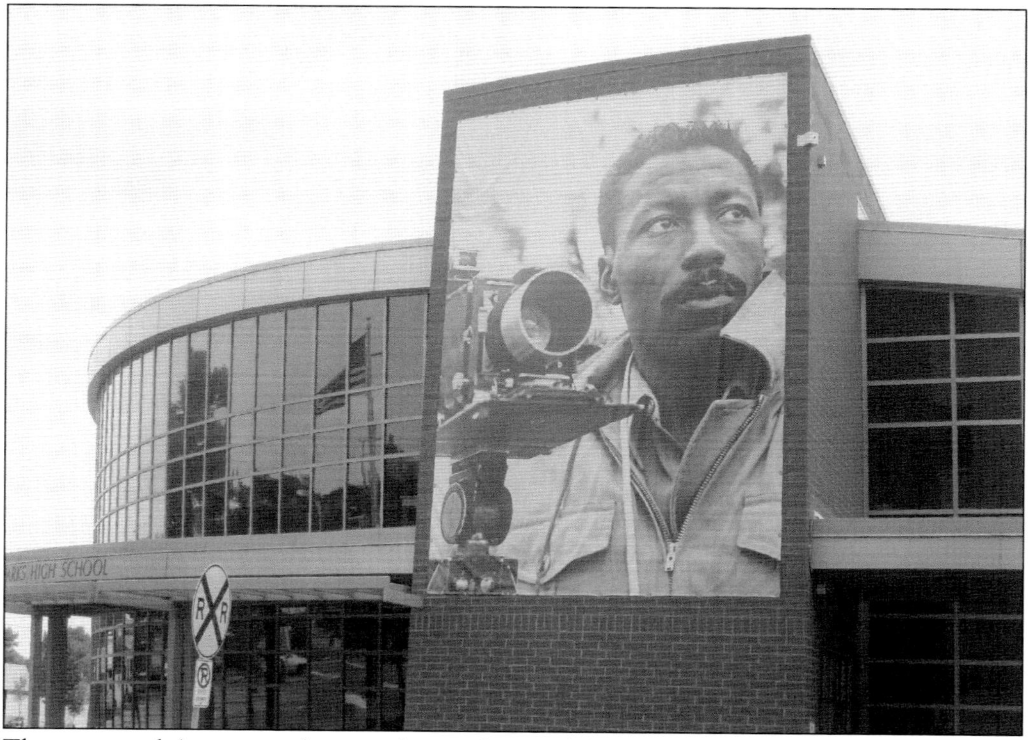

The renowned American photographer, author, and film director Gordon Parks launched his fashion photography career in 1938 when he was able to display his early photographs at the Frank Murphy store. Parks credited Murphy's wife, Madeline, with giving him a chance to prove himself as a fashion photographer. Parks was later honored by the City of St. Paul when it named one of its high schools for him. (Author's collection.)

Roy Wilkins Auditorium was originally known as the St. Paul Auditorium when it was built in 1932. The 5,000-seat civic arena was designed by St. Paul's municipal architect, Clarence Wigington. In 1985, the auditorium was named for the renowned civil rights leader, who had close ties to St. Paul.

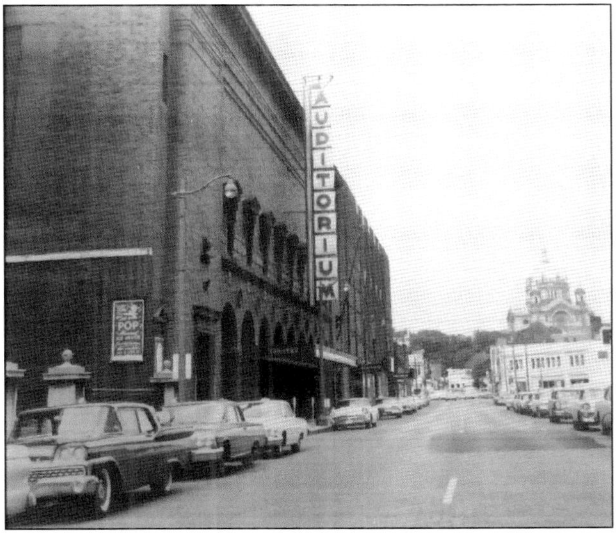

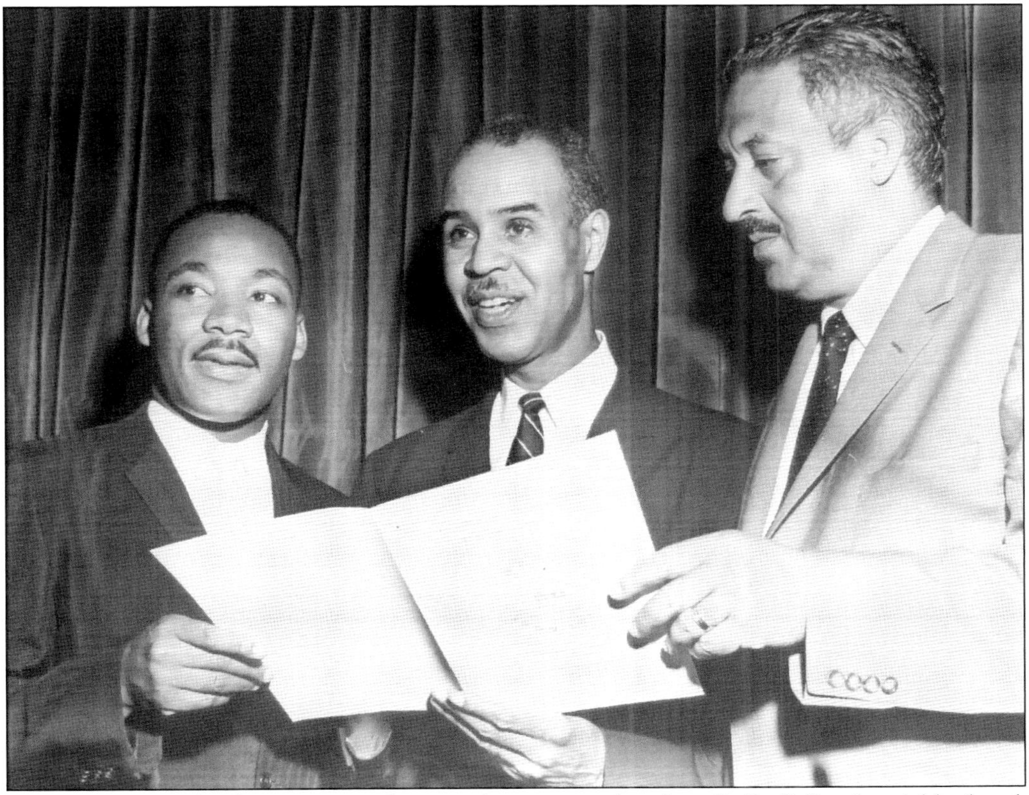

Roy Wilkins spent his formative years living with an aunt and uncle in St. Paul's Rondo neighborhood. He graduated from the University of Minnesota in 1923 and worked as a journalist before moving to New York City and joining the staff of the National Association for the Advancement of Colored People. Wilkins served in leadership roles at the NAACP in the 1950s and 1960s, as the civil rights movement was gaining momentum. He is shown with Martin Luther King Jr. (left) and Thurgood Marshall (right).

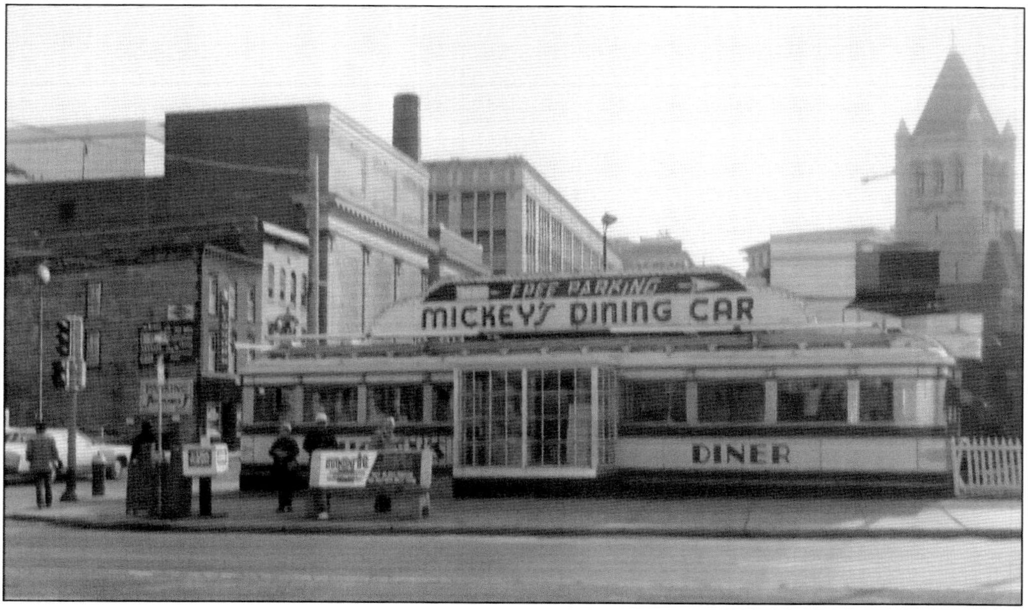

One of downtown St. Paul's most iconic landmarks, Mickey's Diner has occupied the same site on West Seventh Street since 1939. The Art Deco diner, built to resemble a railroad dining car, is open 24 hours a day, 365 days a year. *Gourmet* magazine has named Mickey's one of America's top 10 diners. It has been featured in several Hollywood films, included *The Mighty Ducks*, *Jingle All the Way*, and *A Prairie Home Companion*.

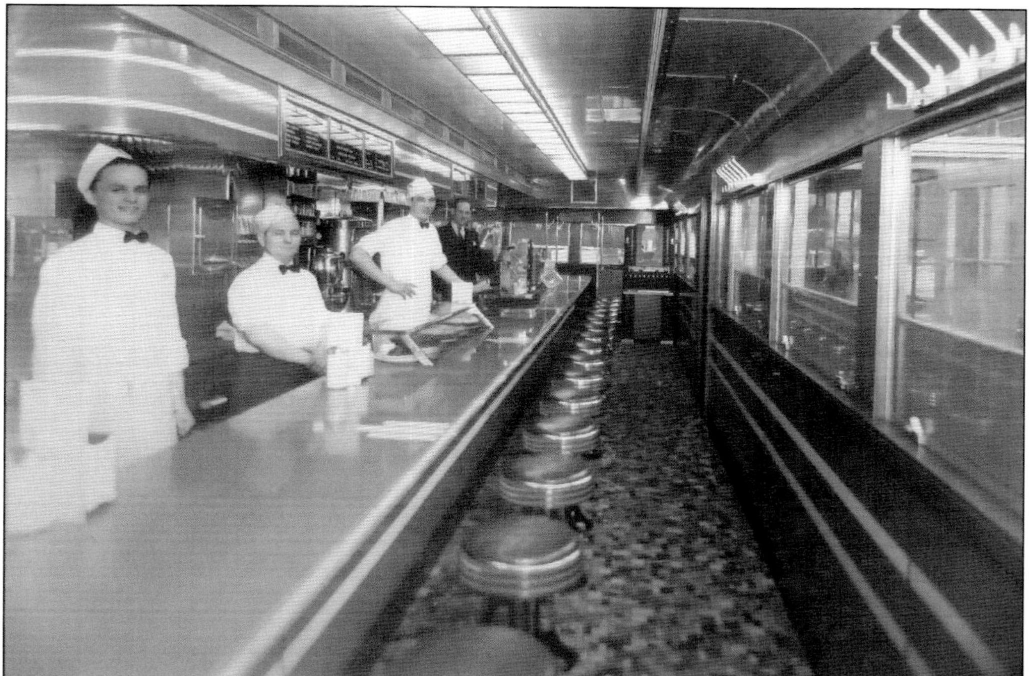

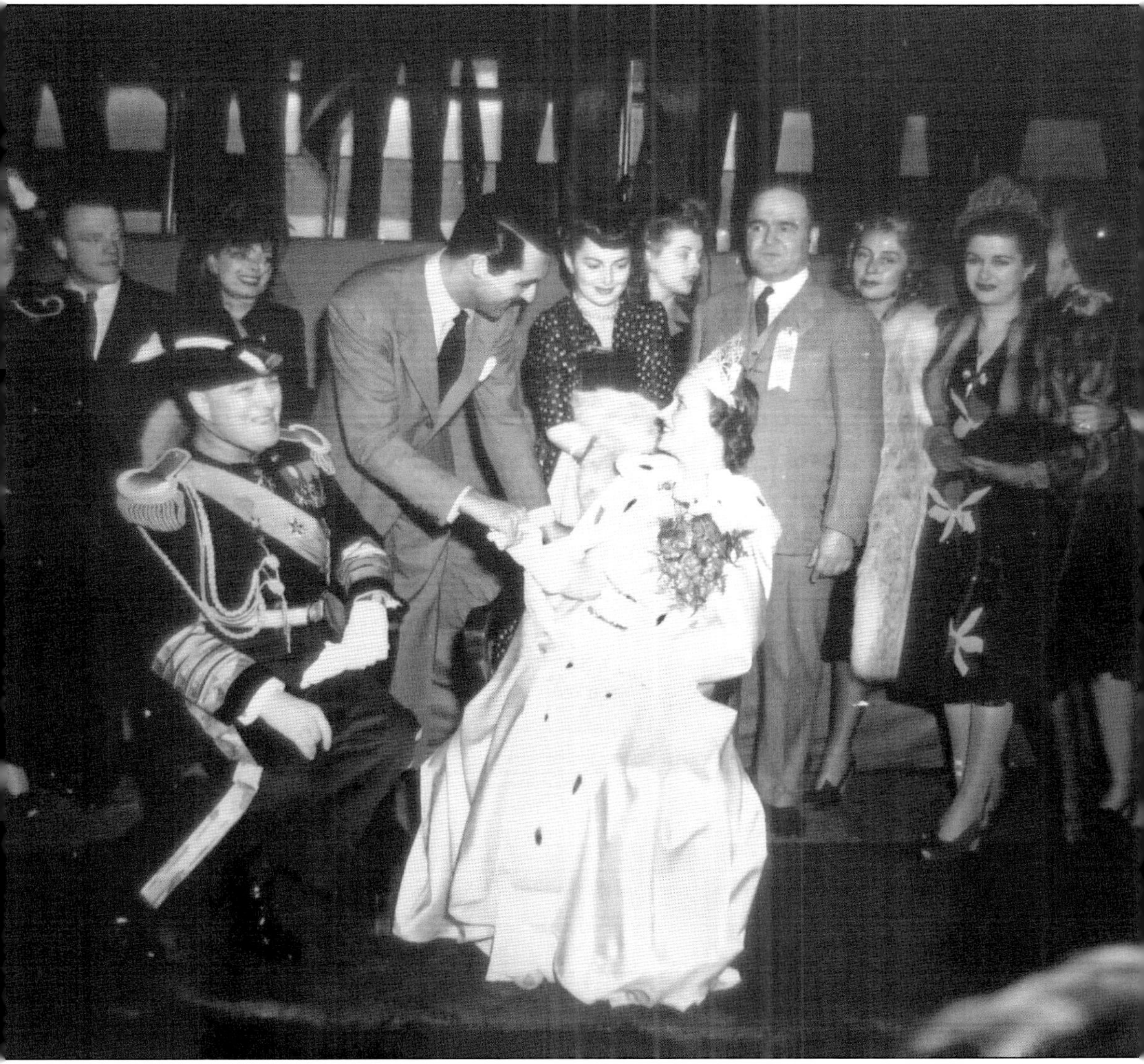

During 1942, a group of Hollywood movie stars toured the country drumming up support for the Red Cross and other World War II home front services. This photograph shows Cary Grant greeting St. Paul's Winter Carnival royalty. Others in Grant's group include Joan Blondell, James Cagney, Claudette Colbert, and Olivia DeHavilland.

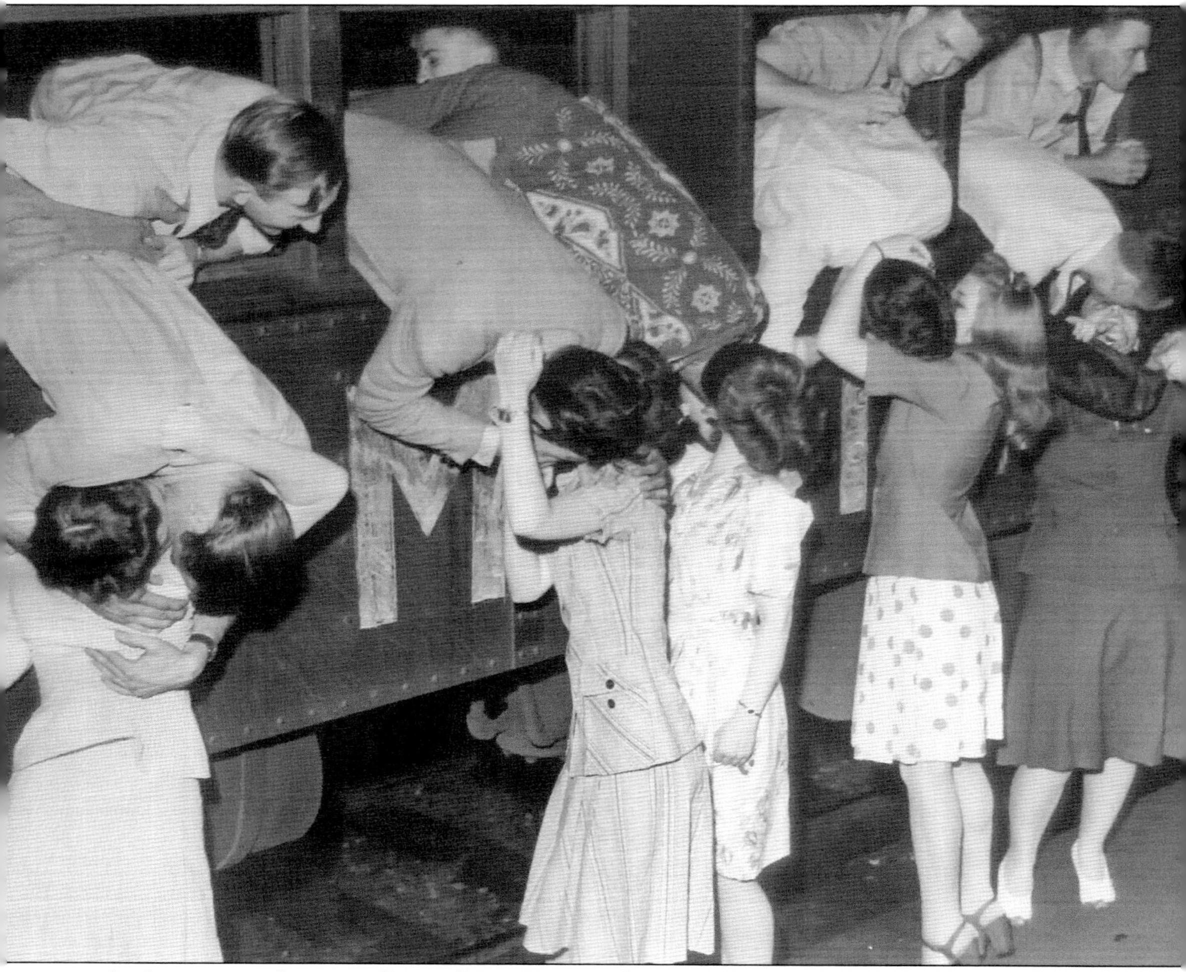

As their train is about to pull out of Union Depot, these Marine recruits are receiving an affectionate sendoff from the members of St. Paul's Semper Fidelis Club. Still dressed in their civilian clothes, these young men have not yet received the standard Marine haircut.

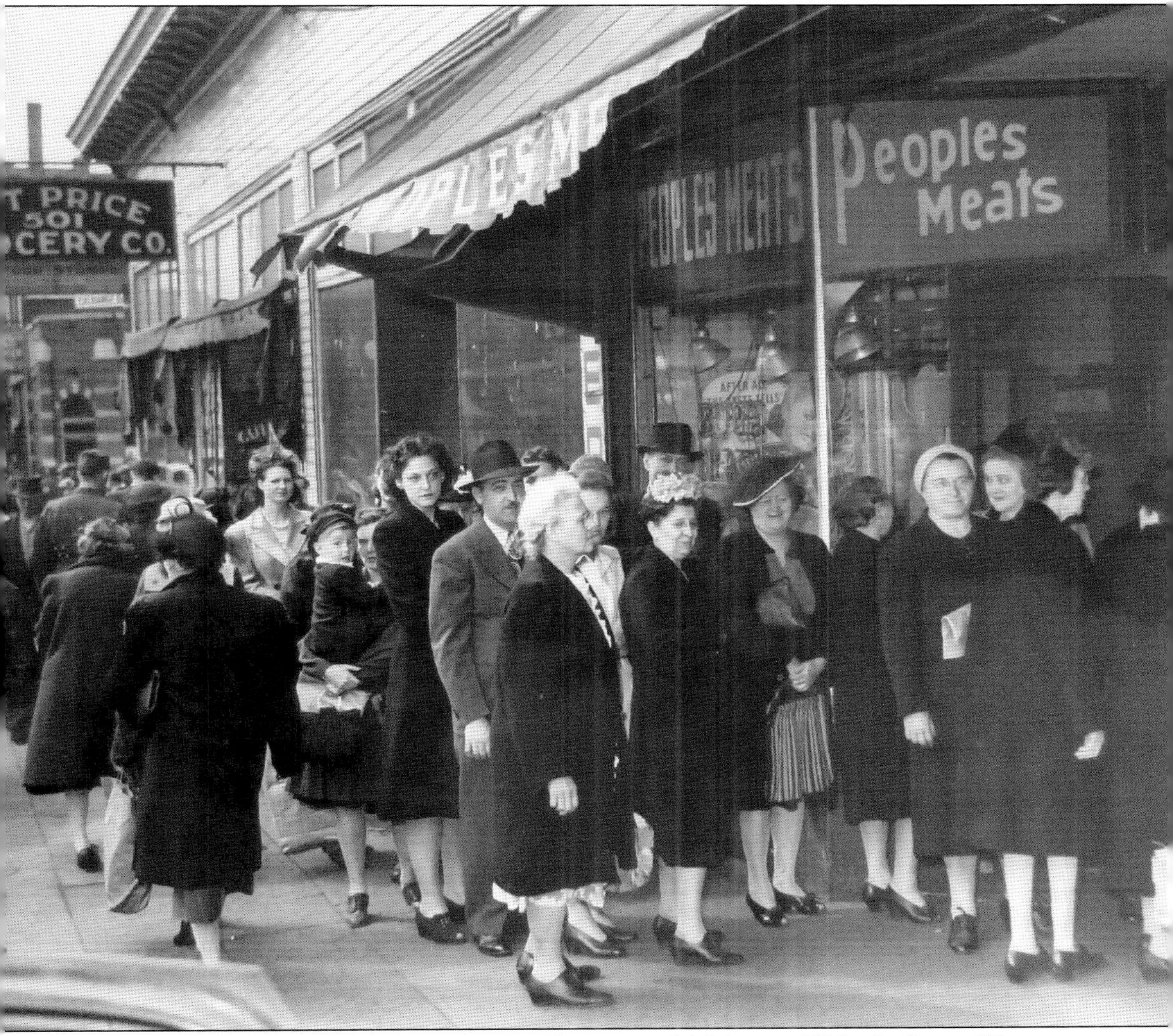

This 1945 photograph shows people lining up to shop at People's Meats on Wabasha Street. Wartime rationing limited the availability of meat for Americans on the home front. The proprietor of People's only let a few customers in his shop at a time to prevent overcrowding. These St. Paulites are waiting patiently for their turn to enter.

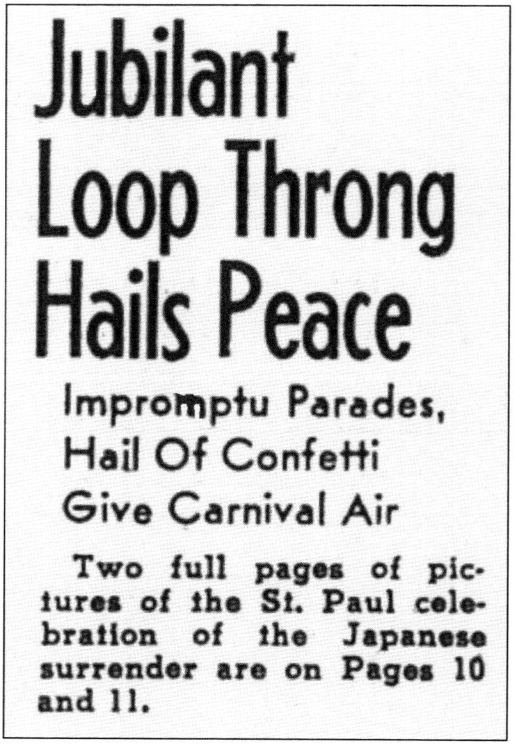
Jubilant Loop Throng Hails Peace

Impromptu Parades, Hail Of Confetti Give Carnival Air

Two full pages of pictures of the St. Paul celebration of the Japanese surrender are on Pages 10 and 11.

At first, the downtown streets were calm when word reached St. Paul that the war was over on VJ Day, August 14, 1945. "But after the first shock of the announcement wore off, the crowd began to thaw out and a carnival spirit took over," the *Pioneer Press* reported. (Courtesy of the University of Minnesota Library.)

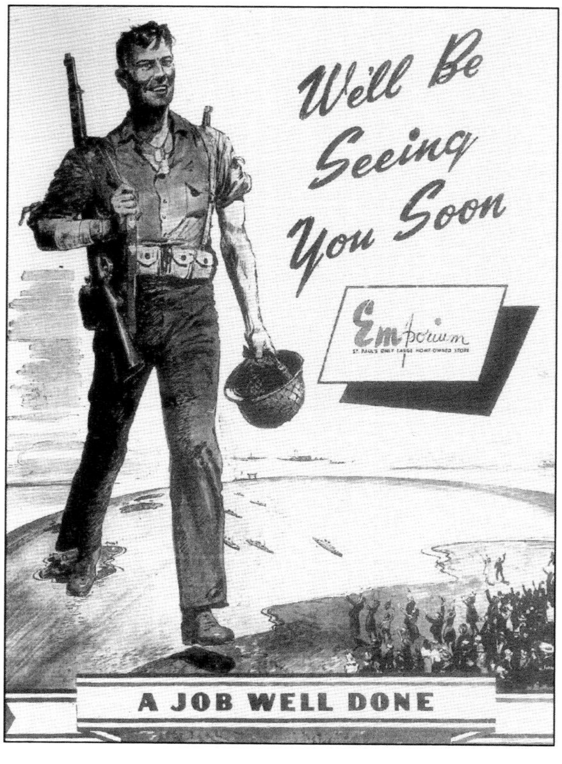

The Emporium Department Store looks forward to the return of St. Paul servicemen in this VJ Day advertisement. Other major St. Paul businesses used their ad space in the city's daily papers on VJ Day to celebrate the end of World War II.

Four

CHALLENGING TIMES

Downtown retained its role as St. Paul's major retail center up through the early postwar years. An economic boom following the end of the war helped fill downtown streets with throngs of shoppers who flocked to the major downtown department stores. But the department store era was about to come to an end. St. Paulites would soon abandon downtown to shop at the new suburban centers that provided acres of free parking.

Downtown's economic decline was exacerbated by St. Paul's negative public image. Civic boosters continued to be embarrassed by a *Fortune* magazine article that described their city as "cramped, hilly and stagnant," with "the atmosphere of a place that had grown old."

By the early 1960s, St. Paul civic leaders finally mobilized in an effort to reverse the negative trends affecting the city's central business district. That effort led to the Capitol Centre development, a federally funded urban renewal project. Capital Centre cleared away many of the aging, obsolete commercial buildings in the heart of downtown.

While Capitol Centre brought new, more modern office buildings to the city's urban core, the new buildings, in and of themselves, did not rejuvenate downtown as many hoped they might. That rejuvenation would not occur until the 1970s, when community leaders found new ways to restore downtown's central role in the city's community life.

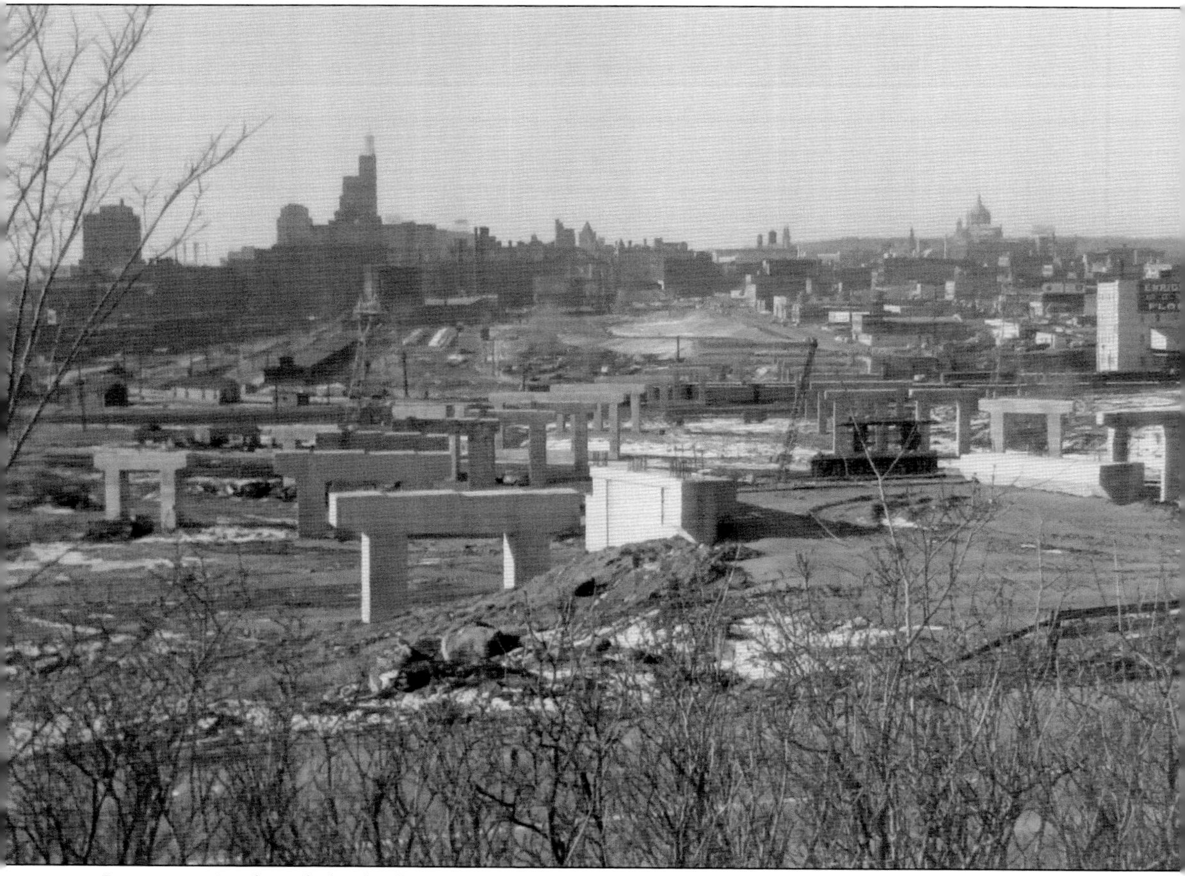

Interstate 94 demolished a large swath of St. Paul's historic commercial core to make room for a freeway link that connected the city's downtown with its counterpart in Minneapolis. The 11-mile link opened in 1968 at a cost of $80 million. Today, I-94 separates the Minnesota State Capitol from St. Paul's commercial core.

Field Schlick, one of St. Paul's most fashionable retailers, got an updated look in 1949 when this new front was installed on its 1920s-era building. The downtown store traced its history to 1856, when Daniel Ingersoll and T.C. Field established a dry goods store at Third and Wabasha Streets. Later, Frank Schlick joined the business as a partner. In 1897, the store became known as Field Schlick.

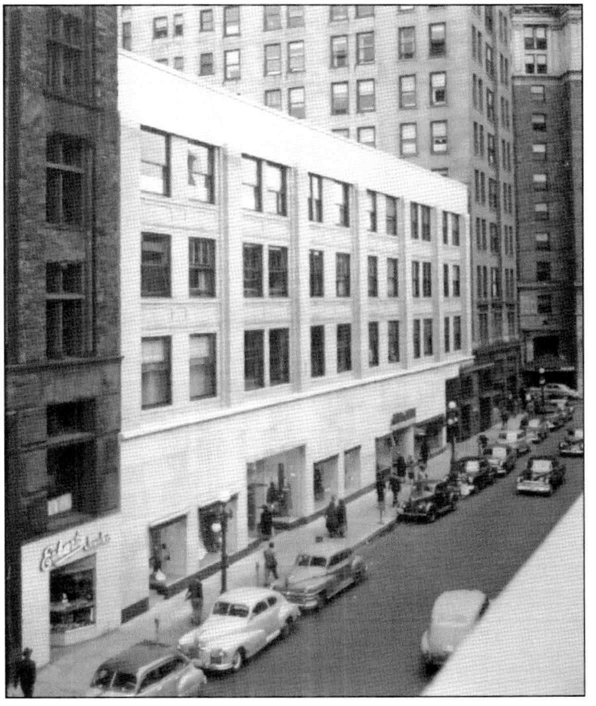

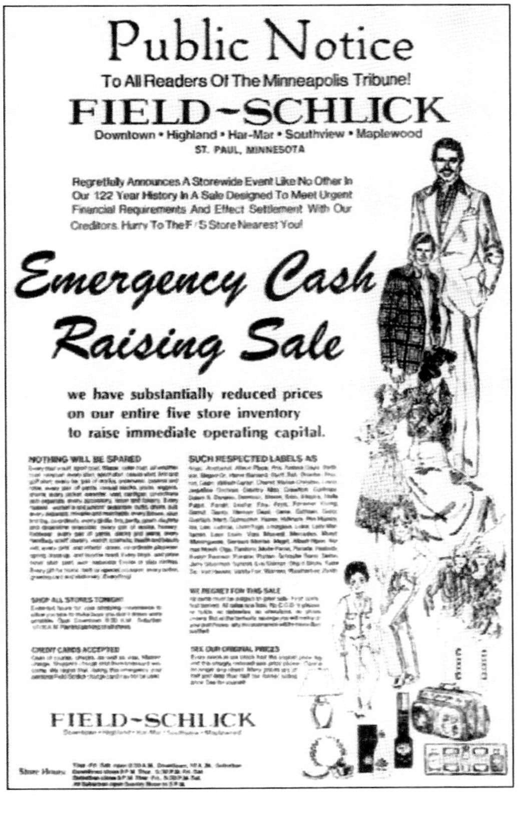

Field Schlick held on through the 1970s. However, by the end of that decade, St. Paul's longtime fashion leader was in deep financial trouble. In April 1979, Field Schlick announced that it was holding an emergency sale to raise cash and settle with its creditors. But the sale did little to help the 120-year-old store make a financial turnaround. By the end of 1979, Field Schlick was gone.

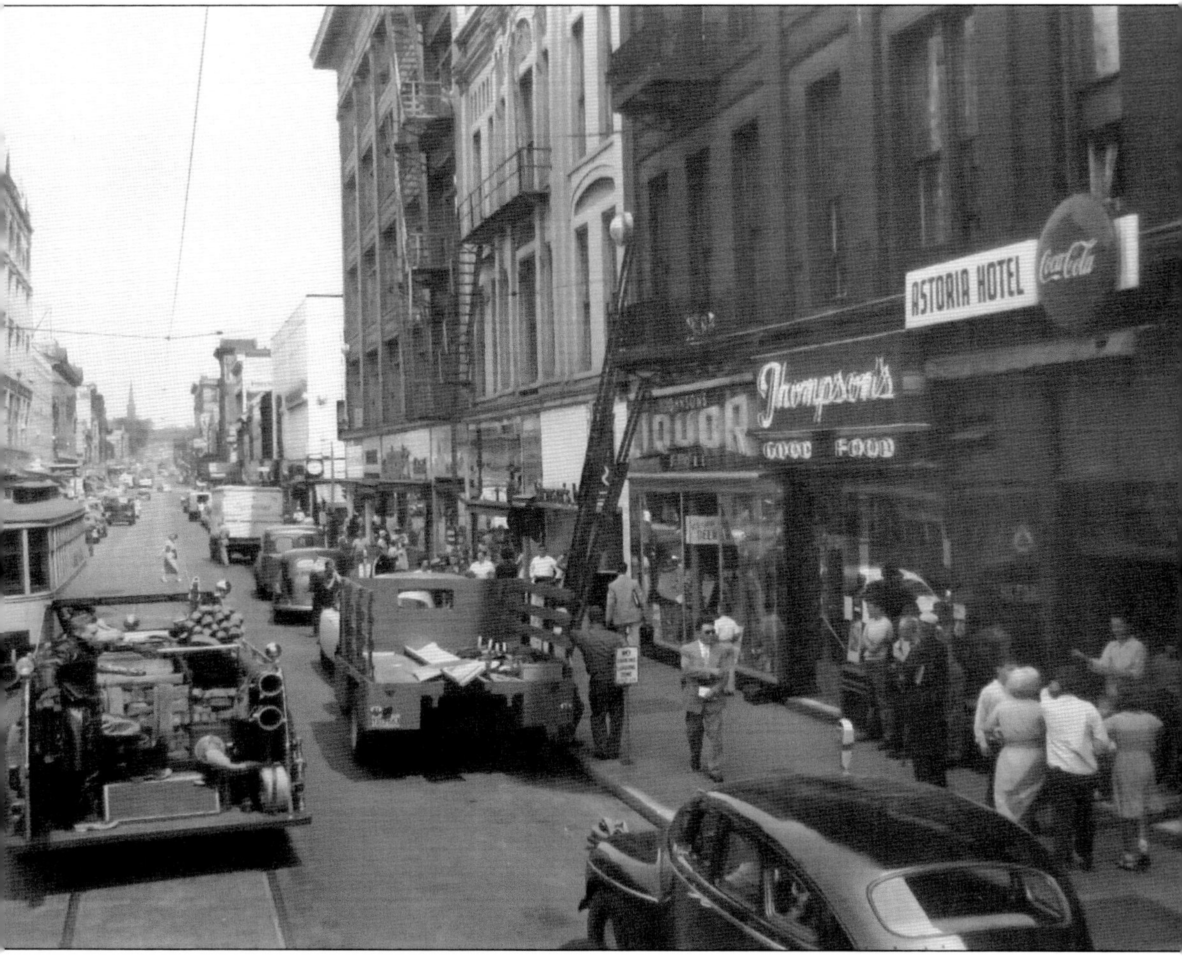

This stretch of Wabasha was already looking down at the heels when this photograph was taken in the early 1940s. The Astoria Hotel, above the liquor store, had seen better days. Later, the hotel and the rest of the block were demolished to make room for the Capitol Centre urban renewal project. Today, this block is part of the plaza in front of the former headquarters for the Ecolab company.

In 1941, downtown was still the place to go to see the latest Hollywood films. That year, moviegoers had their choice of 11 different downtown theaters. The Strand, on the left, opened in 1922. Across the street, the Riviera opened in 1929. But the era of the movie palaces was about to end.

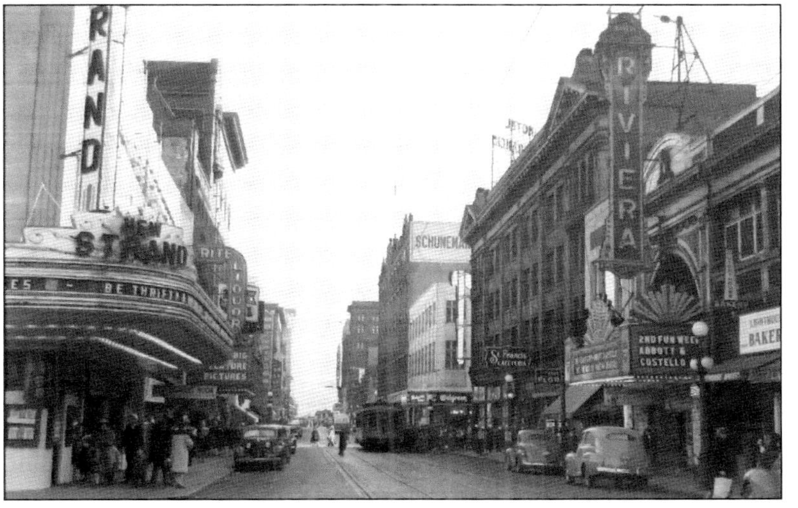

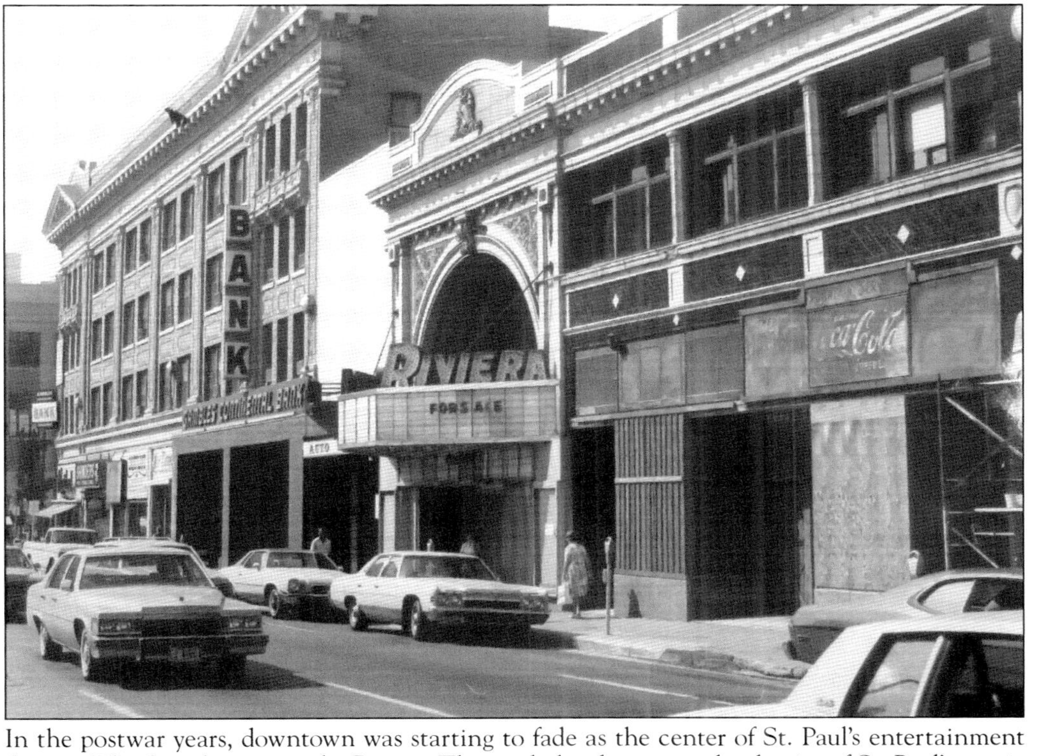

In the postwar years, downtown was starting to fade as the center of St. Paul's entertainment district. The for-sale sign on the Riviera Theater helps document the demise of St. Paul's movie palaces. By 1980, all of the downtown theaters were gone, victims of changing tastes and economics. The empty storefront next to the Riviera points up the economic malaise affecting downtown St. Paul during those years.

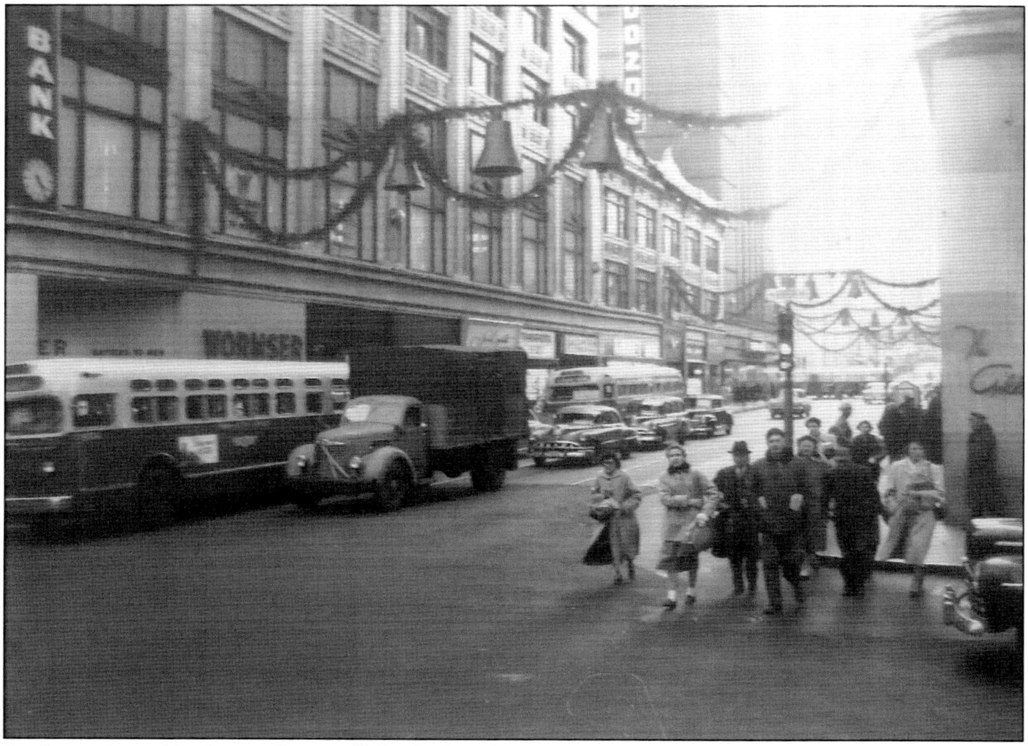

In the early 1950s, St. Paulites still flocked to downtown to do their Christmas shopping. But the allure of the suburban shopping centers would soon reduce the customer base for the downtown department stores. One by one, the downtown stores would close, victims of economic forces beyond their control.

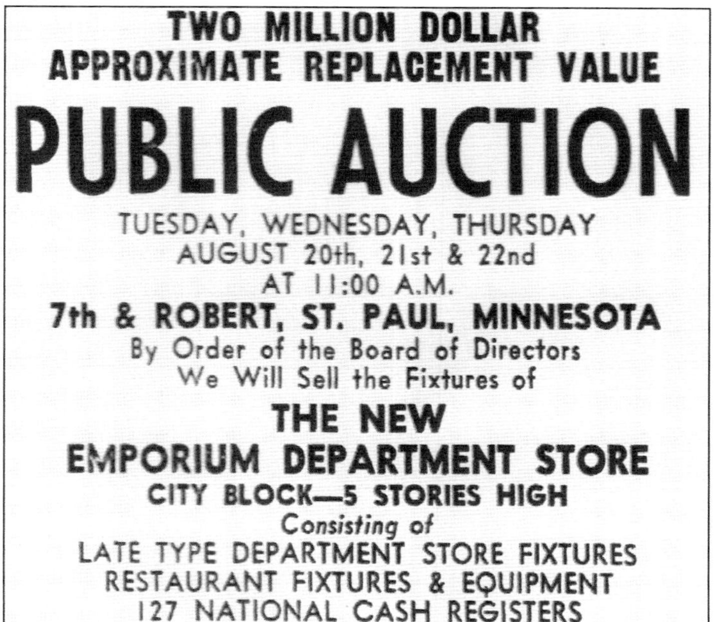

TWO MILLION DOLLAR
APPROXIMATE REPLACEMENT VALUE

PUBLIC AUCTION

TUESDAY, WEDNESDAY, THURSDAY
AUGUST 20th, 21st & 22nd
AT 11:00 A.M.

7th & ROBERT, ST. PAUL, MINNESOTA

By Order of the Board of Directors
We Will Sell the Fixtures of

THE NEW
EMPORIUM DEPARTMENT STORE

CITY BLOCK—5 STORIES HIGH

Consisting of

LATE TYPE DEPARTMENT STORE FIXTURES
RESTAURANT FIXTURES & EQUIPMENT
127 NATIONAL CASH REGISTERS

The Emporium was an early victim of the suburban boom. A group of investors tried rescuing the mammoth downtown store on Robert Street but to no avail. A public auction notice in 1968 documented the demise of this once-mighty retail giant. (Author's collection.)

In 1954, the TCRT decided to eliminate its streetcars and replace them with buses. TCRT's owners maintained that the trolleys were no longer profitable, in part because streetcar track maintenance costs were escalating. The buses that replaced the streetcars on St. Paul's narrow downtown streets only added to traffic congestion.

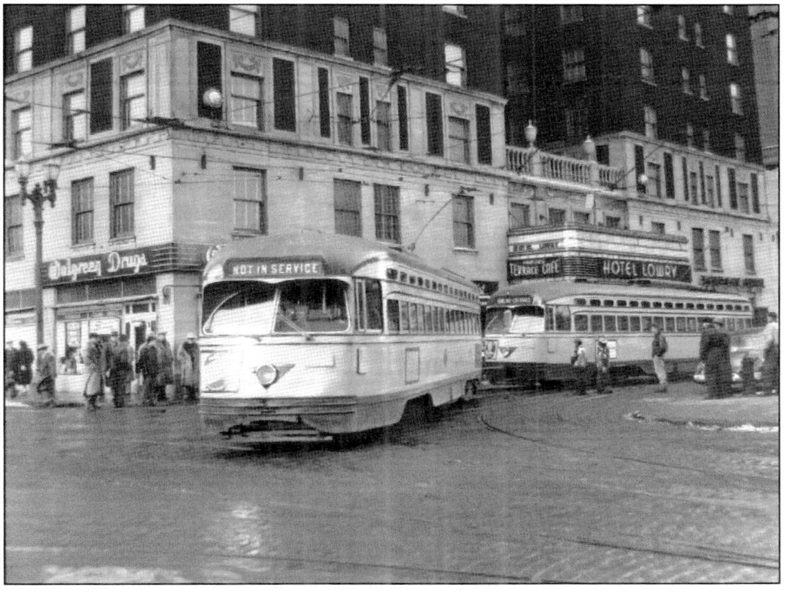

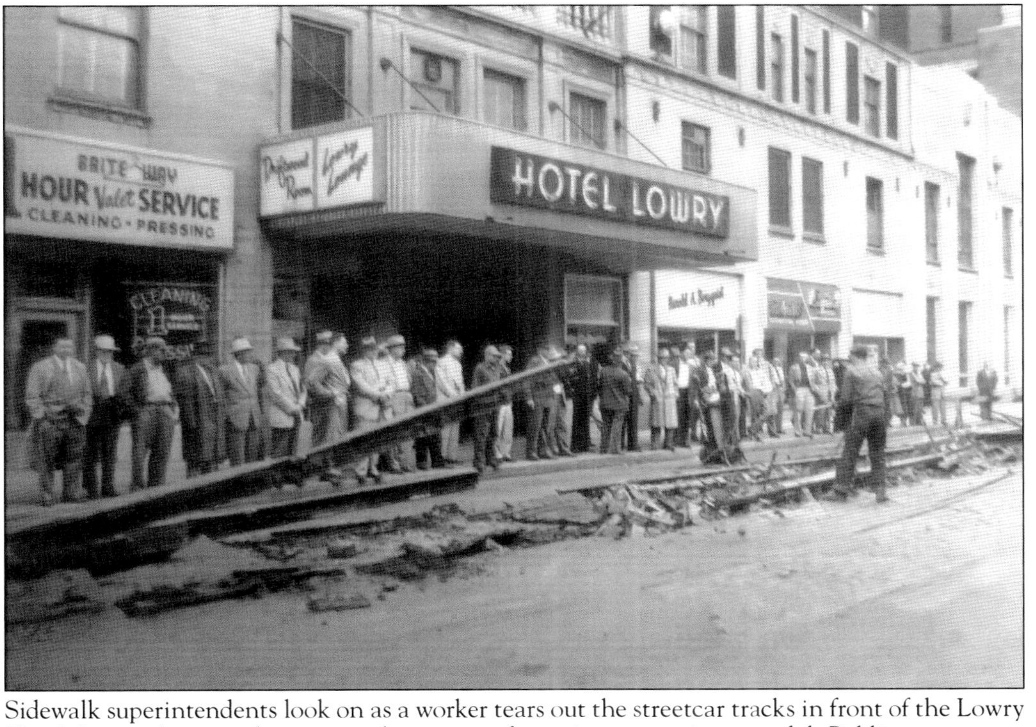

Sidewalk superintendents look on as a worker tears out the streetcar tracks in front of the Lowry Hotel. Later, these tracks were at the center of a major corruption scandal. Public prosecutors learned that TCRT's head, Fred Ossanna, had been receiving kickbacks from a local scrap dealer in exchange for the scrap metal. Ossanna and the dealer both served jail time for their parts in the scheme.

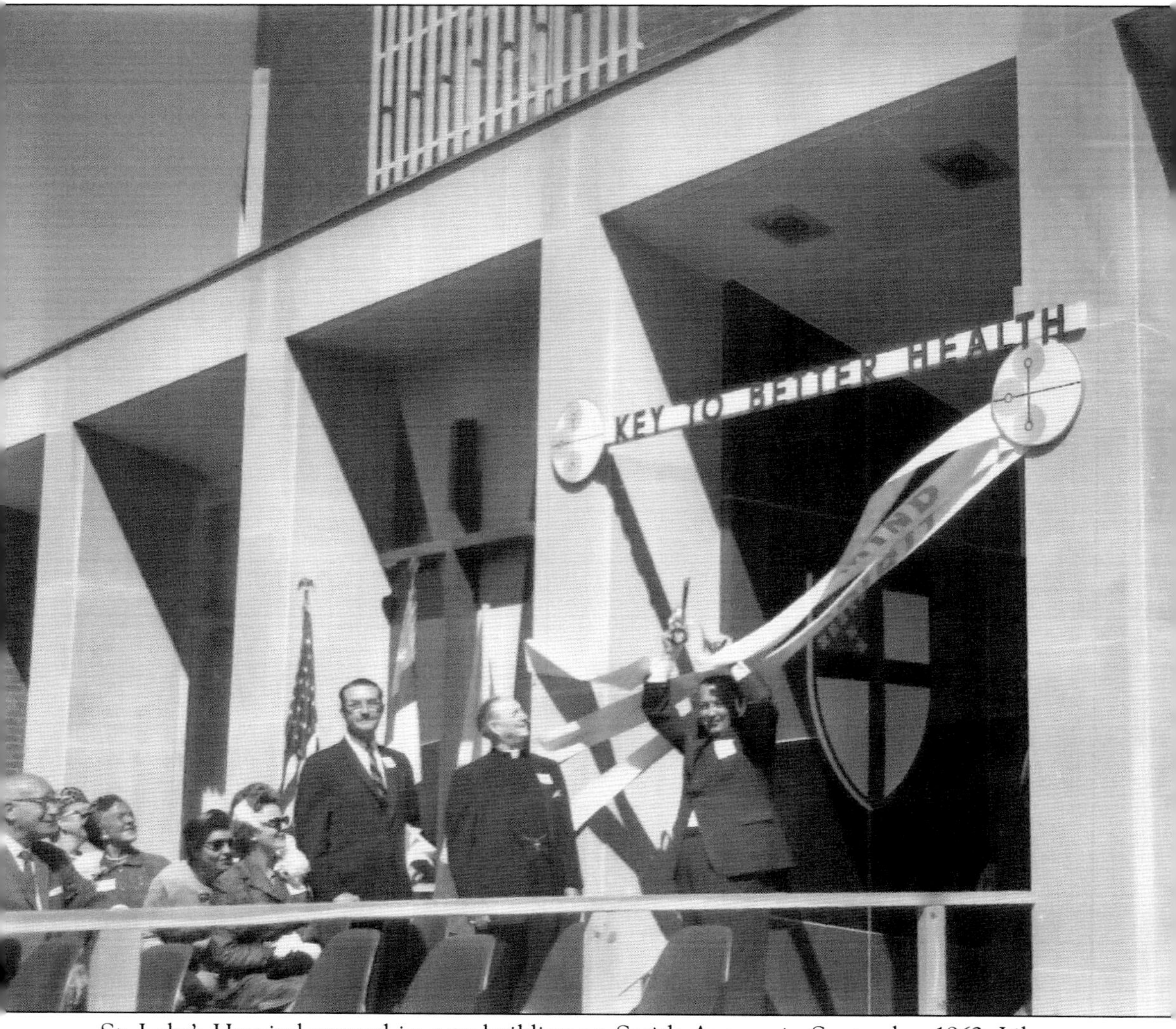

St. Luke's Hospital opened its new building on Smith Avenue in September 1962. Like many modern medical facilities, the downtown hospital underwent a series of organization changes during a history extending across three centuries. Originally known as Church Home and Hospital when it was established in 1857, St. Luke's became United Hospital in 1974, when it merged with Charles T. Miller Hospital. Today, United is part of the Allina hospital system.

This office building at 55 East Fifth Street was built in 1971 as part of St. Paul's Capitol Centre development. Capitol Centre was a federally funded urban renewal project intended to rejuvenate downtown by eliminating physically and economically obsolete structures, many dating to the late 19th century. The project covered a 12-block area in the heart of downtown. (Courtesy of Hennepin County Library Special Collections.)

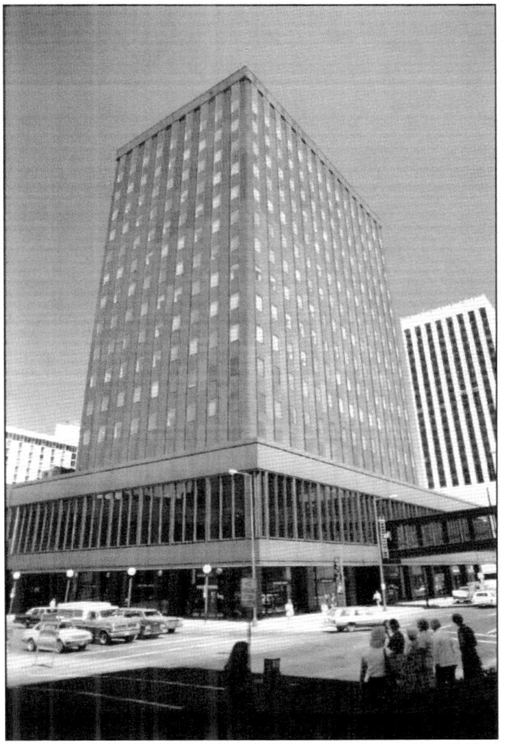

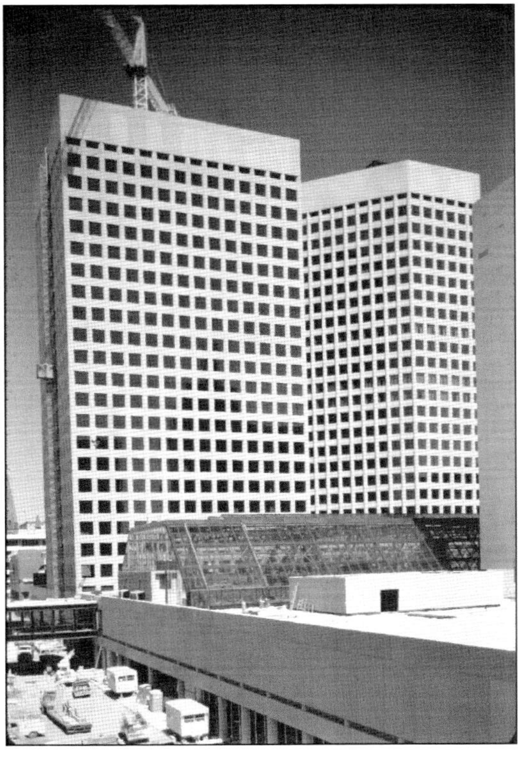

This multi-block development, known as Town Square, was intended to breathe new life into downtown St. Paul when it opened in 1980. The development included two office towers, a shopping mall, and an indoor park. While the office towers continued to attract tenants, the shopping center, anchored by a Donaldson's Department Store, was never successful. Donaldson's, along with most of the mall's other retail shops, eventually closed. (Courtesy of Hennepin County Library Special Collections.)

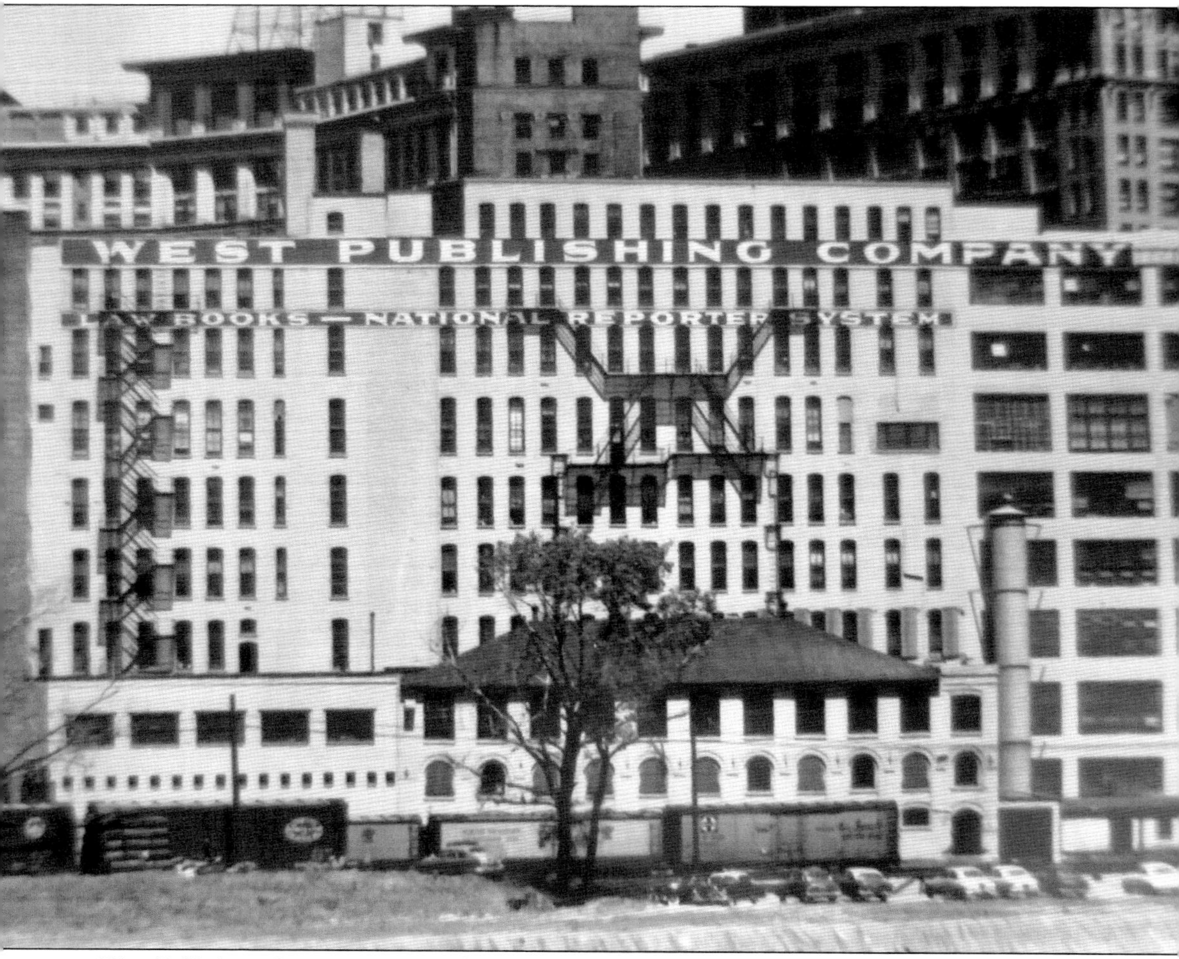

West Publishing Company occupied a prime downtown riverfront site in 1955, when this photograph was taken. At that time, West was the country's leading publisher of law books and other legal materials. When West Publishing was acquired by Canadian-based Thomson Reuters in the late 1990s, the company's headquarters had already relocated to suburban Eagan. The riverfront building later housed Ramsey County offices and was demolished in 2017.

In 1959, Minneapolis-based Dayton's purchased Schuneman's, a longtime St. Paul institution. For a time, the downtown store was known as Dayton's Schuneman's. In 1963, when Dayton's built its new suburban-style store on Wabasha Street, it demolished the original Schuneman's building. Later, Dayton's went through its own ownership and name changes. When the St. Paul store closed in 2013, it was part of the Macy's chain.

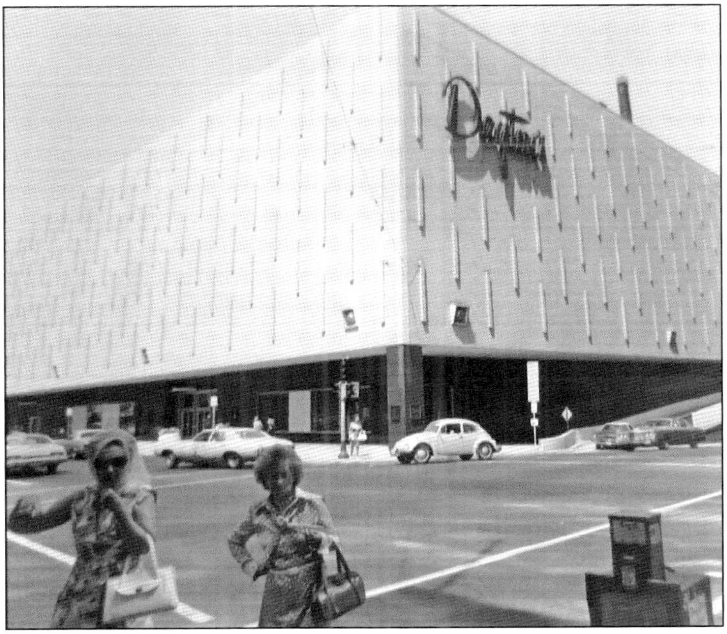

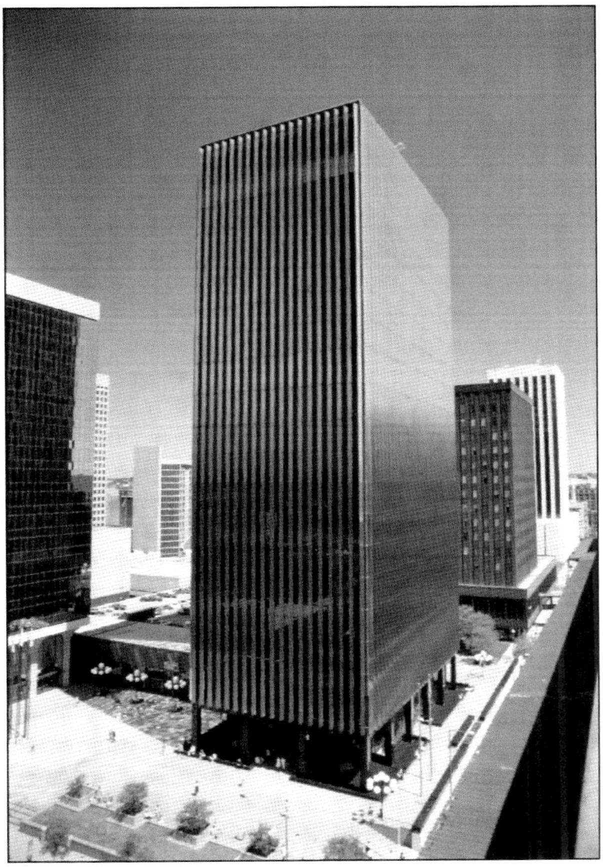

This 20-story office tower was built in 1968 as the headquarters for Ecolab, a St. Paul–based company that provides technology services and products. The company was originally known as Economics Laboratory and changed its name to Ecolab in 1986. In 2017, the building was sold to a local developer who has converted it to a multi-tenant building. Ecolab then relocated to another St. Paul office building. (Courtesy of Hennepin County Library Special Collections.)

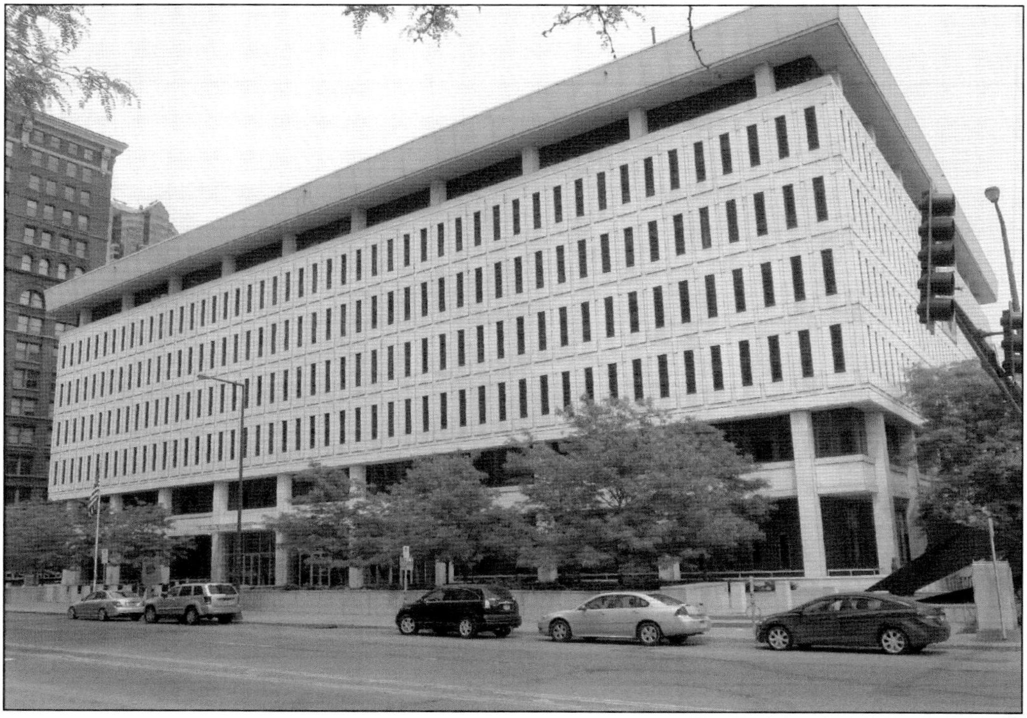

In the 1960s, federal officials decided to replace the aging US courthouse on Rice Park. This new federal court building, completed in 1967, was one of the early redevelopment projects in St. Paul's Capitol Centre urban renewal district. The building is named for Warren Burger, a St. Paul native who served as chief justice of the US Supreme Court from 1969 to 1986. (Author's collection.)

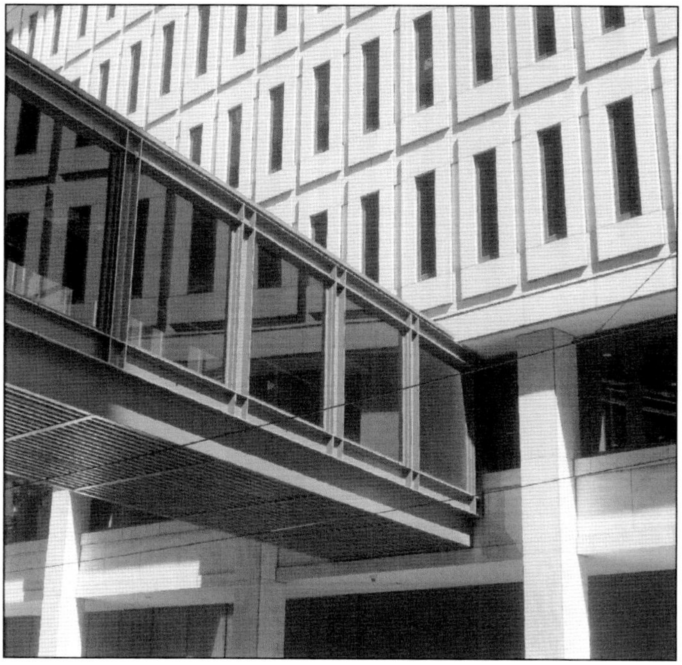

St. Paul built its first skyway in 1967. The second-story covered walkway connected the Burger Federal Building with Pioneer Building across Fourth Street. Unlike Minneapolis, where the skyways are built and maintained by the adjoining property owners, St. Paul's skyways are publicly owned and uniform in appearance. St. Paul's skyway system connects roughly 30 downtown blocks. (Author's collection.)

Five

Urban Revival

The restoration of St. Paul's castle-like federal building in the 1970s marked the start of an urban revival that would rescue downtown from its economic slide. A six-year restoration effort retained the building's distinctive atrium and repurposed the former post office and courthouse as a home for local arts organizations. Renamed Landmark Center, the former federal facility is one of a quartet of architecturally significant buildings facing St. Paul's historic Rice Park. The quartet also includes the Ordway Center for the Performing Arts, the St. Paul Hotel, and the George Latimer Central Library, which shares a site with the James J. Hill Reference Library.

At the north end of downtown, St. Paul's early commercial district, Lowertown, had fallen on hard times. Most of its 19th-century factories and warehouses were partially or completely vacant. A city partnership with a local philanthropic foundation was able to jumpstart a redevelopment effort to convert the still-sturdy buildings in Lowertown to loft apartments and condominiums. An early public square, rebuilt and renamed Mears Park, served as a catalyst for Lowertown's revival. An early overhaul of the historic park was not successful. It converted the square into a sterile, concrete-filled space that came to be known as "the Brickyard." In the 1990s, the Brickyard was replaced with a new plan for Mears Park that added trees, flower gardens, and a water feature in the form of a stream that meandered through the park.

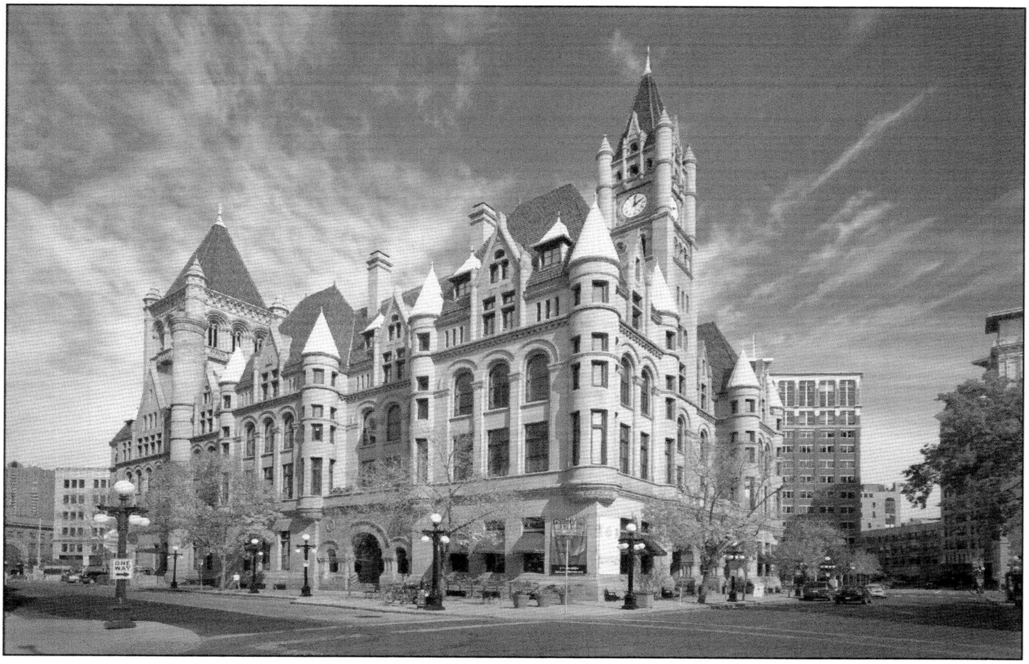

By 1950, the "Old Post Office," as it was then known, was dingy and half-empty. When the building was declared surplus property by the General Services Administration in 1969, plans were in the works to demolish it. Luckily, a group of dedicated preservationists was able to persuade the federal government and the city to save the building. After a multi-year restoration effort, the former federal building was reopened in 1978 and renamed Landmark Center. (Courtesy of Visit St. Paul.)

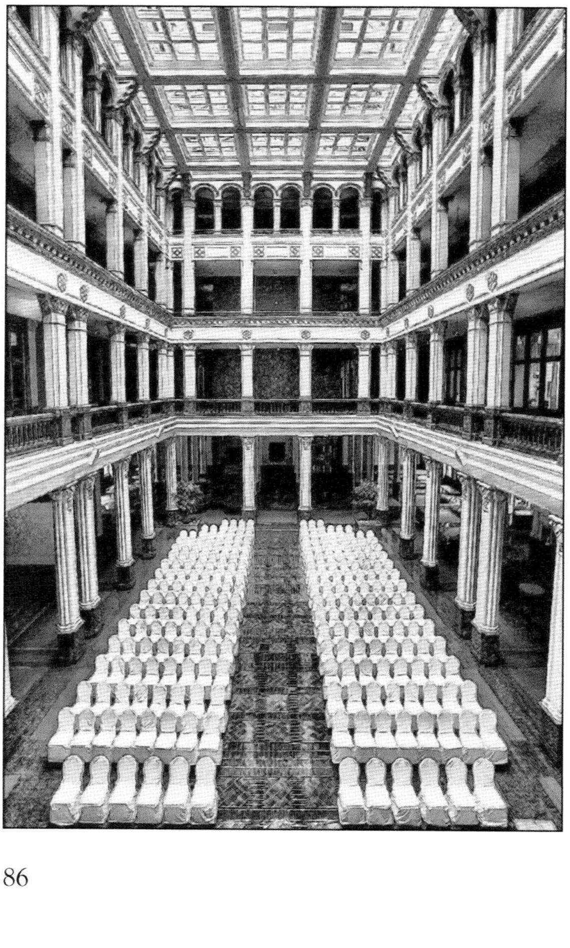

This dramatic atrium in Landmark Center, known as a *cortile*, is used frequently for festivals and other community events. It is also rented out for weddings and other private functions. When the building was a US post office, a drop ceiling was installed in the cortile, and the marble was covered with drab green paint. (Author's collection.)

Elizabeth Musser was the driving force behind the renovation and reuse of Landmark Center. As chair of the St. Paul Council of Arts and Science, she helped raise civic awareness of the need to preserve one of downtown's most significant architectural icons. Later, she oversaw the reconstruction of Landmark as chair of the nonprofit Minnesota Landmarks. This painting honoring Elizabeth Musser is displayed at Landmark Center's main entrance. (Author's collection.)

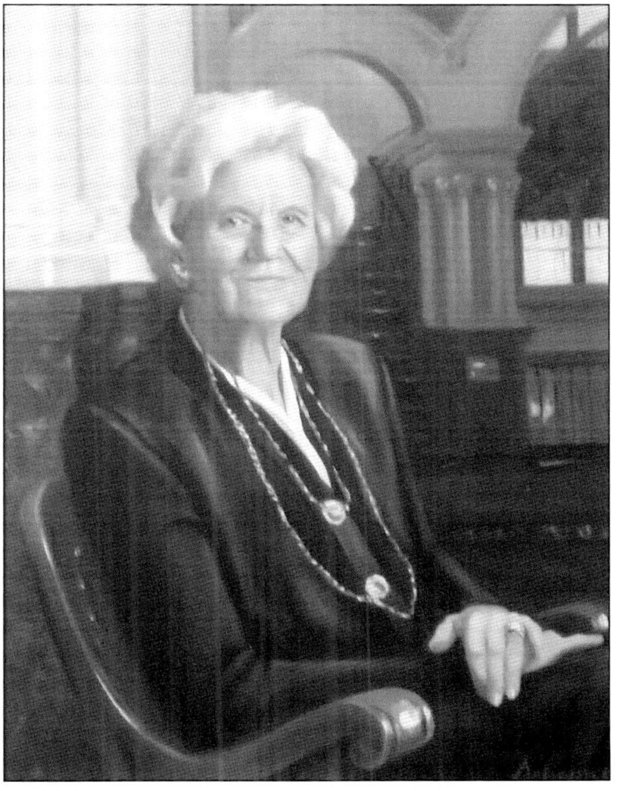

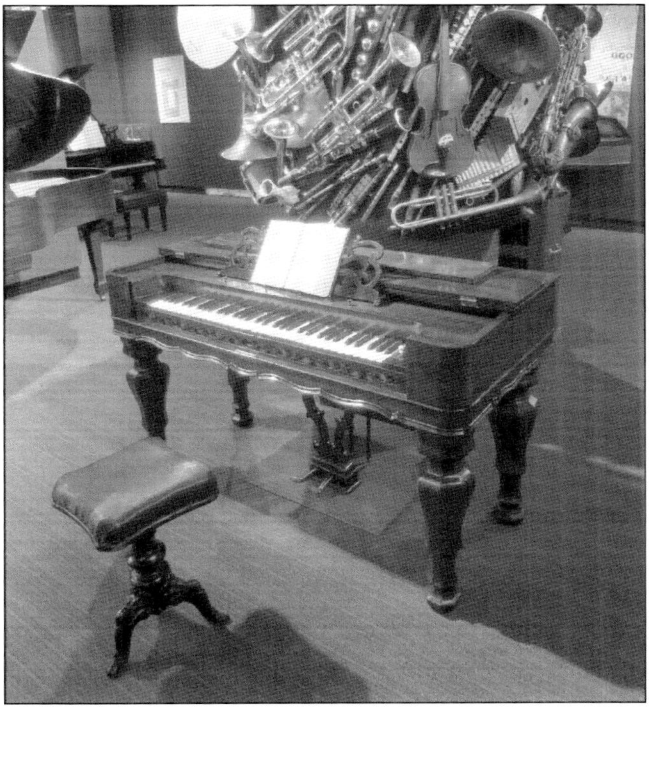

The Schubert Club, St. Paul's oldest musical organization, traces its history to the early 1880s, when a group of local women organized a club known as the Ladies Musicale. The group soon began sponsoring musical performances and changed its name to the Schubert Club to honor the German composer Franz Schubert. Landmark Center houses the club's museum. At the entrance to the museum, a swirl of musical instruments rises up in a dramatic cyclone-shaped sculpture. (Author's collection.)

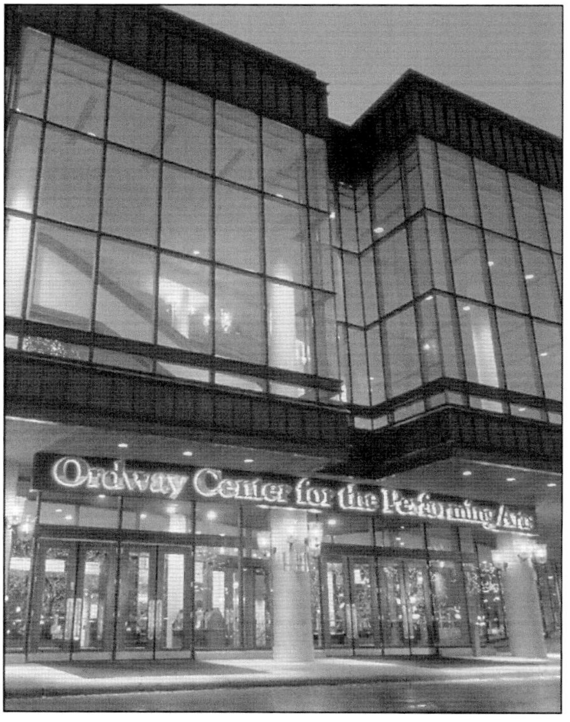

The Ordway Center for the Performing Arts completes the quartet of buildings that surround Rice Park. The building, which opened in 1985, was designed by the Boston architect Benjamin Thompson, a St. Paul native. With its sweeping stairway, the Ordway brings back some of the grandeur associated with the late-19th- and early-20th-century opera houses. The Ordway serves as the home of the St. Paul Chamber Orchestra, the Minnesota Opera, and the Schubert Club. (Courtesy of Visit St. Paul.)

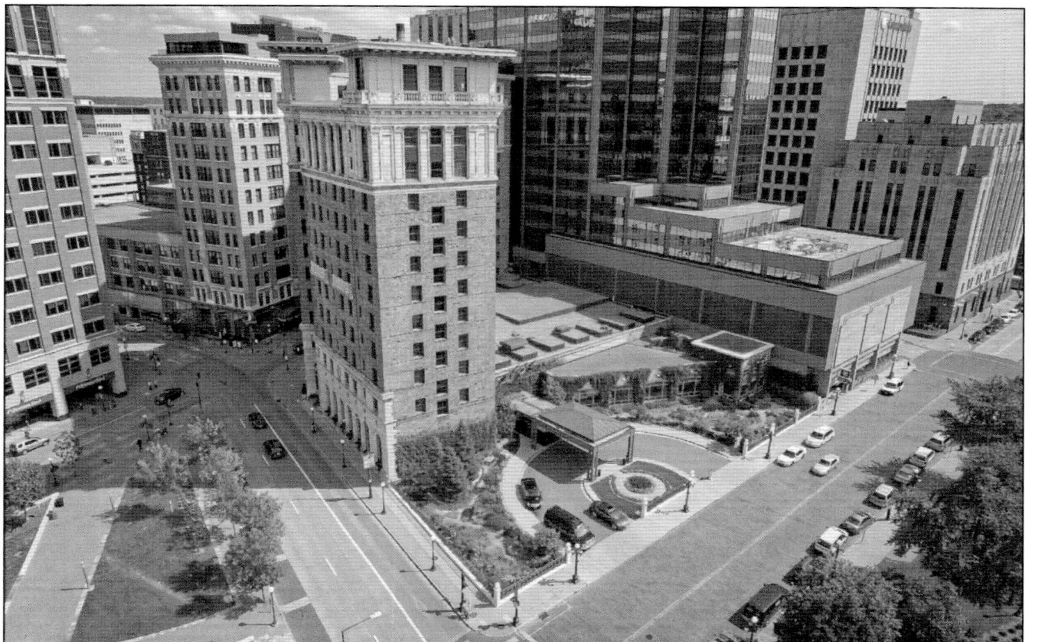

The St. Paul Hotel stood vacant for several years until 1983, when new owners purchased and renovated the downtown St. Paul landmark. As part of the restoration, the hotel's main entrance was moved from its original location on Fifth Street around the corner to Market Street, facing Rice Park. The hotel's St. Paul Grill is a popular gathering spot.

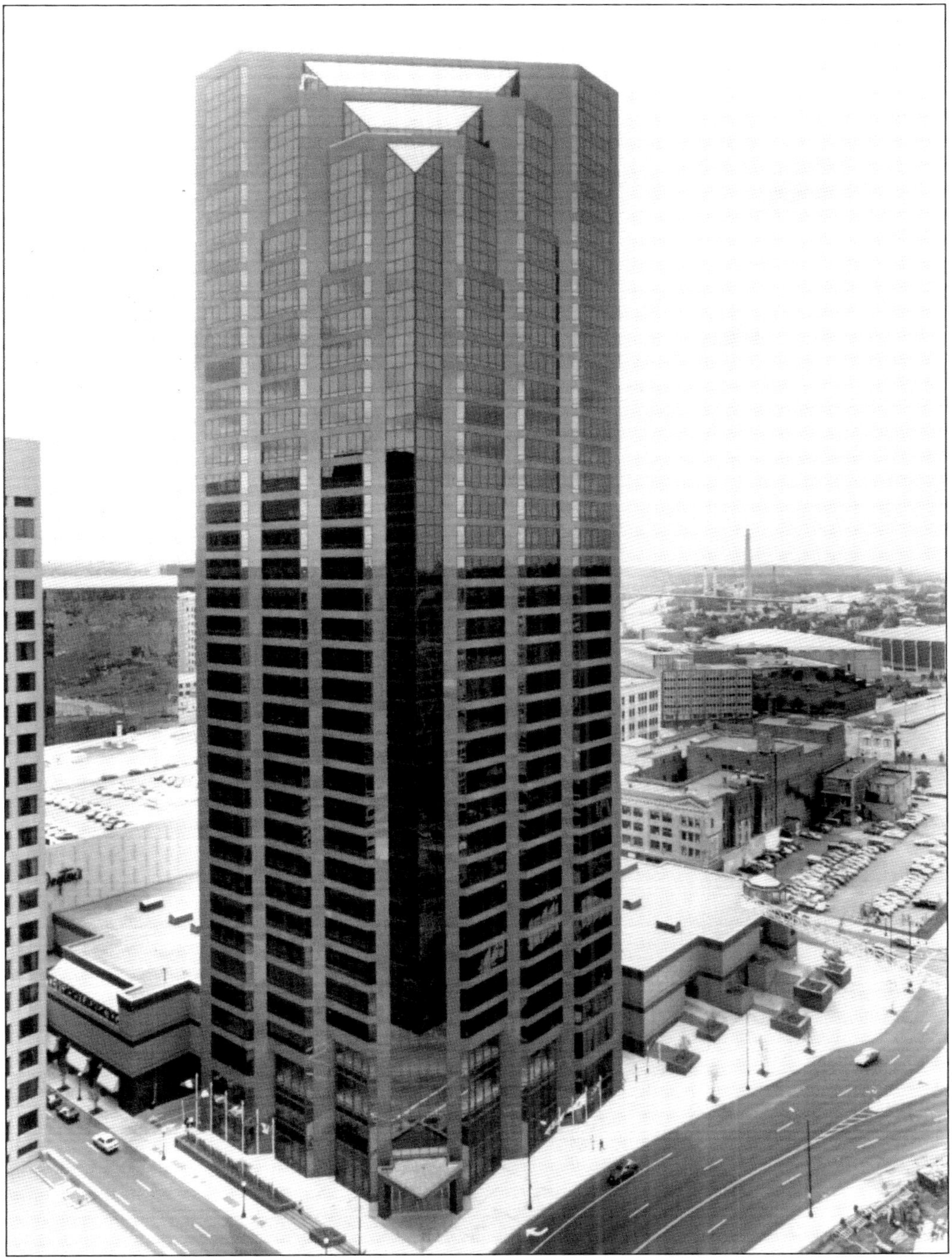

At 471 feet, the Minnesota World Trade Center was downtown St. Paul's tallest building when it opened in 1987. The building was intended to boost the state's role in international commerce, but it never lived up to its original name. In 2003, the building was renamed Wells Fargo Place for its largest tenant, Wells Fargo Bank. The 37-story skyscraper has retained its dominant position on the city's skyline. (Courtesy of the Ramsey County Historical Society.)

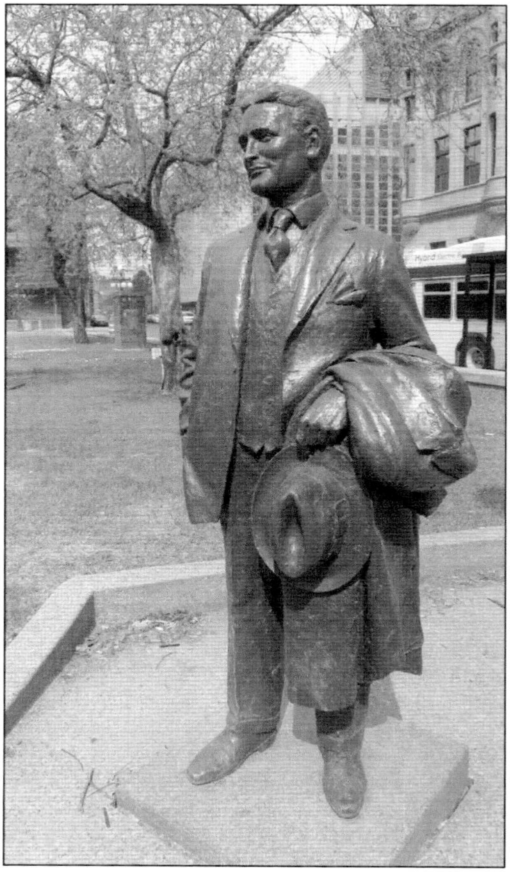

F. Scott Fitzgerald, one of Minnesota's most notable literary figures, launched his career while he was living in St. Paul's Ramsey Hill district. His first successful novel, *This Side of Paradise*, was based on a short story he wrote during his St. Paul days. Fitzgerald, or at least his statue, now has a permanent home in Rice Park. (Author's collection.)

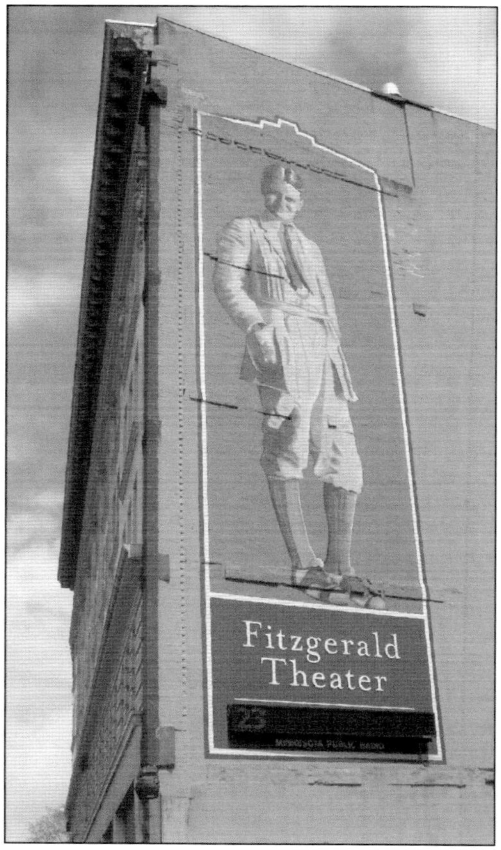

The Fitzgerald Theater, originally known as the Shubert, was renamed for the Minnesota-born author when it became the home of Minnesota Public Radio's *A Prairie Home Companion* show. Fitzgerald, dressed in knickers and saddle shoes, strikes a jaunty pose in this painting on the side of the theater. In recent years, the St. Paul–born author and his work have undergone a nationwide revival. (Author's collection.)

One of Minnesota's best known personalities, Garrison Keillor is a writer and humorist who created the popular *A Prairie Home Companion* for Minnesota Public Radio (MPR). In November 2017, MPR cut its ties with Keillor when he was accused of improper behavior by several staff members. After several months of negotiations, MPR reached a settlement with Keillor that made his radio archives available to the public.

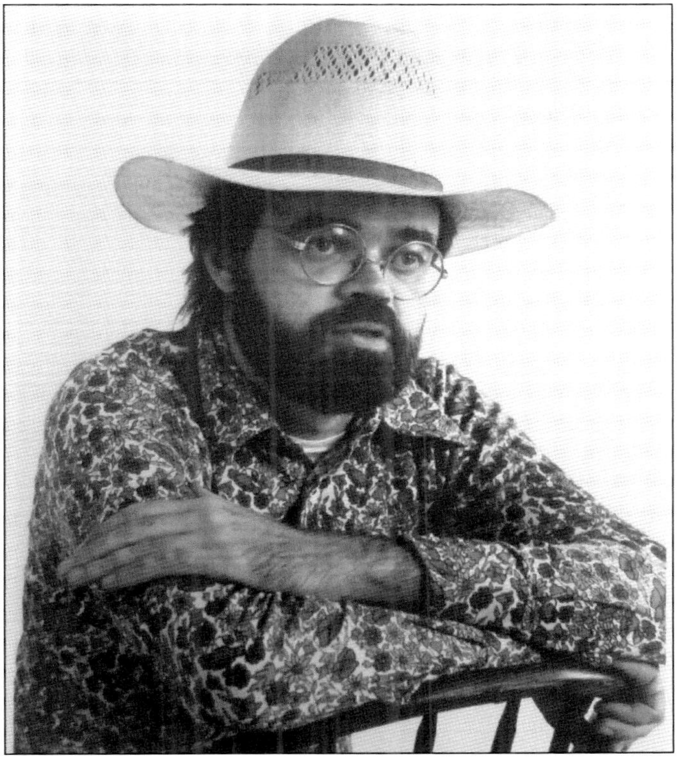

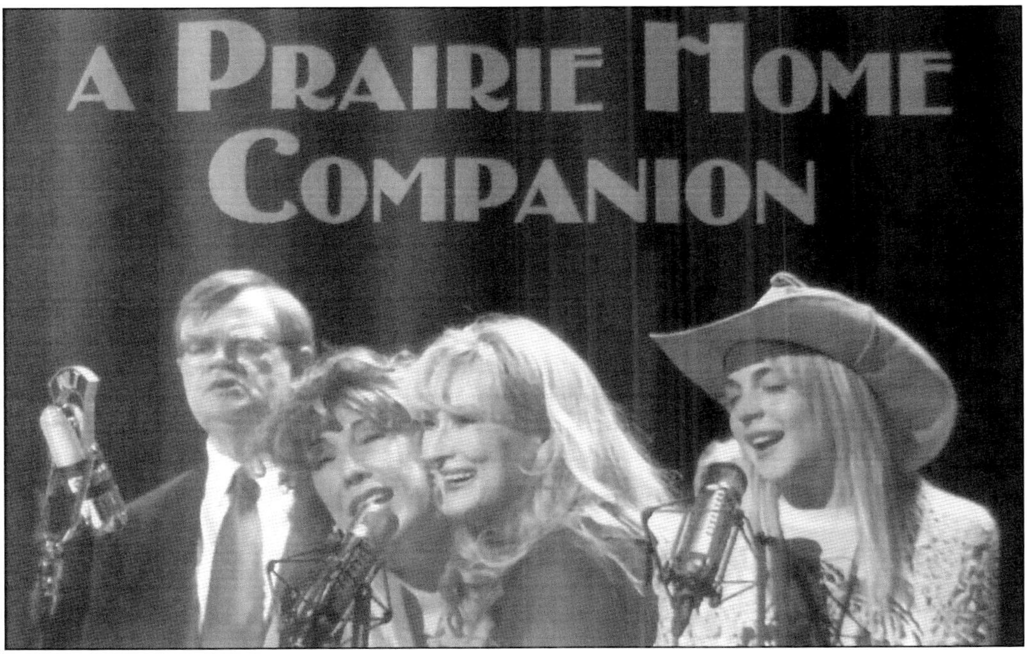

Keillor served as host of *A Prairie Home Companion* from 1974 to 2016. The show was broadcast live from the Fitzgerald Theater and other locations around the country. *A Prairie Home Companion* had feature billing in a film of the same name by the famed American director Robert Altman.

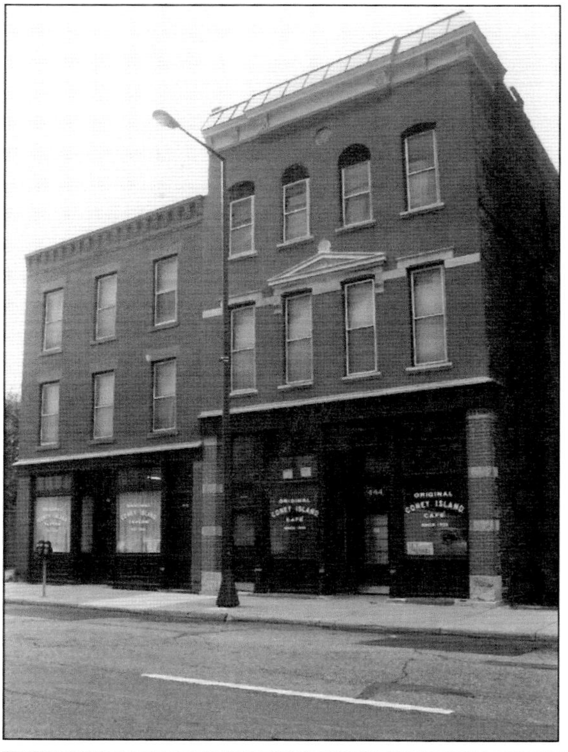

St. Paul's Original Coney Island Tavern and Café is housed in two 19th-century buildings. The earliest of the two, dating to 1858, is St. Paul's oldest commercial structure still currently occupied. In 1920, Greek immigrant Nick Arvanitis became owner of the properties, and by 1923, he established the name of the Original Coney Island. The family business now is owned and operated by Nick's daughter Mary. (Courtesy of Mary Arvanitis.)

Since 1932, hungry customers from all over the Twin Cities have flocked to Candyland for its famous Chicago mix popcorn and its other mouthwatering treats. Candyland's store on Wabasha Street is one of downtown's most popular landmarks. The store's loyal customer base has enabled it to withstand the winds of change buffeting downtown for more than 80 years. (Author's collection.)

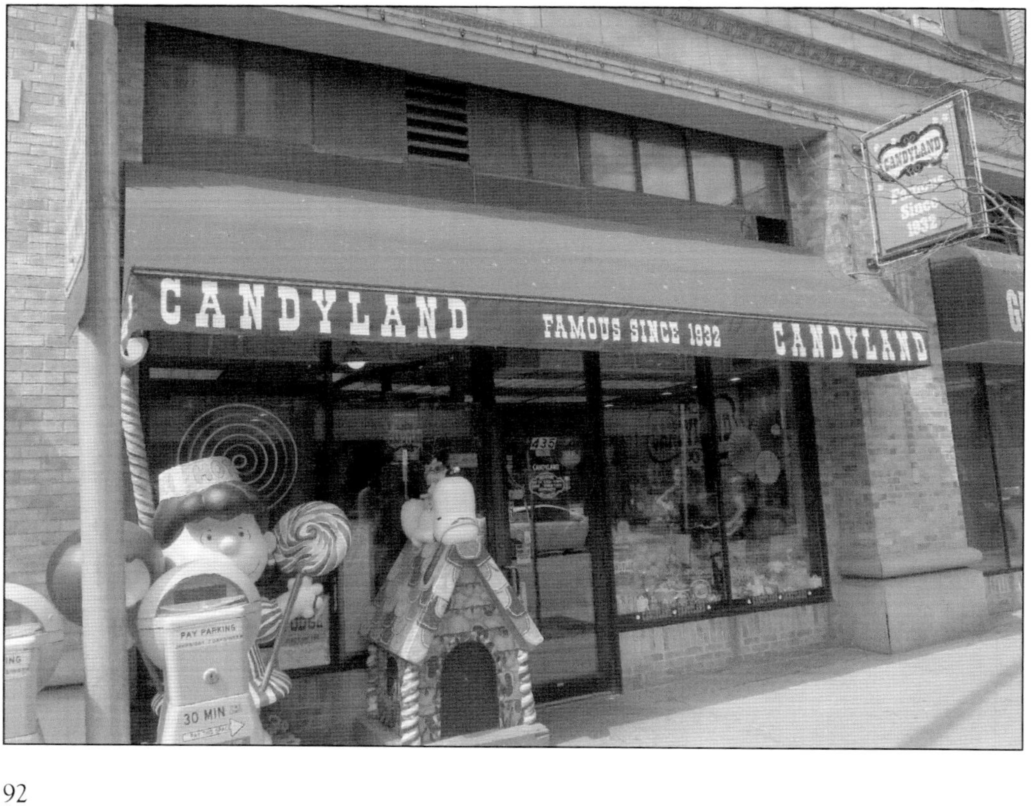

The Park Square Theater has called downtown St. Paul home since it was established in 1975. The theater's early performances were held in the Park Square building. Since 1977, the theater has occupied the 350-seat auditorium in the historic Hamm Building. In 2015, the Park Square added a second stage in the building. (Courtesy of Visit St. Paul.)

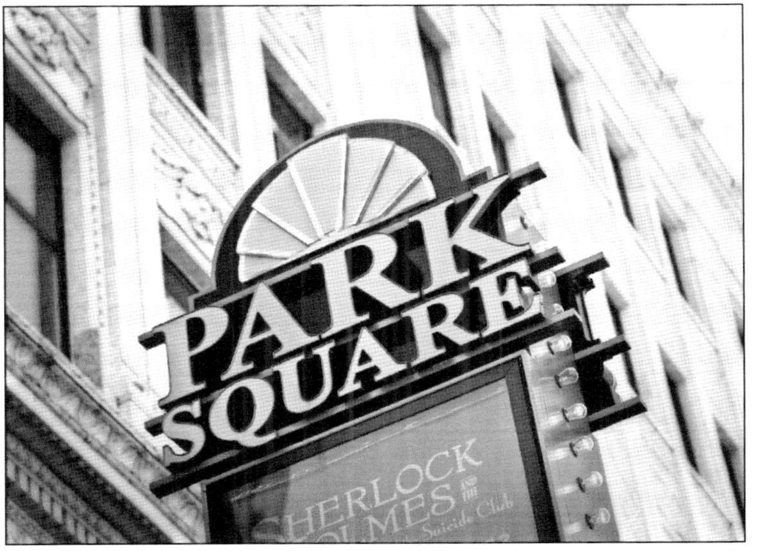

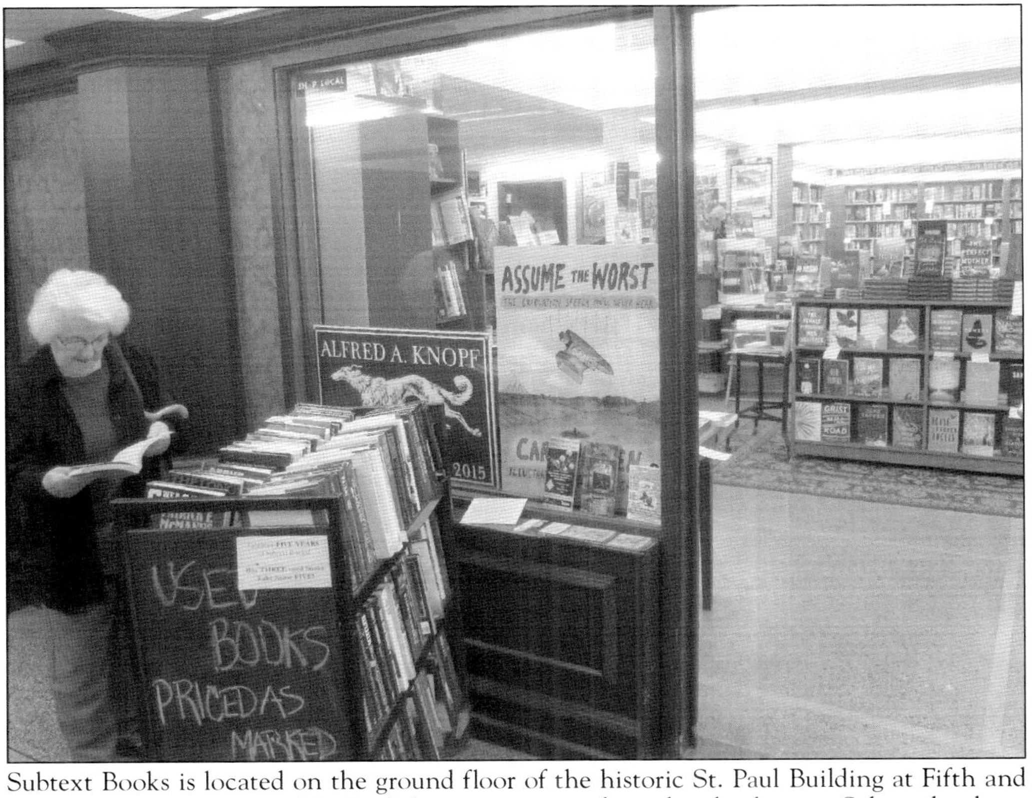

Subtext Books is located on the ground floor of the historic St. Paul Building at Fifth and Wabasha Streets. As one of St. Paul's last remaining independent bookstores, Subtext has been able to draw on a loyal customer base to withstand the current pressures affecting brick-and-mortar retail. The store hosts a regular series of conversations with local and national authors. (Author's collection.)

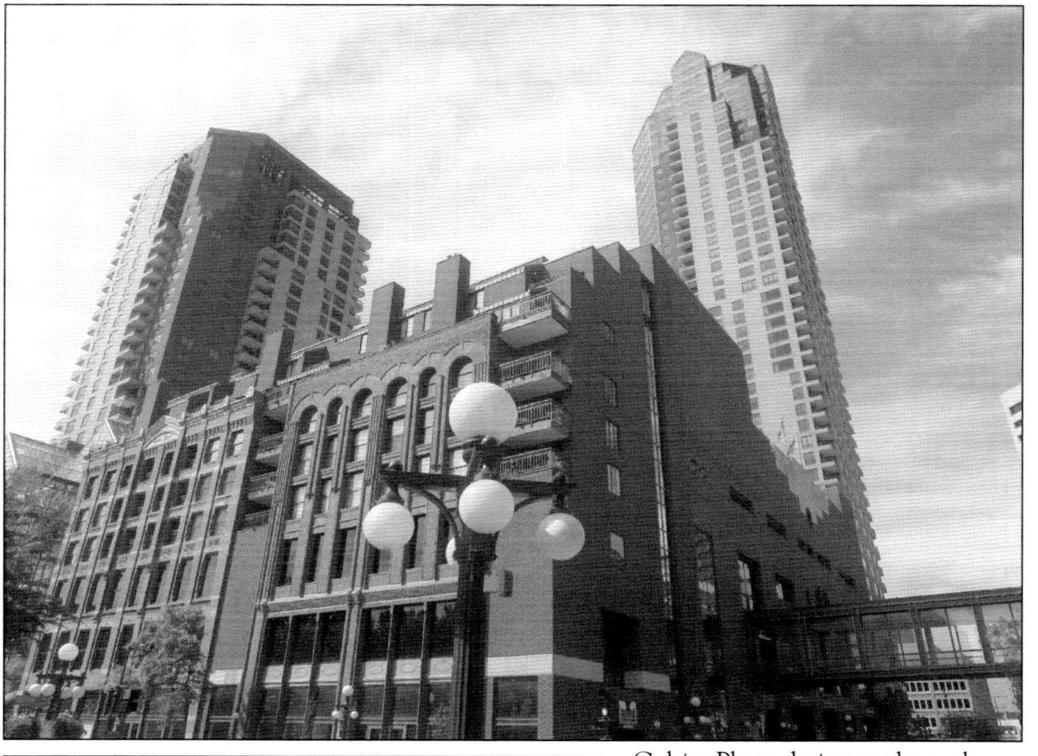

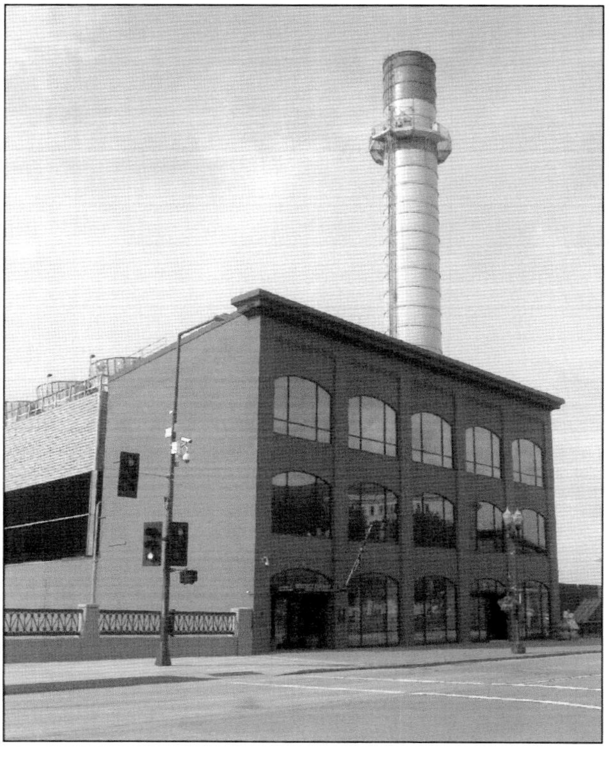

Galtier Plaza, dating to the early 1980s, represents St. Paul's efforts to use a mega-development to rejuvenate its aging downtown. The ambitious project consists of two high-rise residential towers, a new YMCA, and an indoor shopping arcade. While towers continue to attract renters and buyers, the retail phase of Galtier has not been successful. Many of the retail spaces have been converted to offices or remain empty. (Author's collection.)

Downtown's district heating system, known as District Energy St. Paul, was established in 1983 as St. Paul's response to the energy crisis of the 1970s. District Energy provides heating and cooling services on a shared basis to a broad range of downtown buildings. The nonprofit organization increasingly relies on solar energy and other green energy sources to power its operations. (Author's collection.)

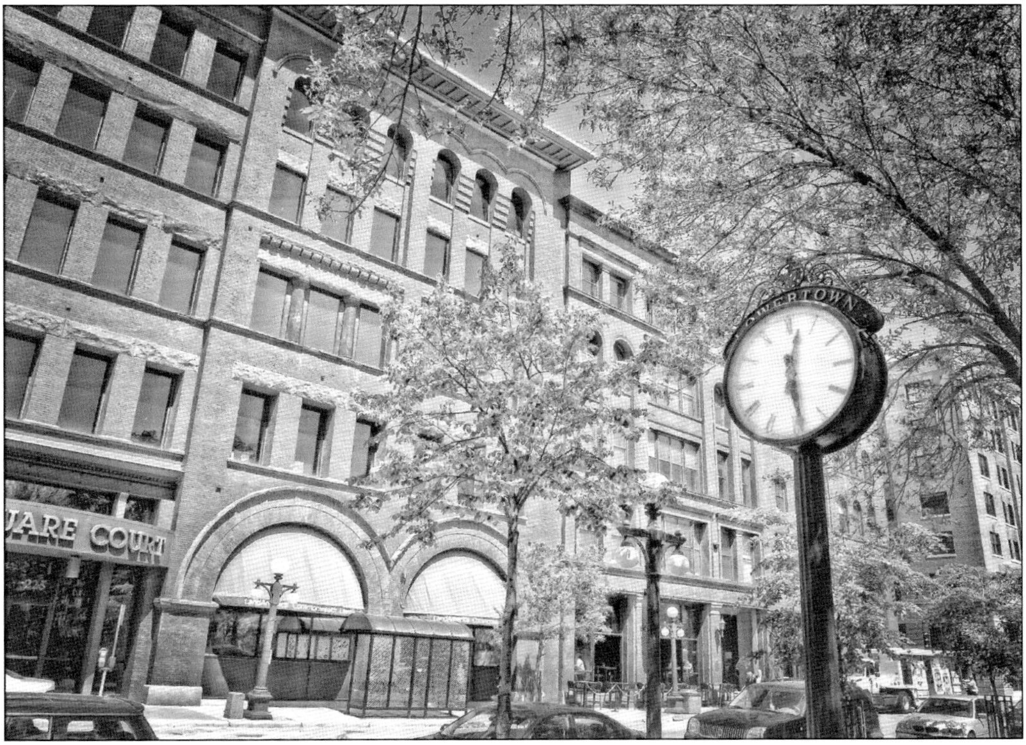

Once a bustling commercial center, Lowertown had become a forgotten corner of downtown St. Paul by the 1950s. Many of the early warehouses and factory buildings were partially or completely vacant. Starting in the 1970s, Lowertown underwent a dramatic turnaround with the creation of the Lowertown Redevelopment Corporation, a partnership between the City of St. Paul and the McKnight Foundation.

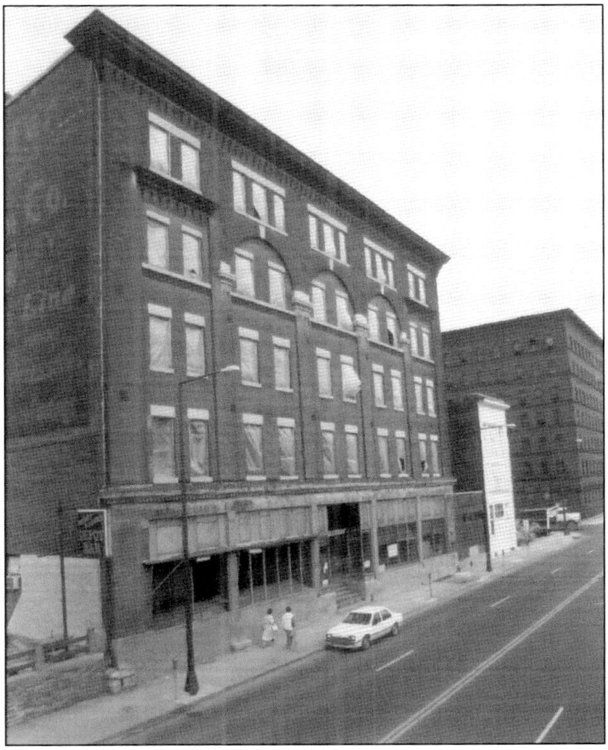

This 19th-century warehouse building was converted to live-work space for artists by the Lowertown Lofts Artists Cooperative in the mid-1980s. Members purchase shares in the cooperative corporation and receive a lease giving them occupancy rights for a particular unit. The cooperative structure is intended to keep the studios affordable for artists, many of whom find themselves priced out of gentrifying neighborhoods.

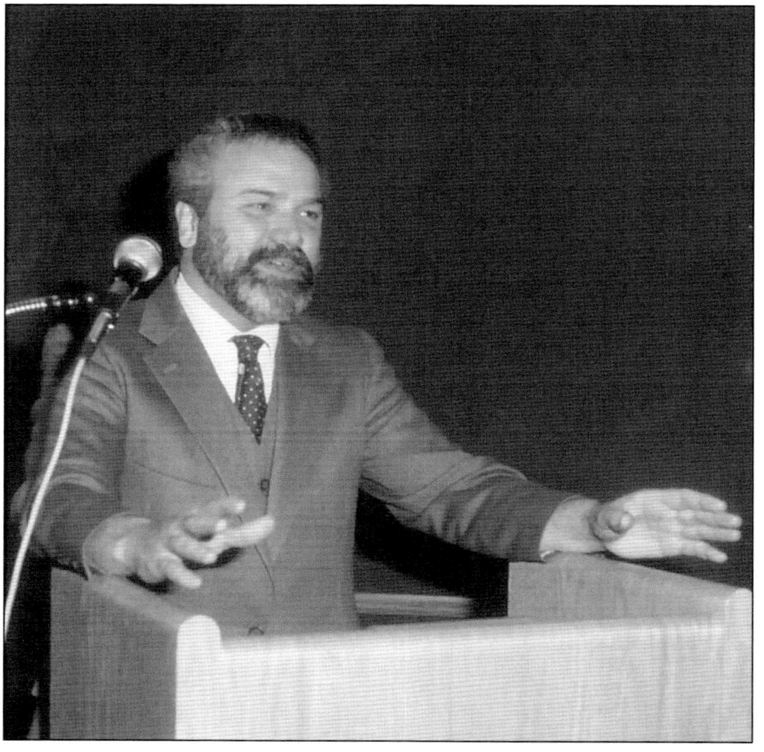

George Latimer served as mayor of St. Paul from 1976 to 1990. During his years as mayor, Latimer helped guide a series of public-private efforts aimed at revitalizing St. Paul's downtown. He played a leading role in the creation of St. Paul's district heating system and the Lowertown Redevelopment Corporation (LRC). (Courtesy of the Ramsey County Historical Society.)

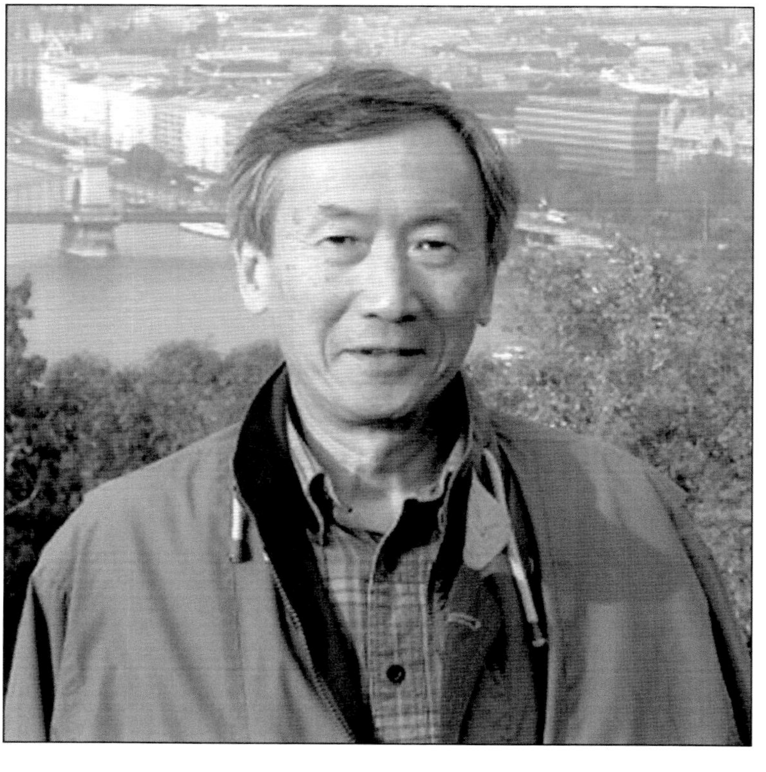

Weiming Lu served as the longtime executive director of the Lowertown Redevelopment Corporation. In that post, he helped guide the redevelopment of the historic Lowertown district. LRC helped leverage private investments in the district by providing front-end loans and grants for targeted projects. After retiring from LRC, Lu has continued to write about central city revitalization and the role of public-private partnerships. (Courtesy of Weiming Lu.)

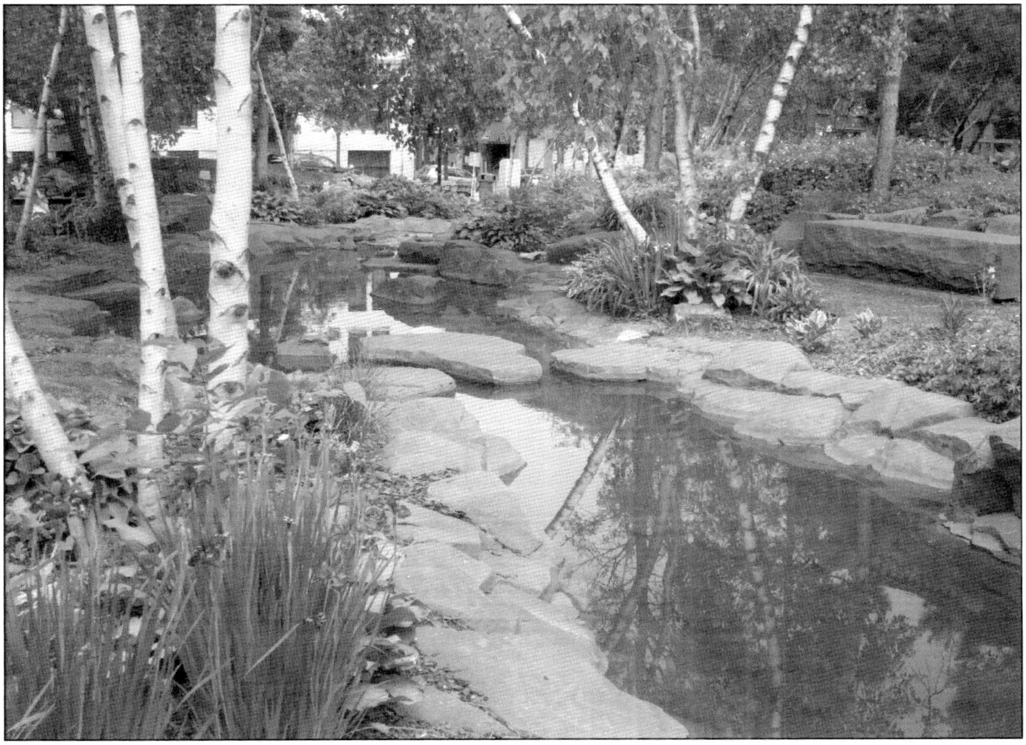

Mears Park, a Lowertown landmark, adds a touch of nature to this densely developed urban district. The park incorporates a water feature in the form of a stream that bisects the block. The stream is surrounded by a series of gardens, many of which are maintained by neighborhood residents who live in the nearby condos and apartments. Rebuilt in the early 1990s, the current version of Mears Park replaced an earlier remake dating from the early 1970s that was known derisively as the Brickyard. (Author's collection.)

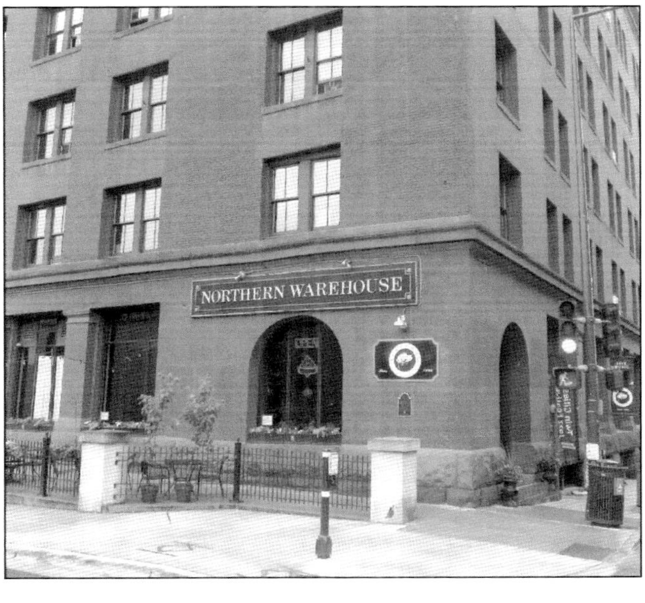

Minnesota-based Art Space developed its first live-work project, the Northern Warehouse Artists Cooperative, in 1990. This Lowertown development provides affordable housing and studio space for people engaged in creative pursuits. Over the last 30 years, Art Space has expanded its scope to include projects in more than 20 states.

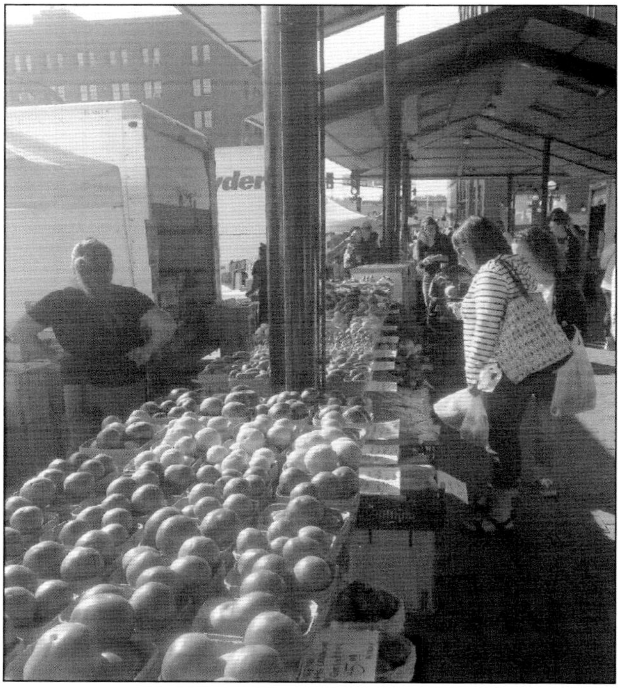

The St. Paul Farmers Market covers a full square block in Lowertown. A popular gathering spot for families from all over the Twin Cities, the outdoor market is open on weekends from late April to mid-November. Growers from around the Twin Cities, many from the local Hmong community, provide the plants, flowers, and vegetables offered for sale at the market. (Both, author's collection.)

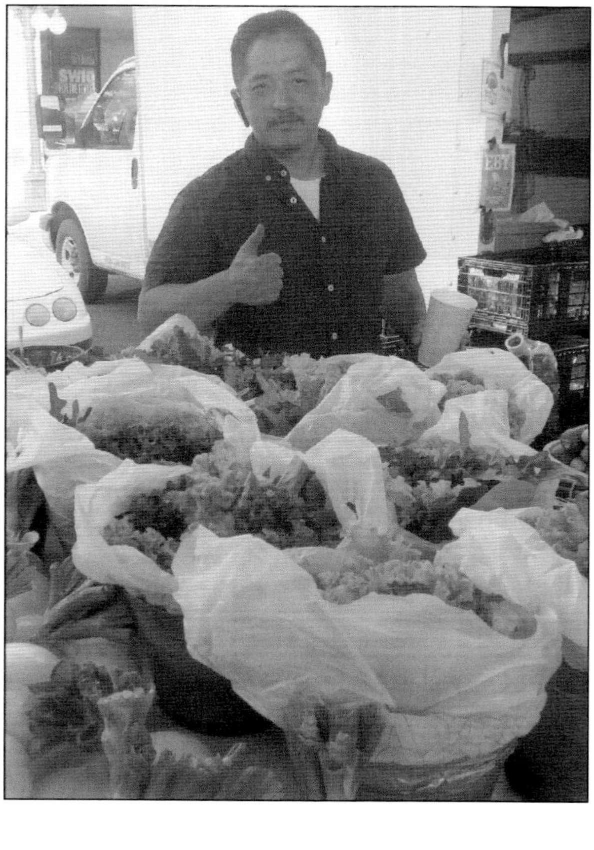

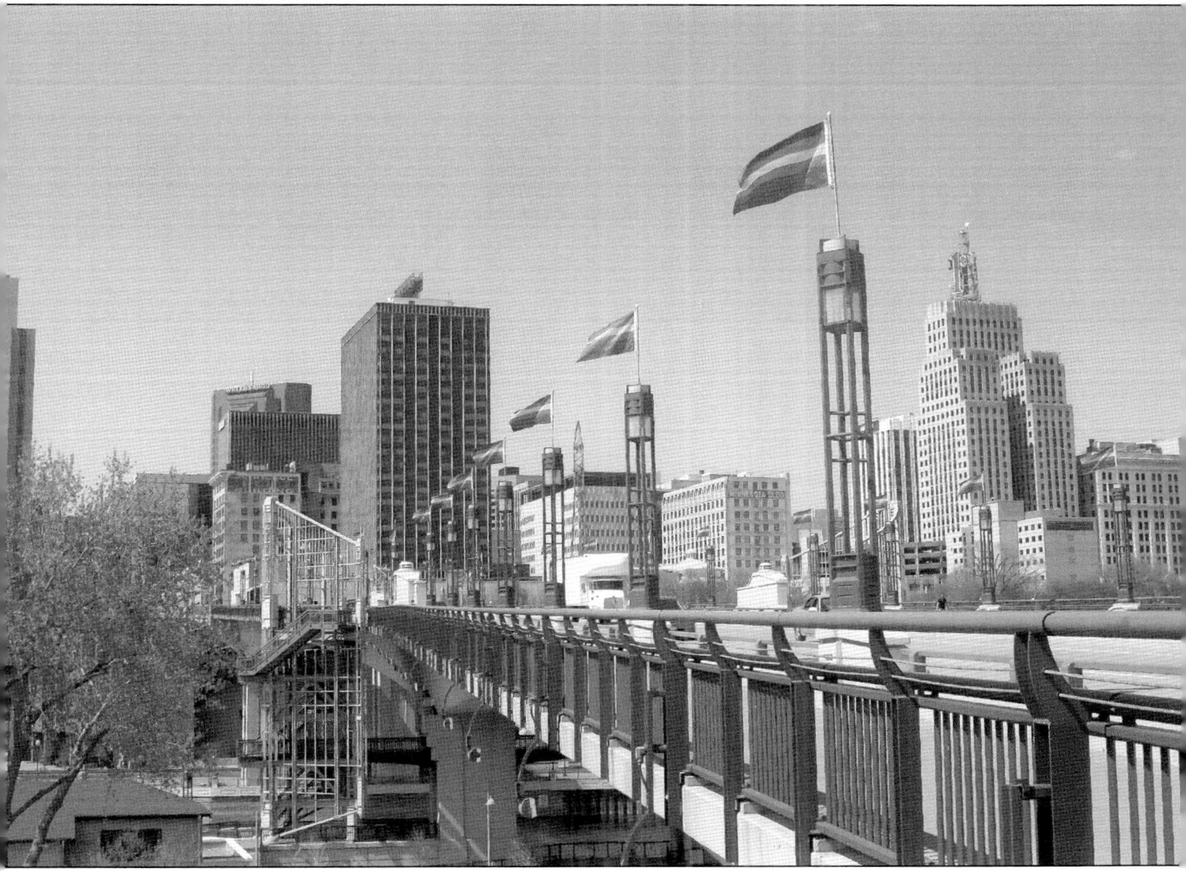

The flag-bedecked Wabasha Bridge is the third river span at this location. The current bridge, which opened in 1998, was intended to bring a modern touch to downtown St. Paul. An original plan called for a suspension bridge supported by cables extending from a V-shaped mast. But the earlier plan was rejected by city officials because of cost considerations. A stairway from the bridge leads down to Raspberry Island, named for the wild raspberries that once grew there. (Courtesy of Visit St. Paul.)

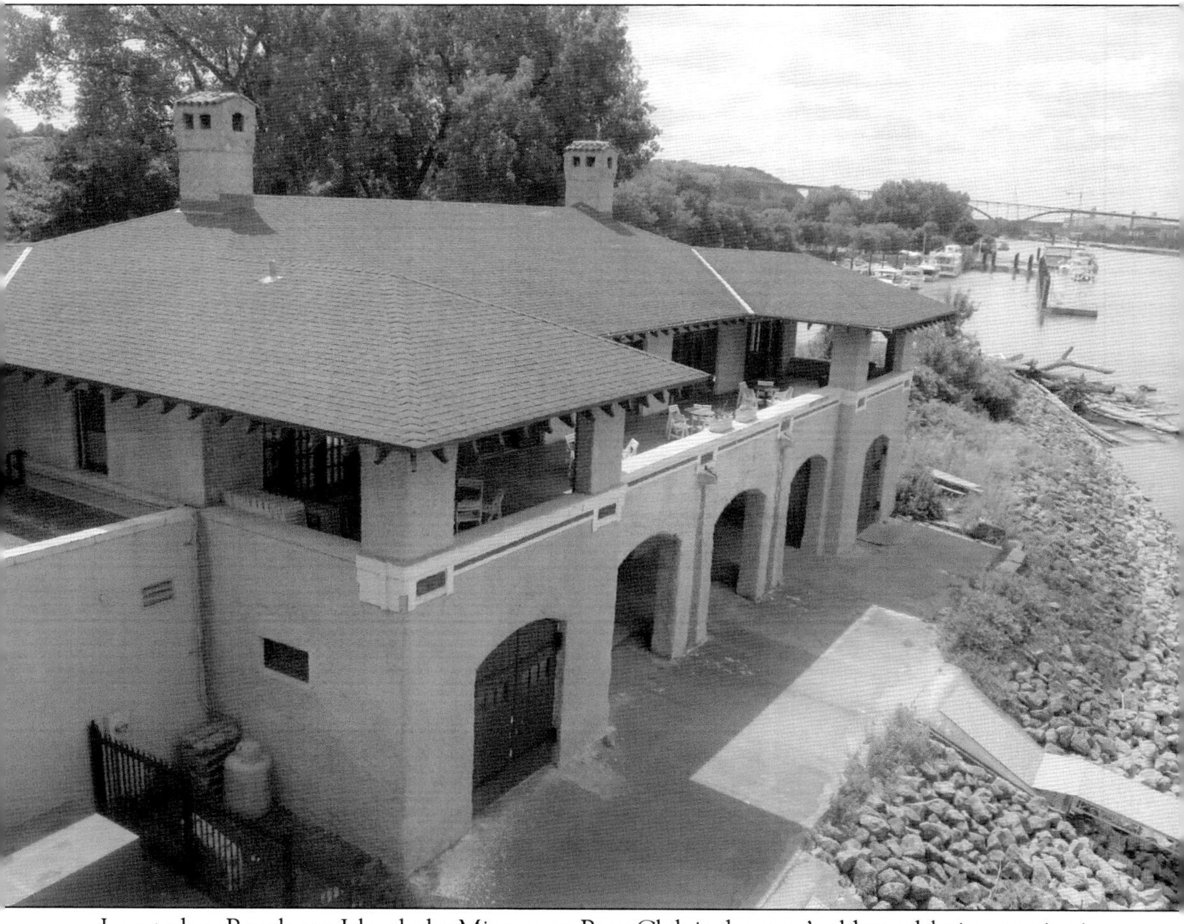

Located on Raspberry Island, the Minnesota Boat Club is the state's oldest athletic organization, dating to 1870. The group's Spanish Revival–style clubhouse was built in 1910. It houses the rowing equipment that is put to good use by club members during the spring, summer, and fall rowing seasons. (Author's collection.)

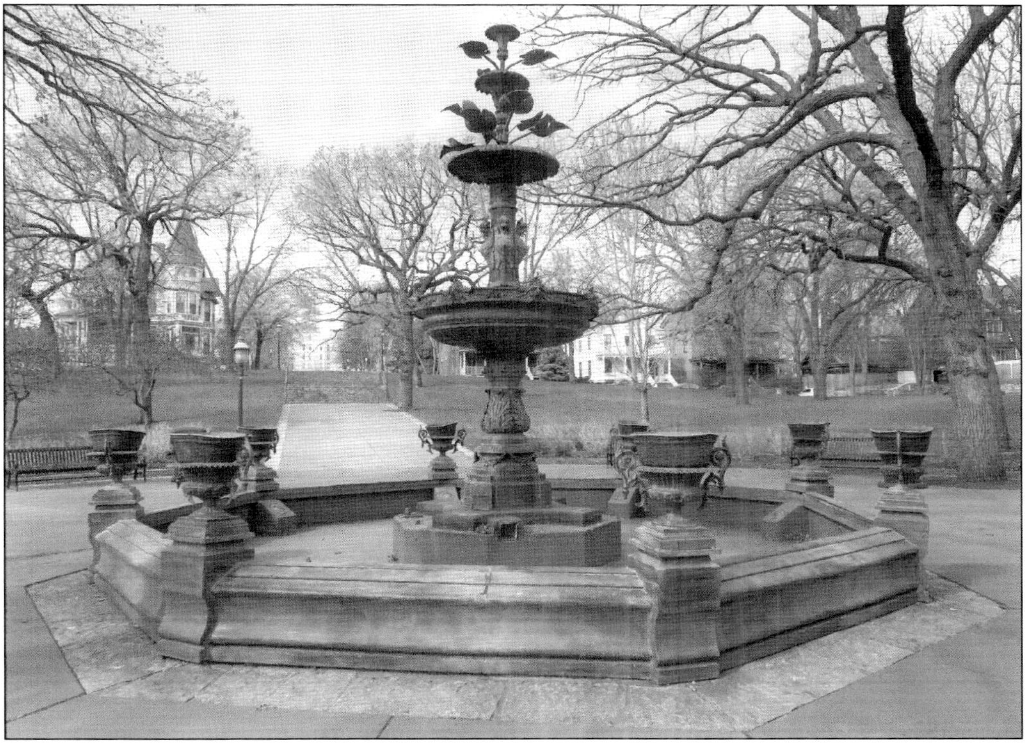

This elegant fountain serves as the focal point of the restored Irvine Park neighborhood. Ignored and severely blighted by the mid-20th century, the neighborhood was rescued and rebuilt starting in the 1970s through a partnership of neighborhood activists and the City of St. Paul. While certain homes in the area remain at their original site, others were moved into the neighborhood to recreate a bucolic Victorian enclave at the edge of downtown. (Author's collection.)

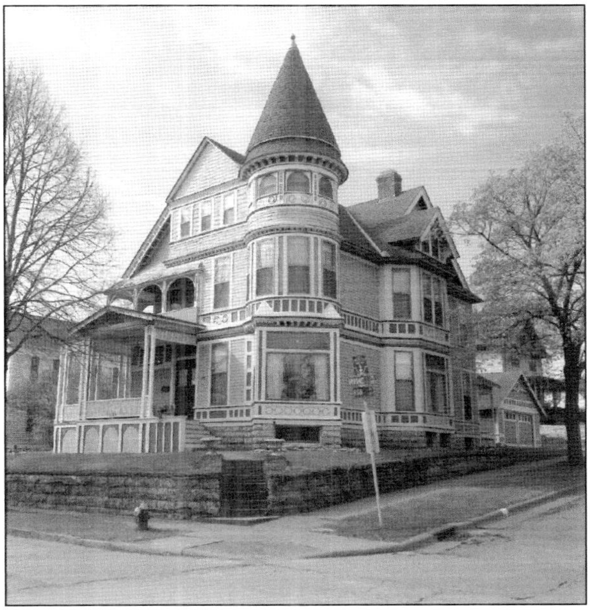

Known as Irvine Park's "Grand Victorian Dame," the Murray Lampher house dates from 1886. The structure had fallen on hard times before it was renovated in the 1970s. Now restored to its late-19th-century grandeur, "it is probably what most people have in mind when they dream of a Queen Anne house," historian Larry Millett has observed. (Author's collection.)

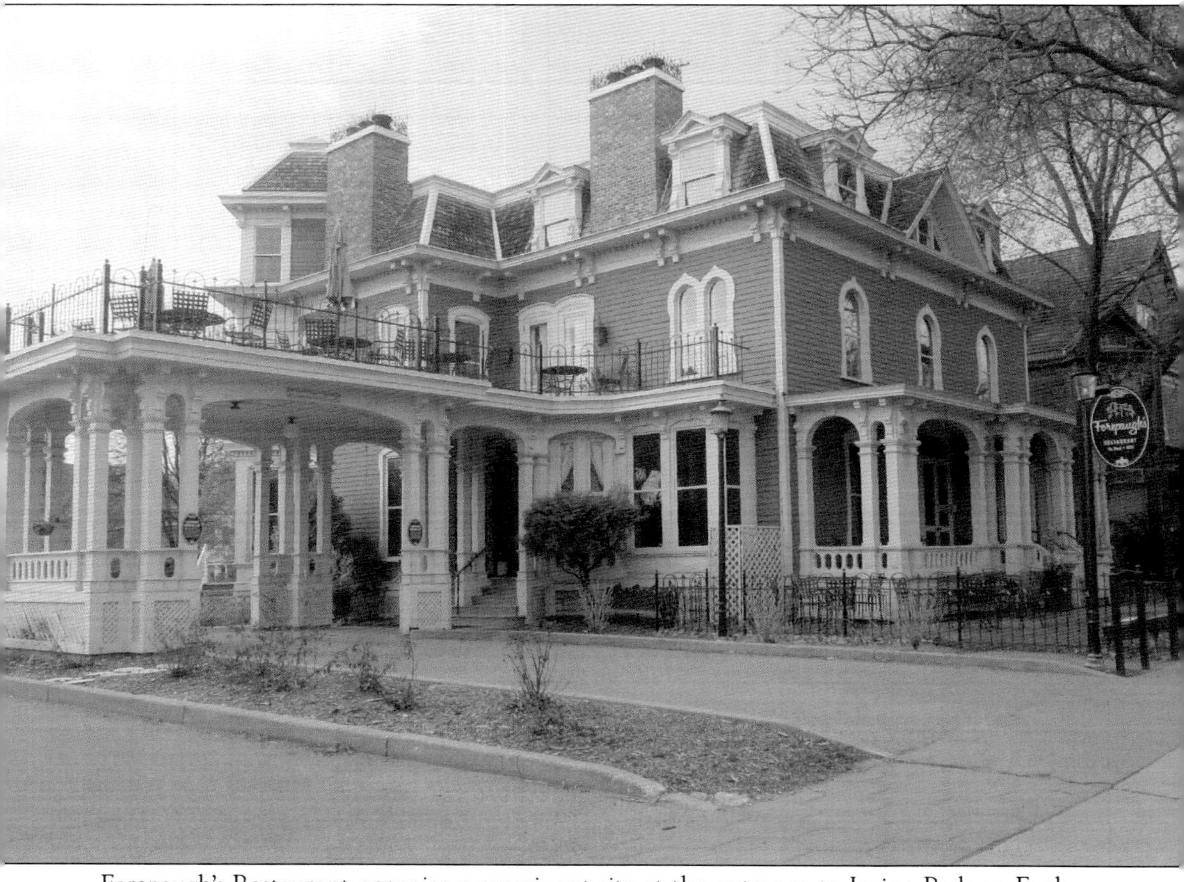

Forepaugh's Restaurant occupies a prominent site at the entrance to Irvine Park on Exchange Street. The building was originally the home of Joseph Forepaugh, a wealthy St. Paul businessman. It had sat vacant and was badly deteriorated before it was rebuilt by the restaurant's original owners in 1976. (Author's collection.)

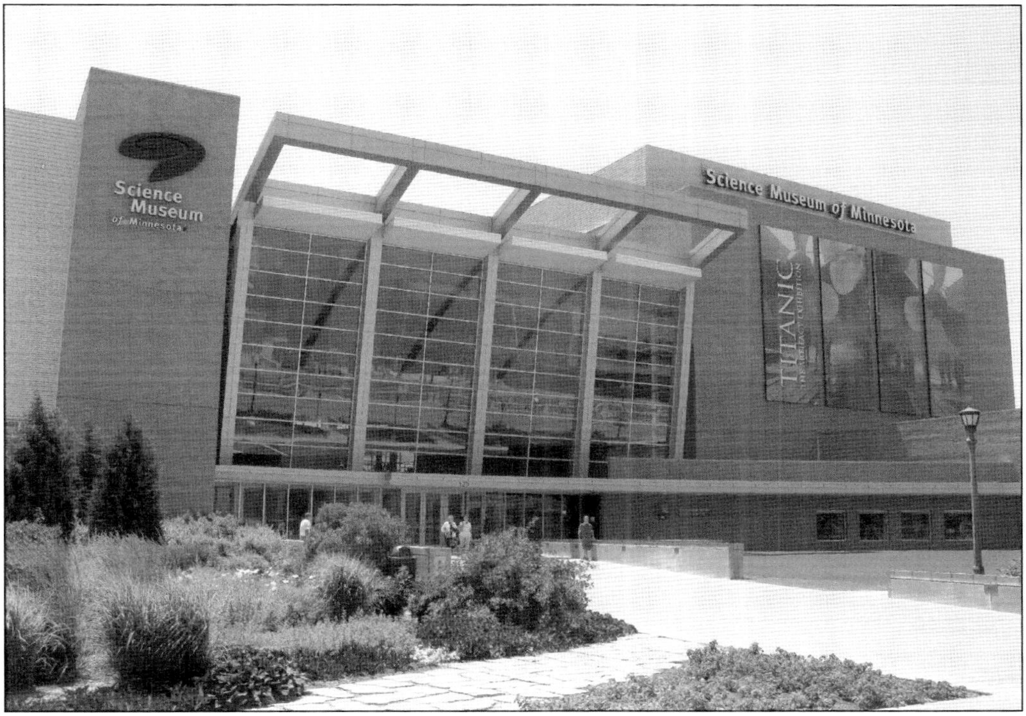

The Science Museum of Minnesota traces its history to 1906, when it was established as the St. Paul Institute of Science and Letters. Now a major St. Paul institution, the museum has had several homes over the last 100 years. In 1999, the Science Museum of Minnesota moved into its current building on Kellogg Boulevard. (Both, courtesy of Visit St. Paul.)

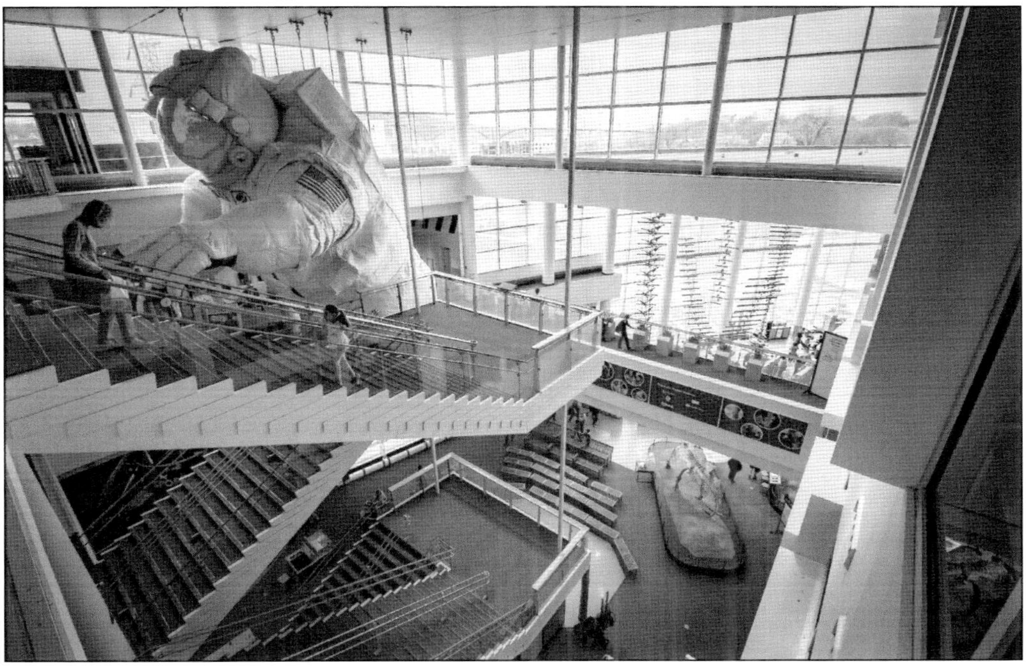

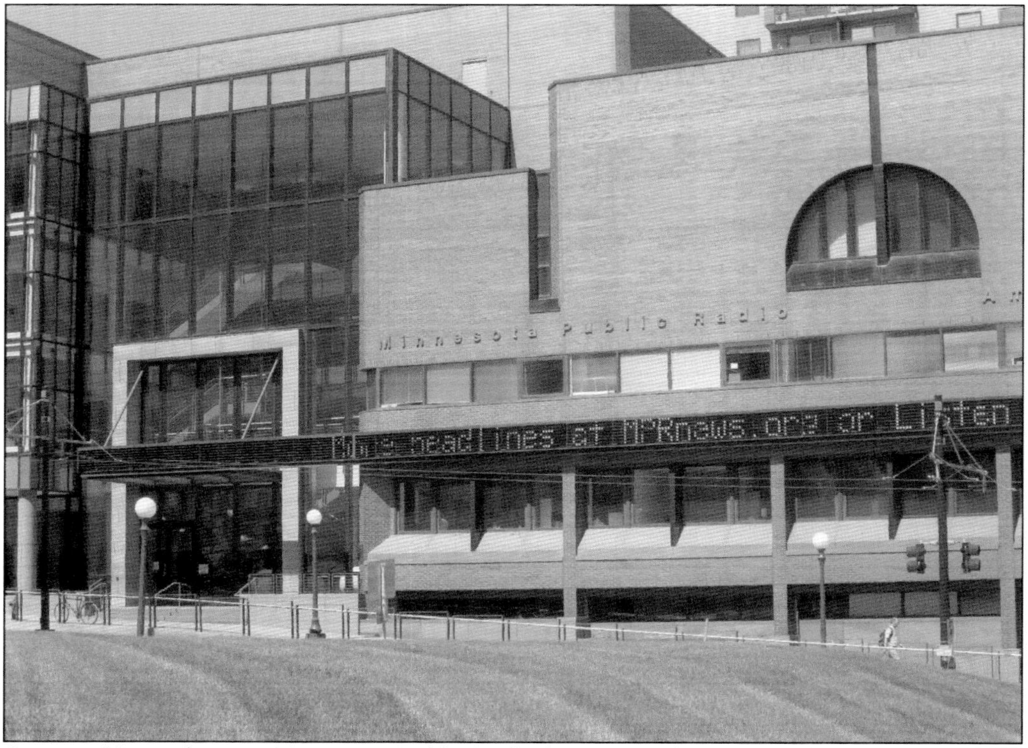

Over its 50-year history, Minnesota Public Radio has emerged as one of the country's leading public broadcasting organizations. *A Prairie Home Companion* helped the organization reach a national audience. MPR's current home on Cedar Street dates to the mid-1960s. The building was enlarged and substantially remodeled in the 1980s. (Author's collection.)

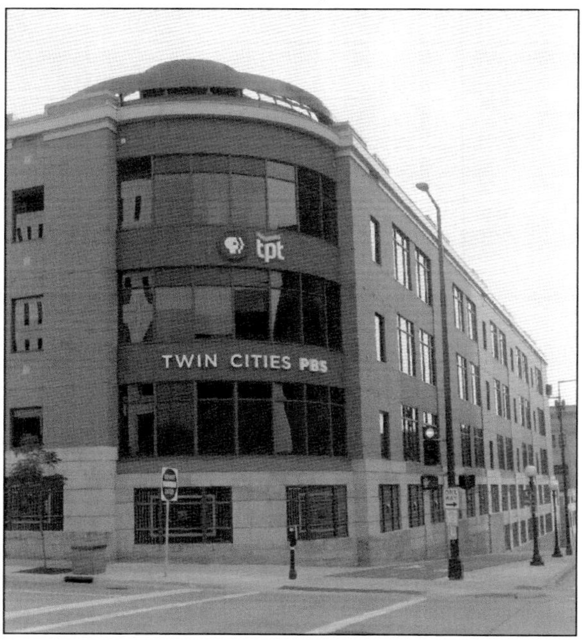

Twin Cities Public Television, Minnesota's oldest noncommercial television system, began broadcasting in 1957 on KTCA Channel 2. Then known as Twin Cities Area Public Television, the station was originally located on the University of Minnesota's St. Paul campus. Now renamed Twin Cities PBS, the public television system moved to its current Lowertown location in 1989. (Author's collection.)

Six

21st Century

The new century saw a revival of downtown St. Paul's historic role as a transportation hub. In 2012, Union Depot reopened following a $245-million renovation. Two years later, rail passenger service returned after a 43-year hiatus when Amtrak made the depot the Twin Cities stop for its *Empire Builder* train. In 2016, the depot became the eastern terminus of the light rail transit Green Line, which connects downtown Minneapolis with downtown St. Paul.

During the early years of the 21st century, downtown created a new identify for itself as a sports and entertainment center. In 2000, the new Xcel Energy Center at Seven Corners became the home of the Minnesota Wild, St. Paul's professional hockey team. The Xcel Center also doubles as a concert venue that draws the biggest names in the pop music world to St. Paul. In 2015, the city's professional baseball team, the Saints, also got a new home with the opening of CHS Field in Lowertown.

At the southern edge of downtown, adjacent to the historic Upper Landing, a dismal industrial site was rebuilt as a new residential district overlooking the riverfront. The Upper Landing helped develop downtown into a new urban neighborhood attracting both empty nesters and millennials. While many of downtown's new residents occupy upscale loft apartments and condominiums, St. Paulites dealing with social and economic challenges are also able to find a place to live downtown. Catholic Charities' Opportunity Center and Dorothy Day Residences offer affordable housing and support services for people experiencing long-term homelessness.

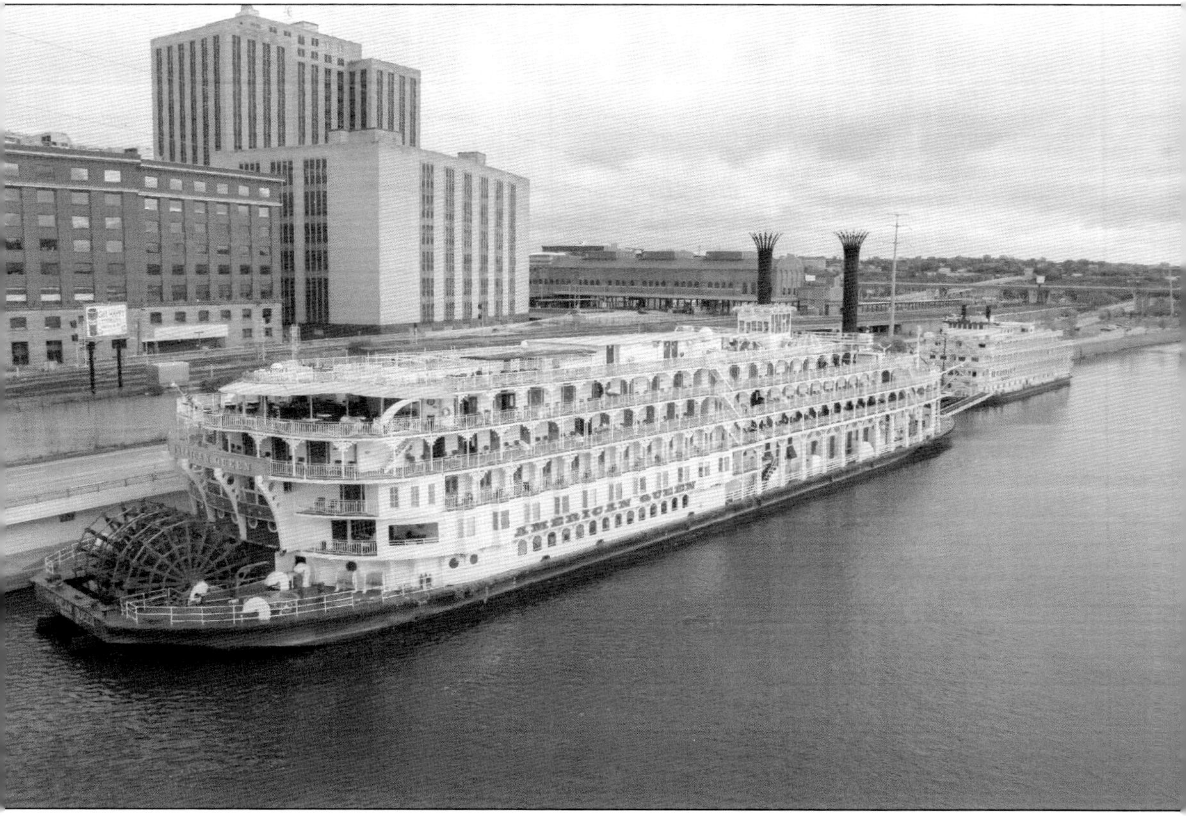

The *American Queen* evokes St. Paul's early history, when the Minnesota town was an important port for steamboats traveling up and down the Mississippi. The *American Queen* now docks at St. Paul's Lower Landing, just as its predecessors did in the mid-19th century. A modern recreation of a 19th-century steamboat, the *American Queen* sails between St. Paul and St. Louis. (Courtesy of Visit St. Paul.)

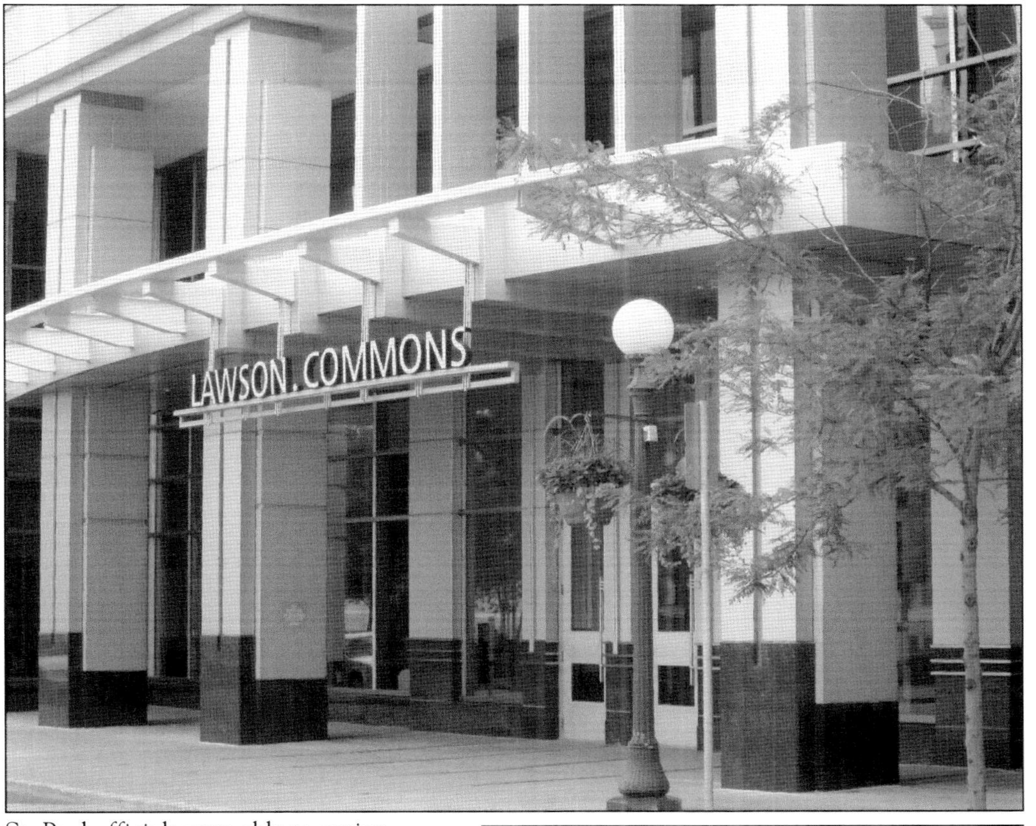

St. Paul officials were able to entice Lawson Software to leave Minneapolis and relocate in downtown St. Paul by providing city assistance for the company's new headquarters. The headquarters building, known as Lawson Commons, opened in 2000. Lawson was later sold to a New York–based multinational firm but continues to occupy space in the downtown building that bears its name. (Author's collection.)

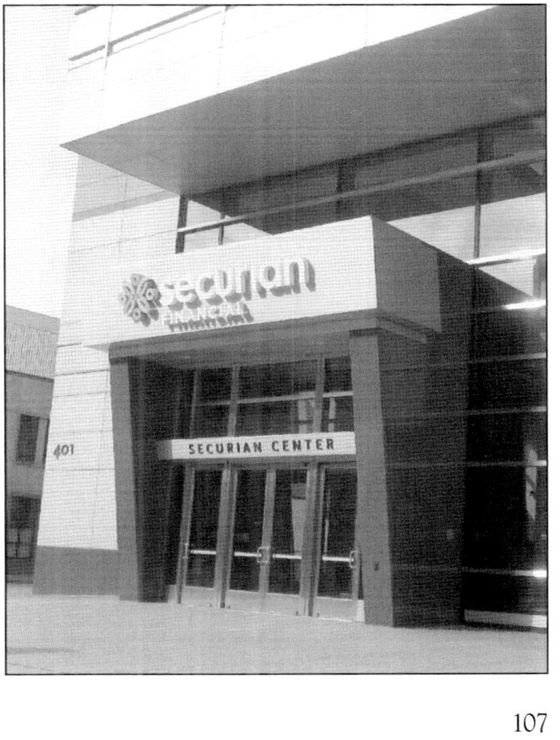

One of downtown's oldest businesses traces its history to 1880, when it was established as Bankers Association of Minnesota. In 1901, Bankers Association became Minnesota Mutual Life Insurance, a name the company retained through the remainder of the 20th century. In 2005, Minnesota Mutual was renamed Securian Financial. (Author's collection.)

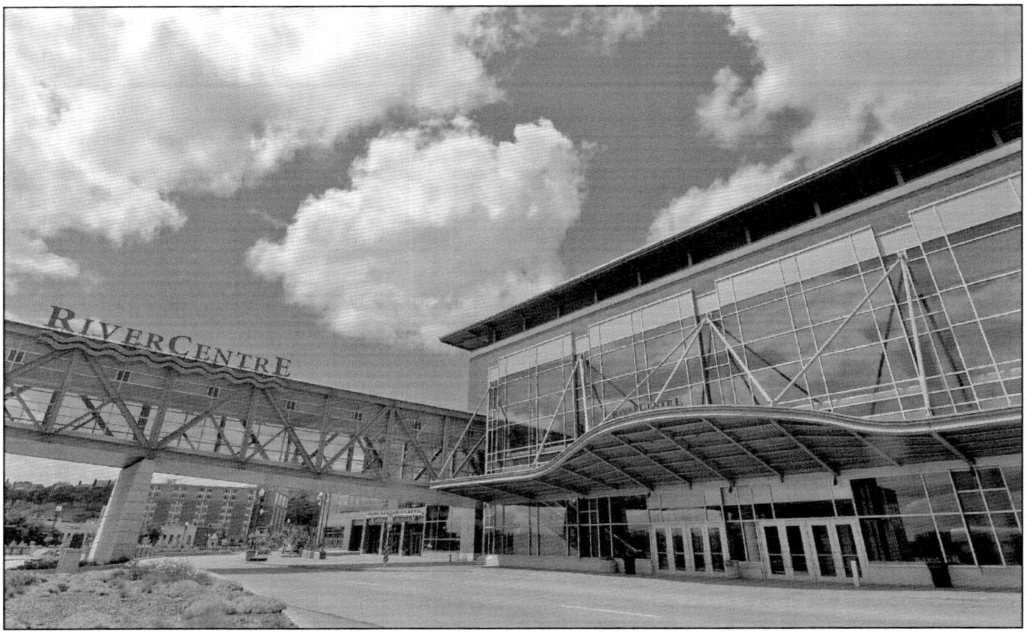

RiverCentre represents St. Paul's effort to attract major regional and national conventions. The center is part of a complex that includes the Xcel Center, a sports and entertainment venue, and the historical Roy Wilkins Auditorium, dating to 1936. RiverCentre was built in 1998 at a cost of $75 million. (Courtesy of Visit St. Paul.)

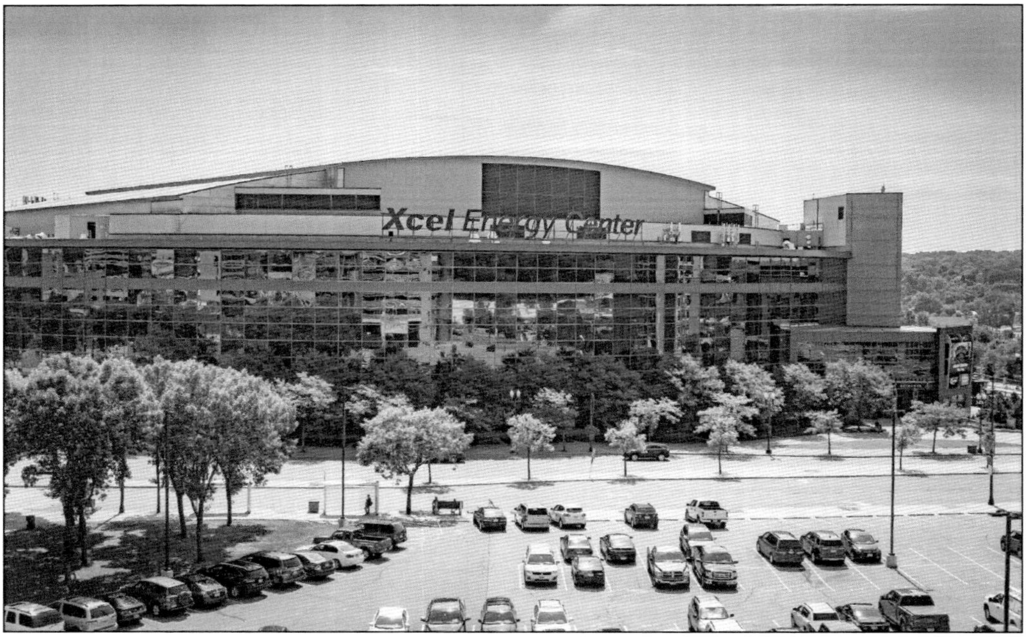

The Xcel Energy Center, which opened in 2000, is the home of the Minnesota Wild, St. Paul's NHL hockey team. The Wild's 40 home games bring throngs of fans to downtown St. Paul during the hockey season, which extends from October through early April. RiverCentre and Xcel also serve as concert venues. (Courtesy of Visit St. Paul.)

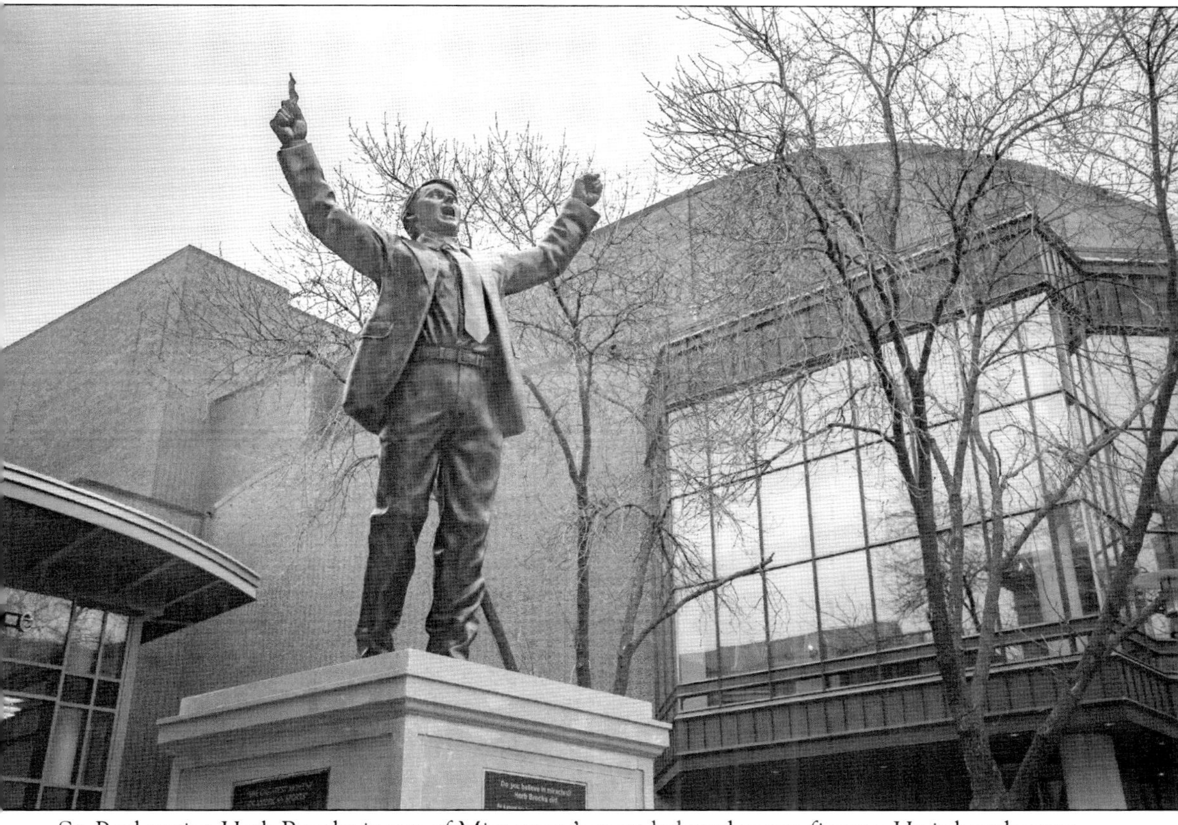

St. Paul native Herb Brooks is one of Minnesota's most beloved sports figures. He is best known as the coach of the US hockey team that defeated the favored Soviet team at the 1980 Winter Olympics on their way to winning the gold medal. That game came to be known as the "Miracle on Ice." Brooks, who died in 2003, has been immortalized in this statue facing Rice Park. (Courtesy of Visit St. Paul.)

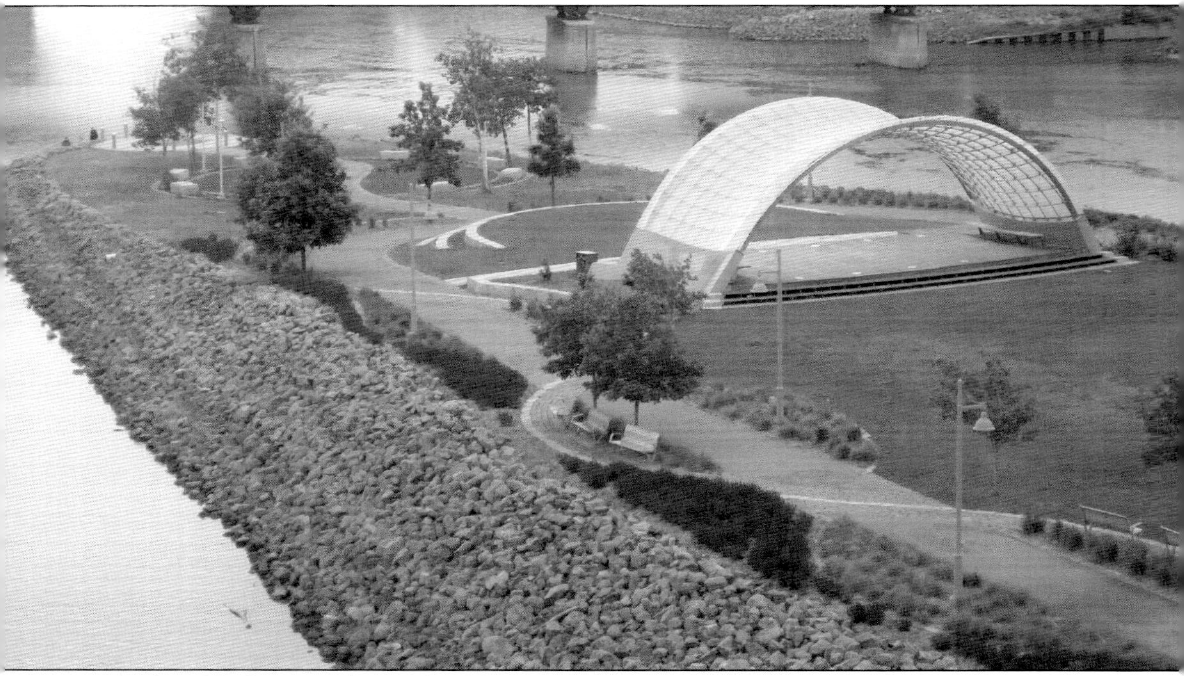

This bandshell on Raspberry Island, built by the Schubert Club in 2002, has been called the "most poetic object on St. Paul's riverfront" by architectural historian Larry Millett. The saddle-shaped structure, made of stainless steel and laminated glass, is known technically as a hyperbolic paraboloid. A popular venue for summer concerts and other outdoor arts events, the Schubert Club bandshell has become one of downtown's most widely admired landmarks. (Author's collection.)

This loft-style condominium is located in the former Lowry Medical Arts Building. In 2005, the building was converted to condominiums that retain many of the Lowry's 1912 architectural features. In recent years, downtown has attracted a growing number of residents seeking an urban lifestyle. In 2017, downtown's population was nearly 9,000. (Author's collection.)

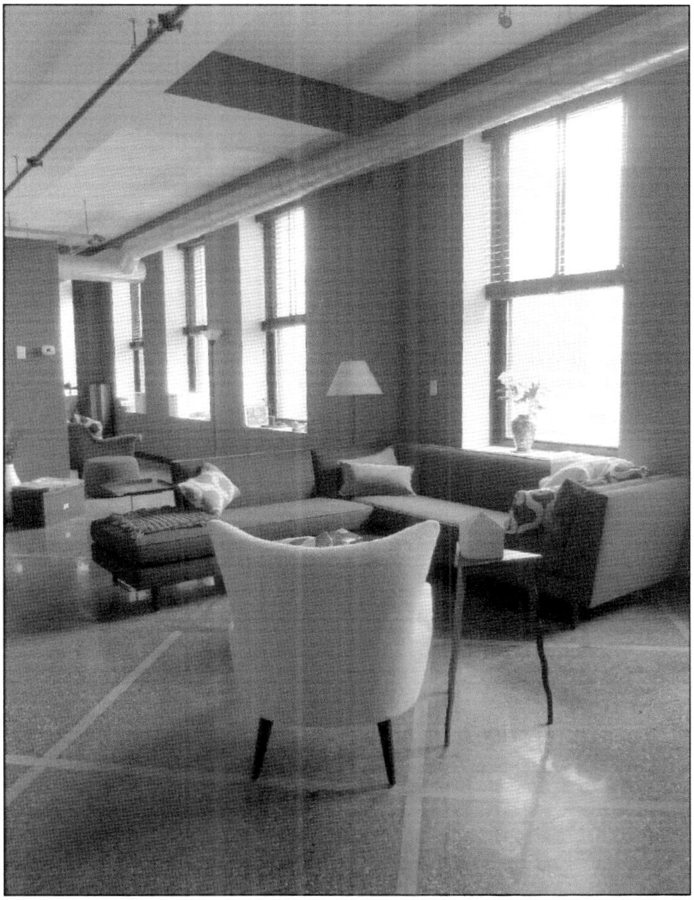

The Metro Transit Green Line is the second of the Twin Cities' first two light rail transit projects. The 11-mile Green Line, which opened in 2014, connects downtown St. Paul with downtown Minneapolis. The Green Line has four stations in downtown St. Paul, including this one at the Union Depot. (Courtesy of Visit St. Paul.)

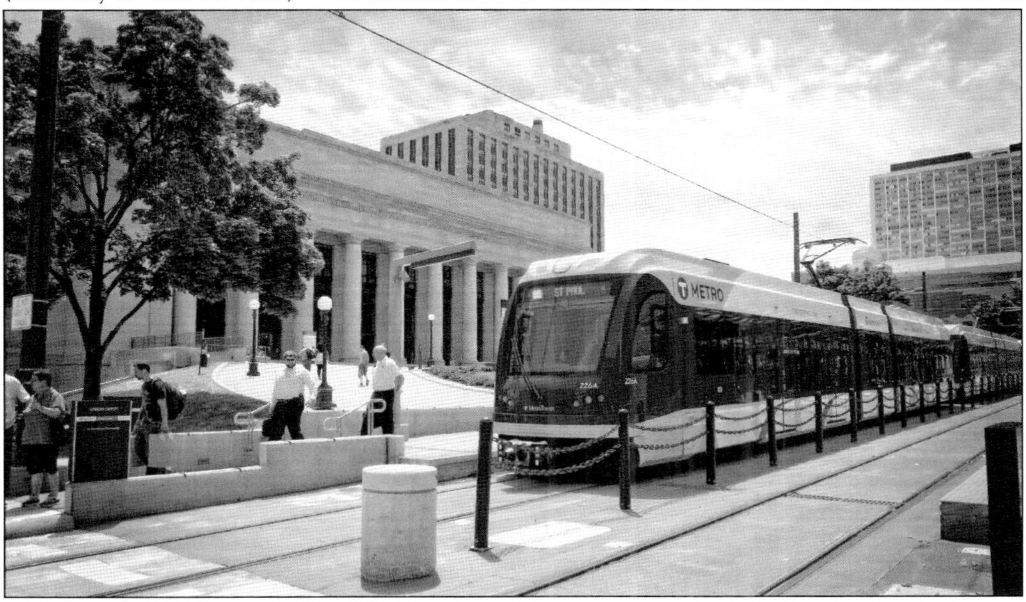

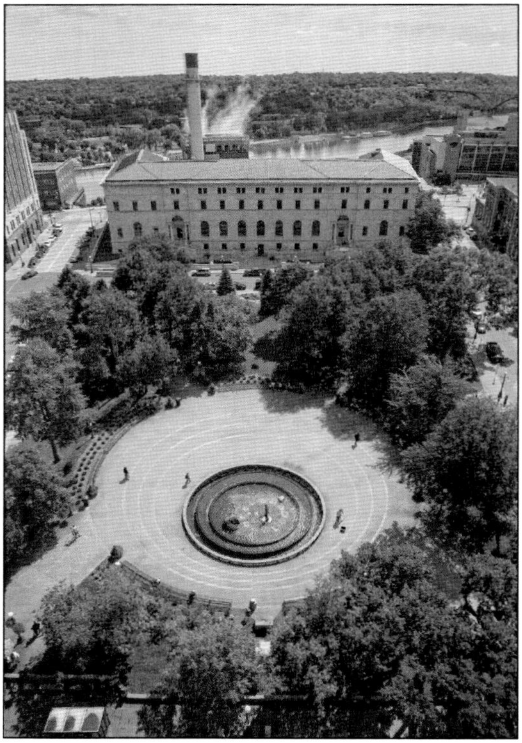

Rice Park continues to be an attractive gathering spot for St. Paulites. The park provides a green space in the heart of downtown that has a very European feel. During January, the park is the site of the Winter Carnival's annual ice sculpture display. In 2018, Rice Park underwent a $2.42-million renovation that included expanded gardens, new walkways, and new park lighting. (Both, courtesy of Visit St. Paul.)

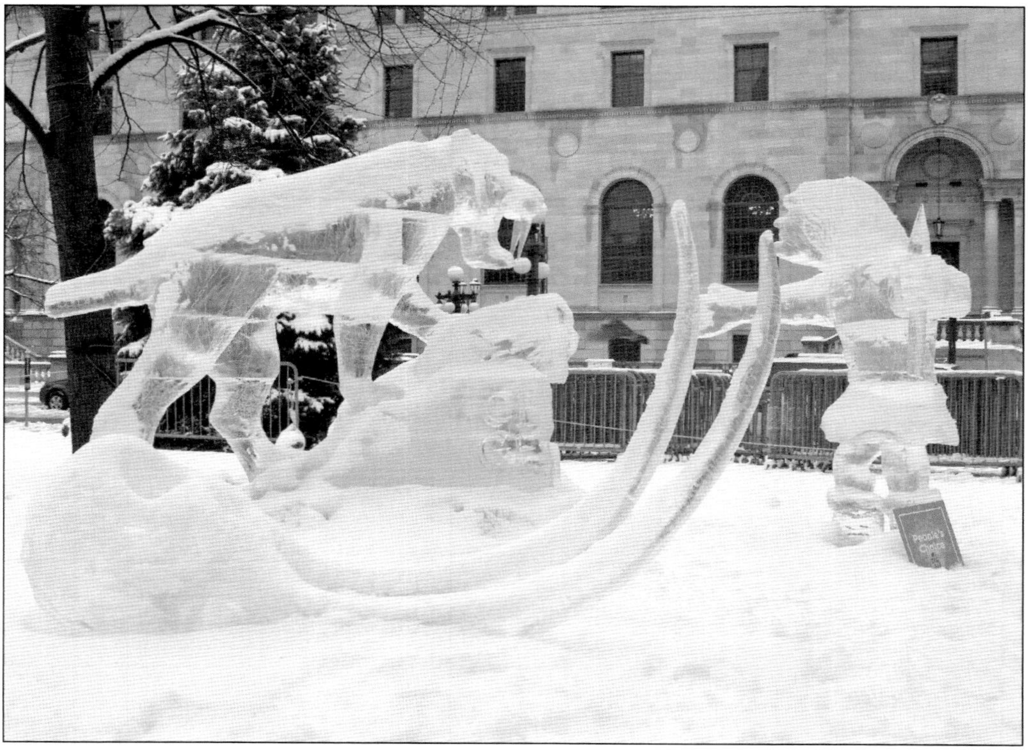

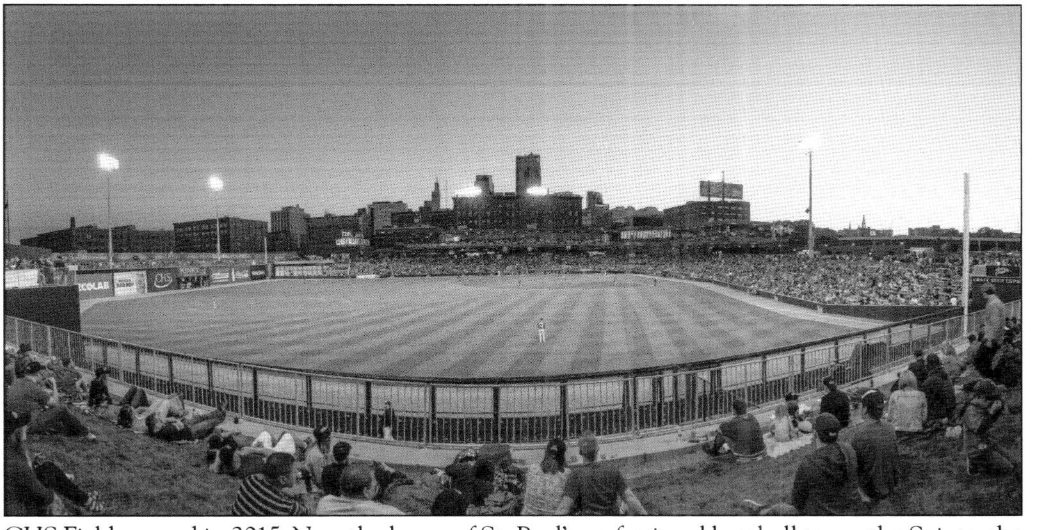

CHS Field opened in 2015. Now the home of St. Paul's professional baseball team, the Saints, the ballpark was built by the City of St. Paul at a cost of $65 million. The stadium's low-rise profile does not overpower its Lowertown neighbors. (Courtesy of Visit St. Paul.)

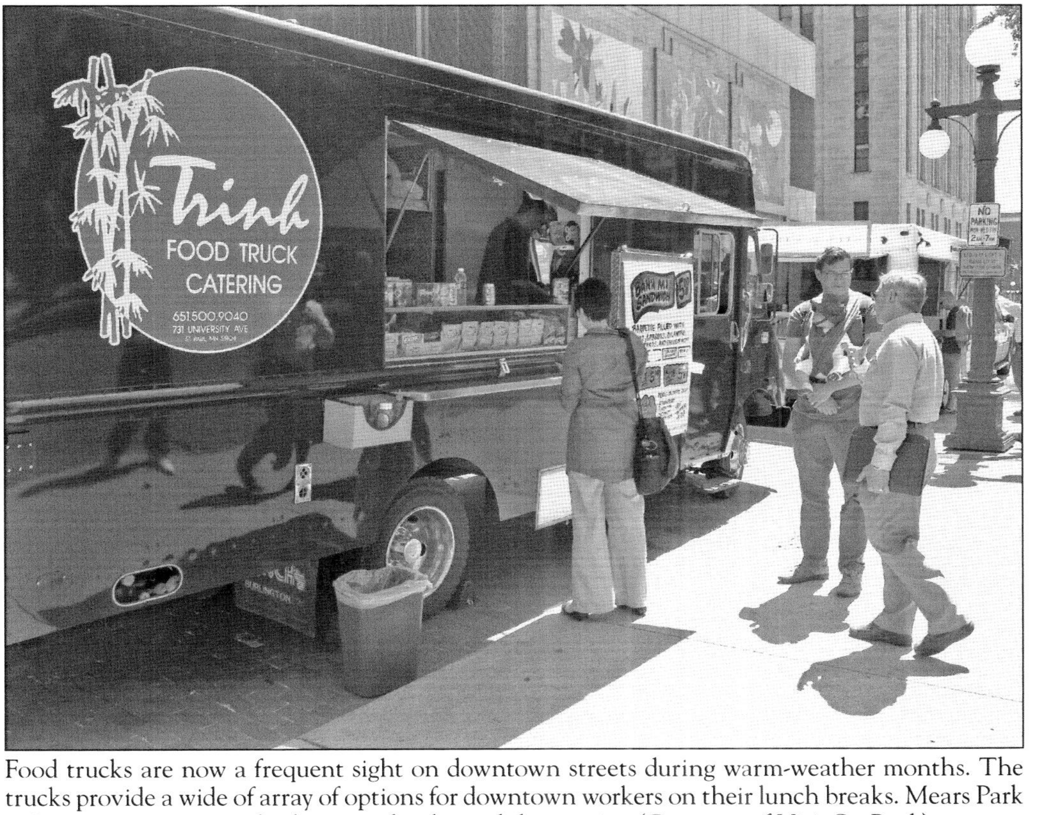

Food trucks are now a frequent sight on downtown streets during warm-weather months. The trucks provide a wide of array of options for downtown workers on their lunch breaks. Mears Park in Lowertown is a popular location for the mobile eateries. (Courtesy of Visit St. Paul.)

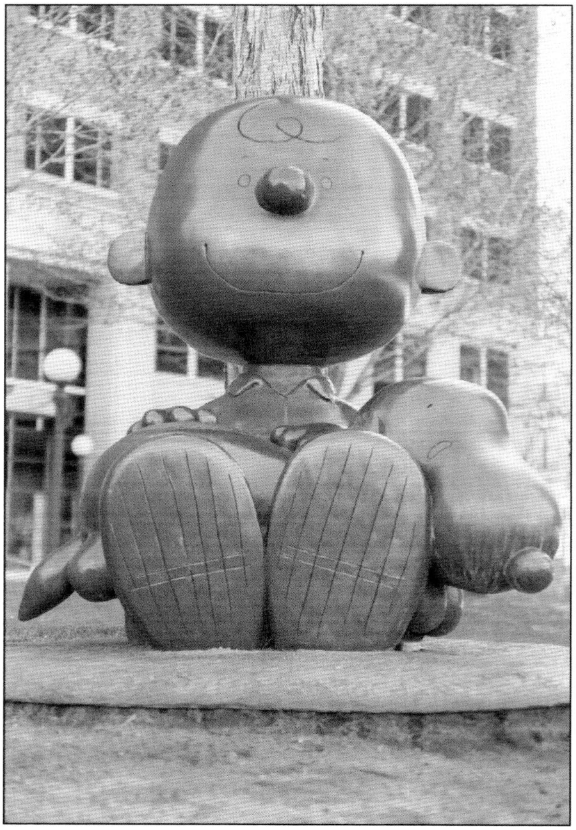

These small sculptures honor St. Paul native Charles Schulz, who created the comic strip *Peanuts*. Several of Schultz's loveable characters now have a permanent home in Landmark Plaza. The proceeds from past *Peanuts* promotions in St. Paul help maintain these bronze sculptures. (Both, courtesy of Visit St. Paul.)

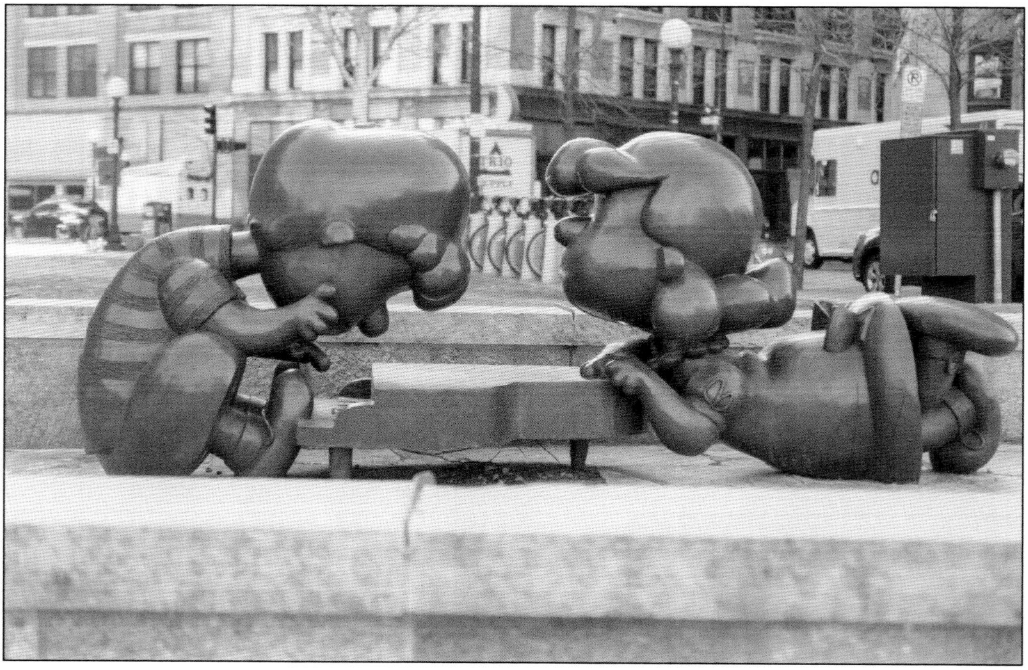

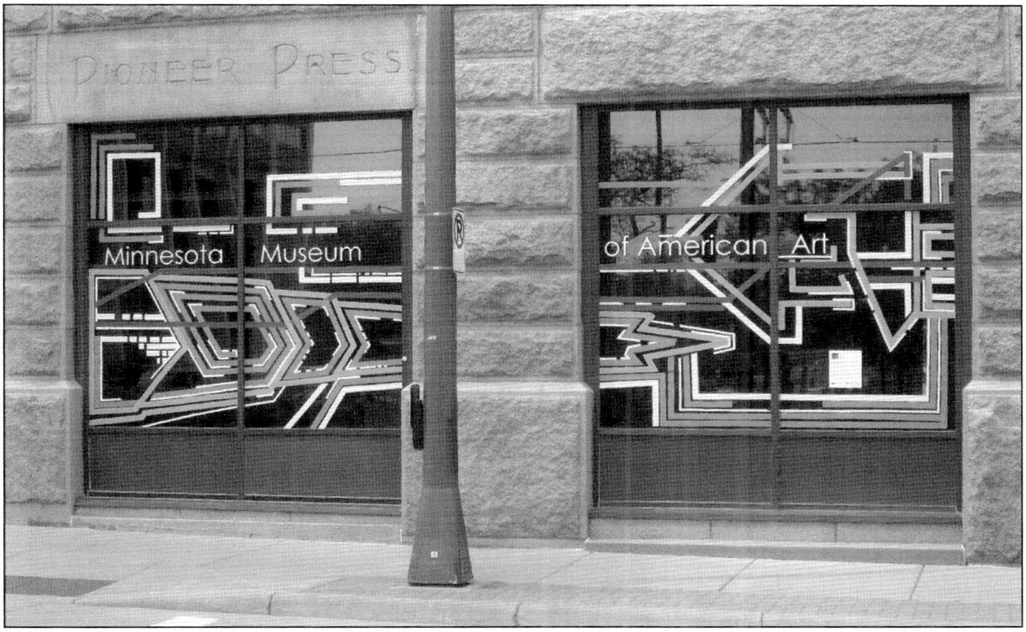

The origins of the Minnesota Museum of American Art extend to the 1890s, when the organization was known as the St. Paul School of Fine Arts. The museum specializes in works by American artists. Now located in the historic Pioneer Endicott Building, the museum has rebranded itself as "the M." (Author's collection.)

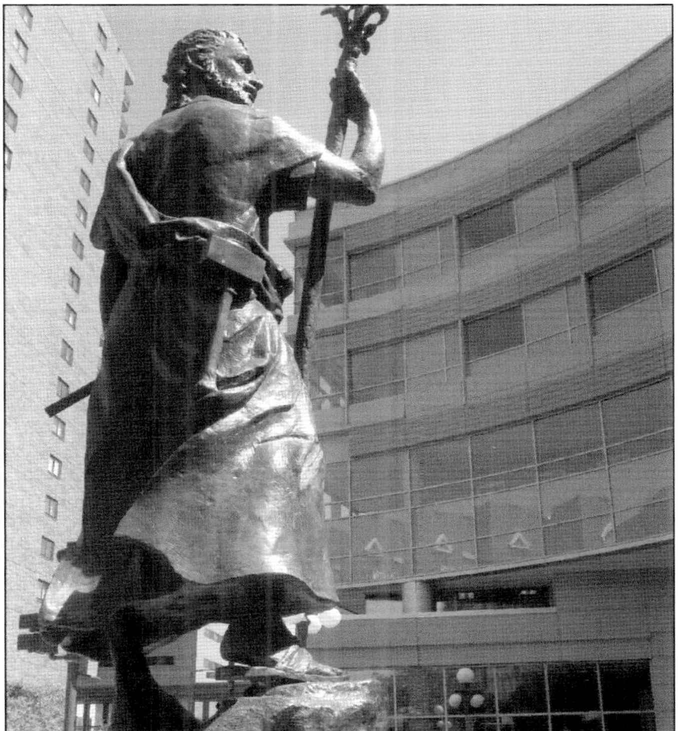

This 17-foot-tall statue of St. Joseph was created by Minnesota sculptor Nicolas Legeros. It was installed in the plaza in front of St. Joseph's Hospital in 2009. Legeros works in the traditional lost wax method of bronze casting. His statue is one of a number of public artworks installed in downtown St. Paul in recent years. (Author's collection.)

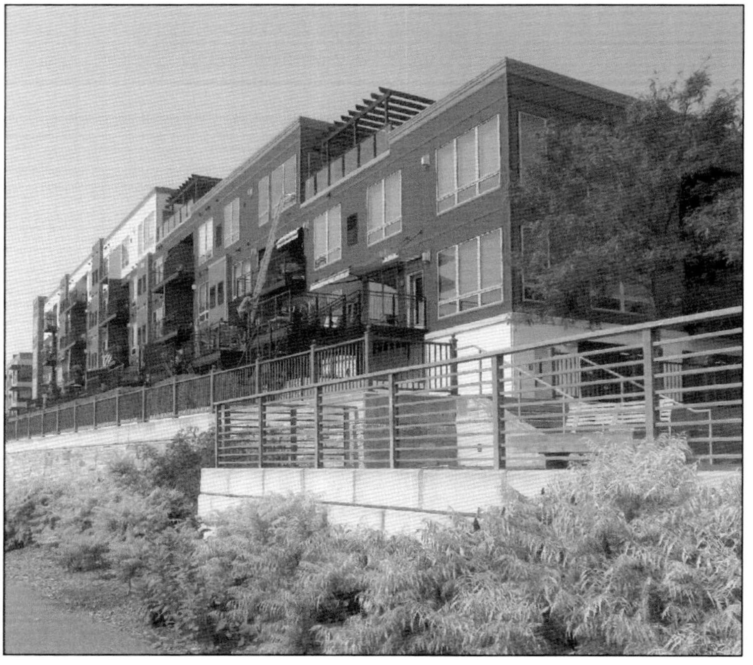

St. Paul's historic Upper Landing was once the site of a small immigrant neighborhood known as Little Italy. In the 1950s, the flood-prone neighborhood was converted to industrial uses. Then, starting in the late 1990s, the Upper Landing underwent another wave of redevelopment when an upscale residential enclave was created on the 22-acre riverfront site. (Author's collection.)

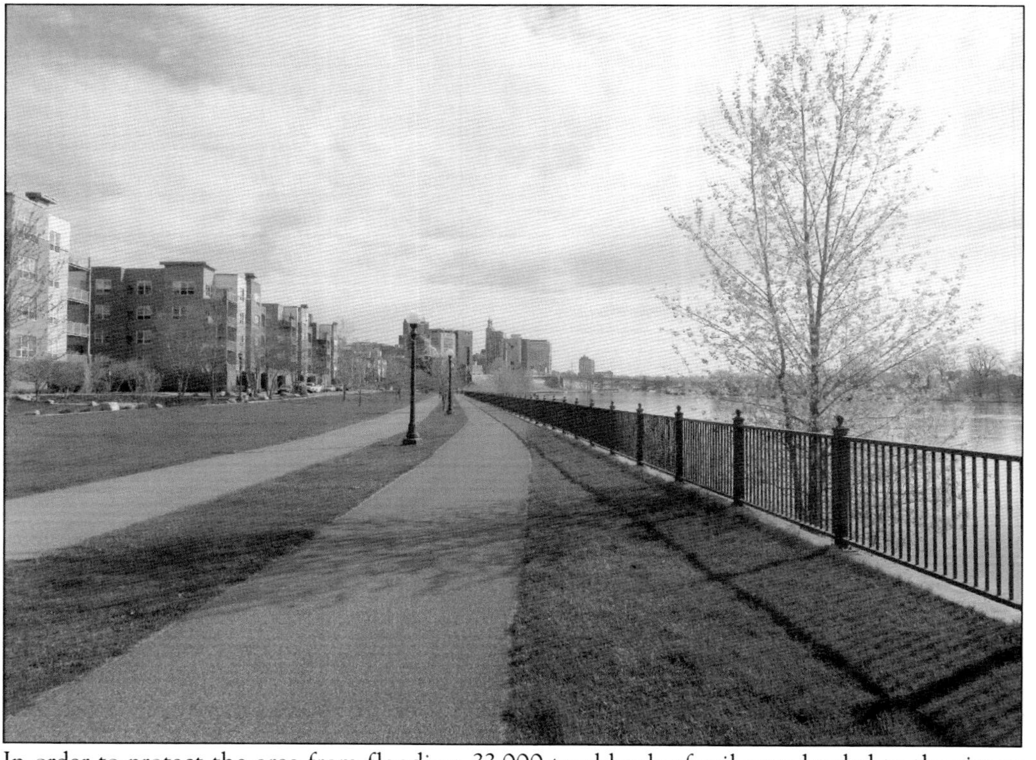

In order to protect the area from flooding, 33,000 truckloads of soil were hauled to the site to raise its elevation. The Upper Landing's new residents received assurance that their homes and apartments were at least nine feet above the highest recorded flood level. (Author's collection.)

The municipal grain terminal is a riverfront landmark dating to 1931. It operated as a distribution center for St. Paul's grain industry up through the 1980s. Trains would arrive at the terminal, where spring wheat and other grains would be loaded onto barges for shipment down the river. No longer in operation, the grain terminal now serves as a historic site and Upper Landing focal point. (Author's collection.)

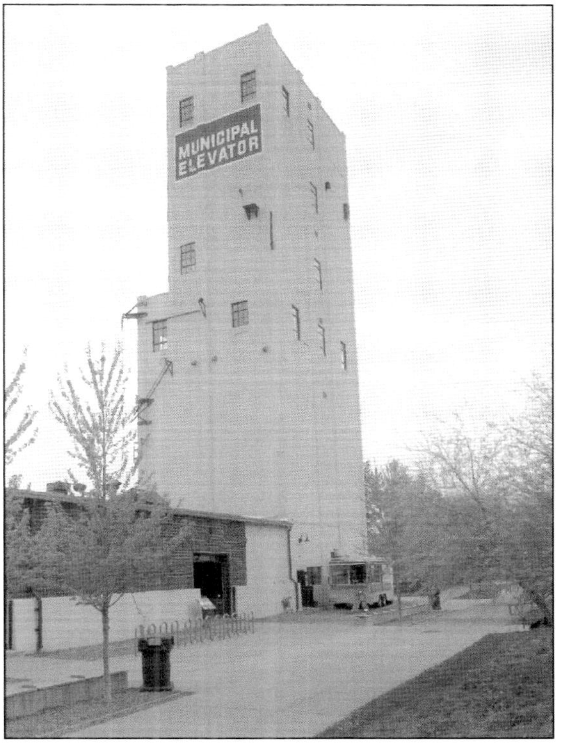

The Sam Morgan Trail is a bike and pedestrian pathway that spans the downtown riverfront. The trail is named for Samuel H. Morgan, a prominent Twin Cities attorney and environmental activist. Morgan was the longtime president of the Minnesota Parks Foundation and a staunch advocate for parks and trails throughout the state. (Author's collection.)

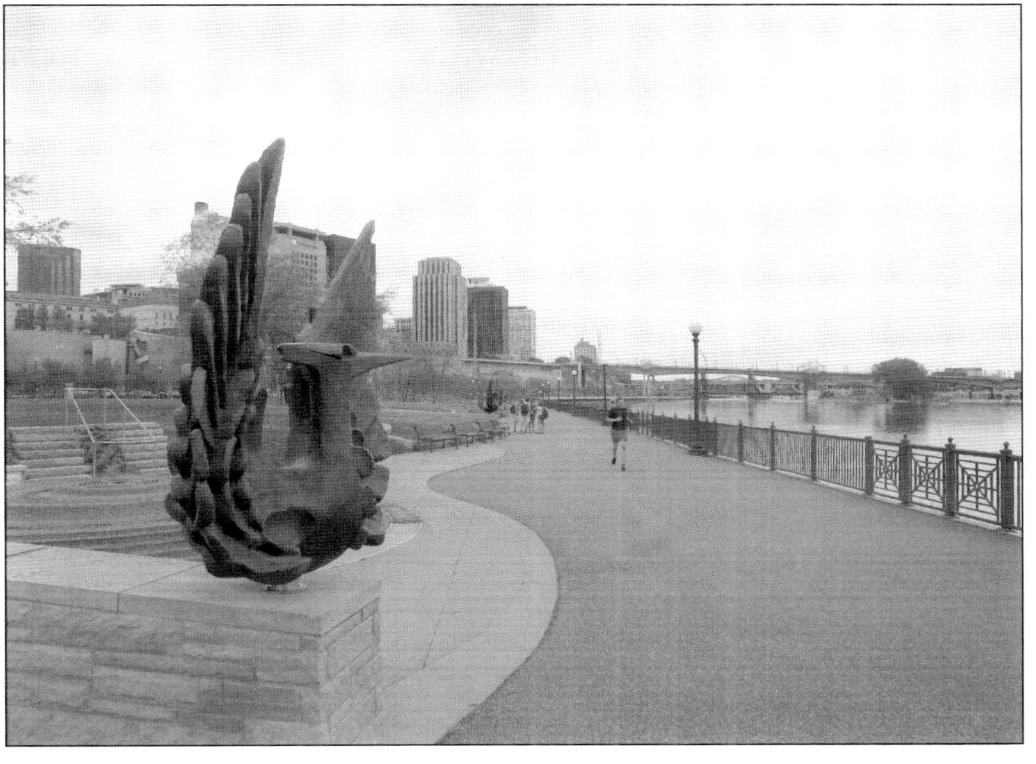

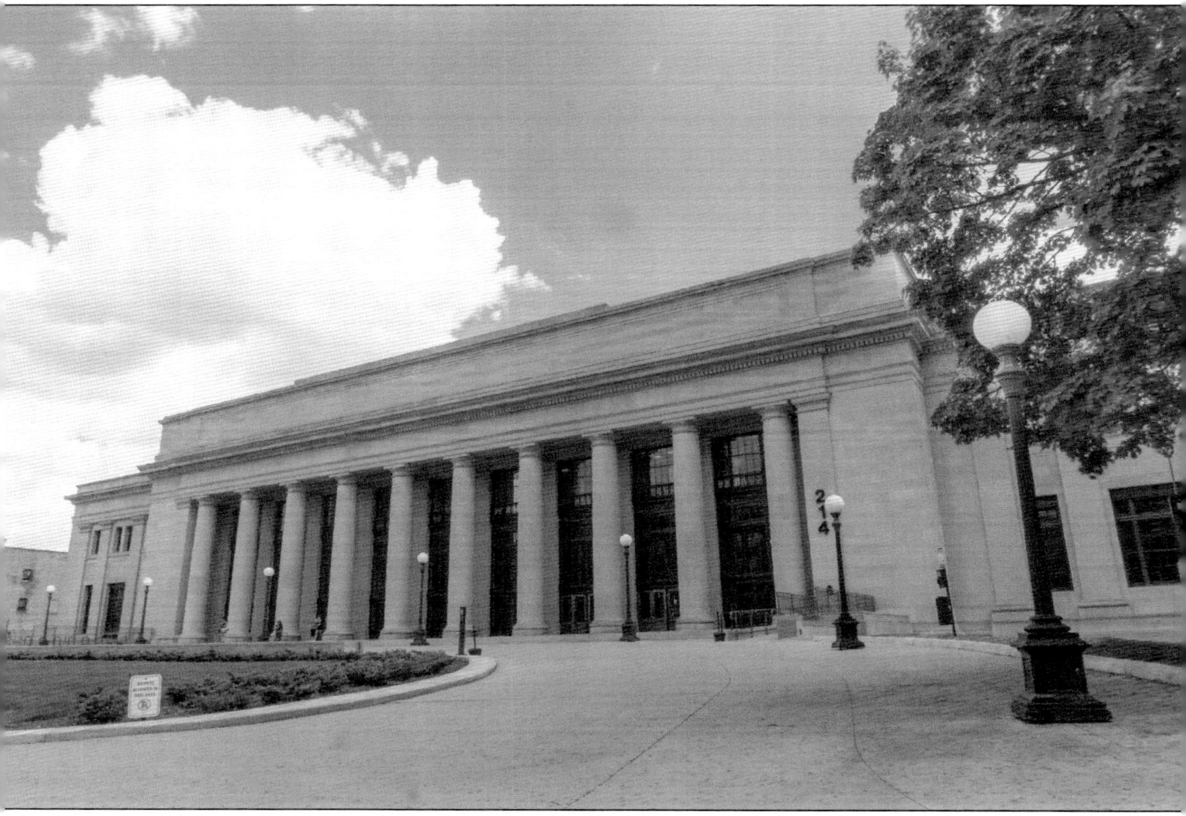

St. Paul's historic Union Depot reopened in 2012 after a major renovation costing $245 million. The depot now serves as Amtrak's passenger station for the Twin Cities. Union Depot also operates as a hub for light rail transit and intercity bus service. (Courtesy of Visit St. Paul.)

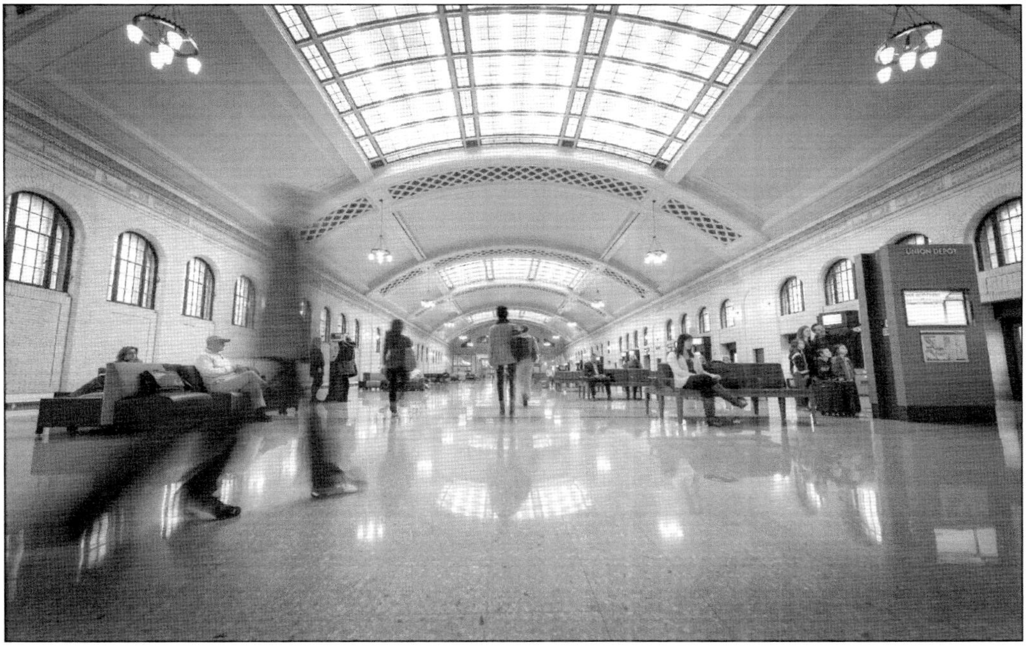

The depot's expansive waiting room is now used for weddings, private parties, and other special events. The waiting room also provides a respite for passengers coming and going on Amtrak's *Empire Builder* train between Chicago and Seattle. (Courtesy of Visit St. Paul.)

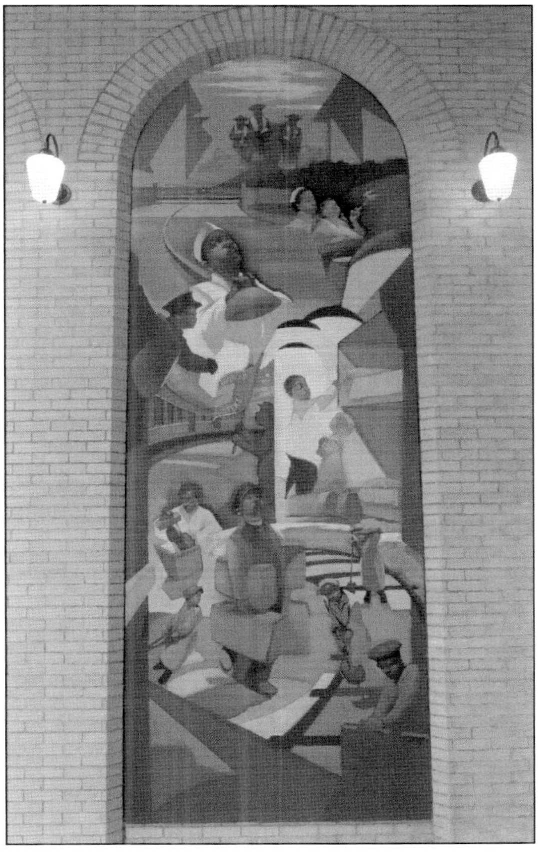

This Union Depot painting, one of six by muralist Ralph Gilbert, highlights the role of the "red caps" in St. Paul's transportation history. These mainly African American railroad workers assisted passengers with their luggage and provided other services in the busy train station. They played an important leadership role in St. Paul's historic African American community in the Rondo district. (Author's collection.)

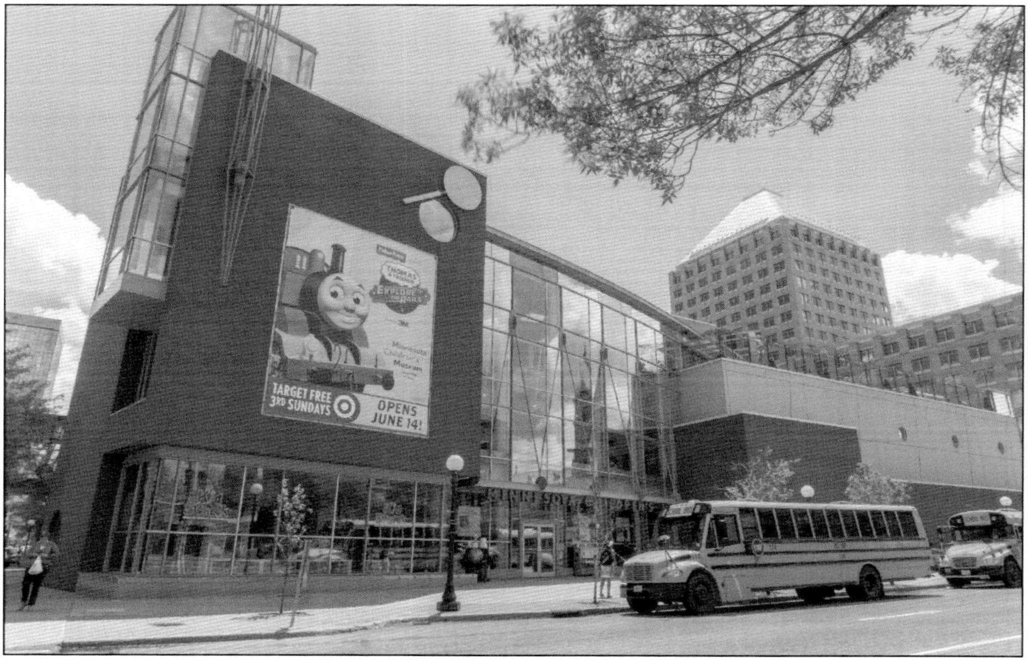

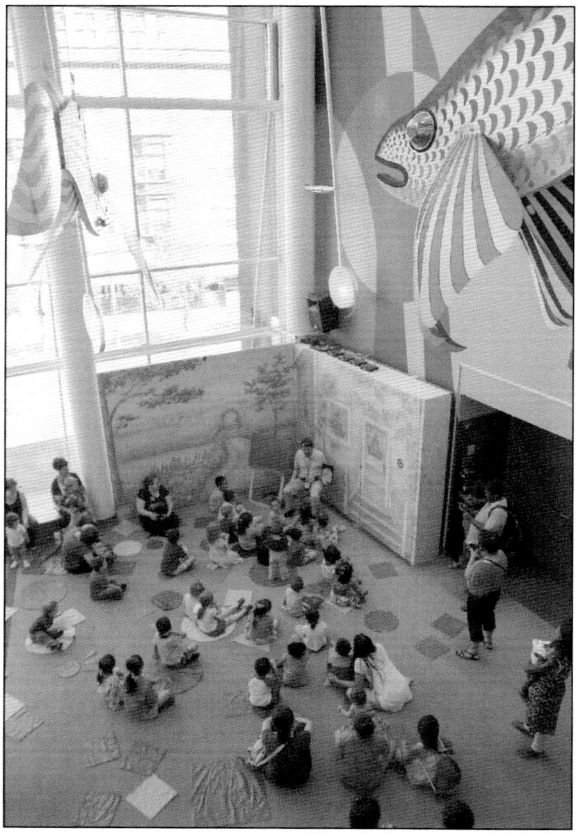

Originally known as the Minnesota AwareHouse, the Minnesota Children's Museum provides a playful hands-on learning environment for young people. In 1995, the museum moved from its earlier site in Bandana Square to a new home on West Seventh Street. The Minnesota Children's Museum has been described as a "jolly pirate ship . . . in downtown's sea of sober, gray, brown and beige buildings." (Both, courtesy of Visit St. Paul.)

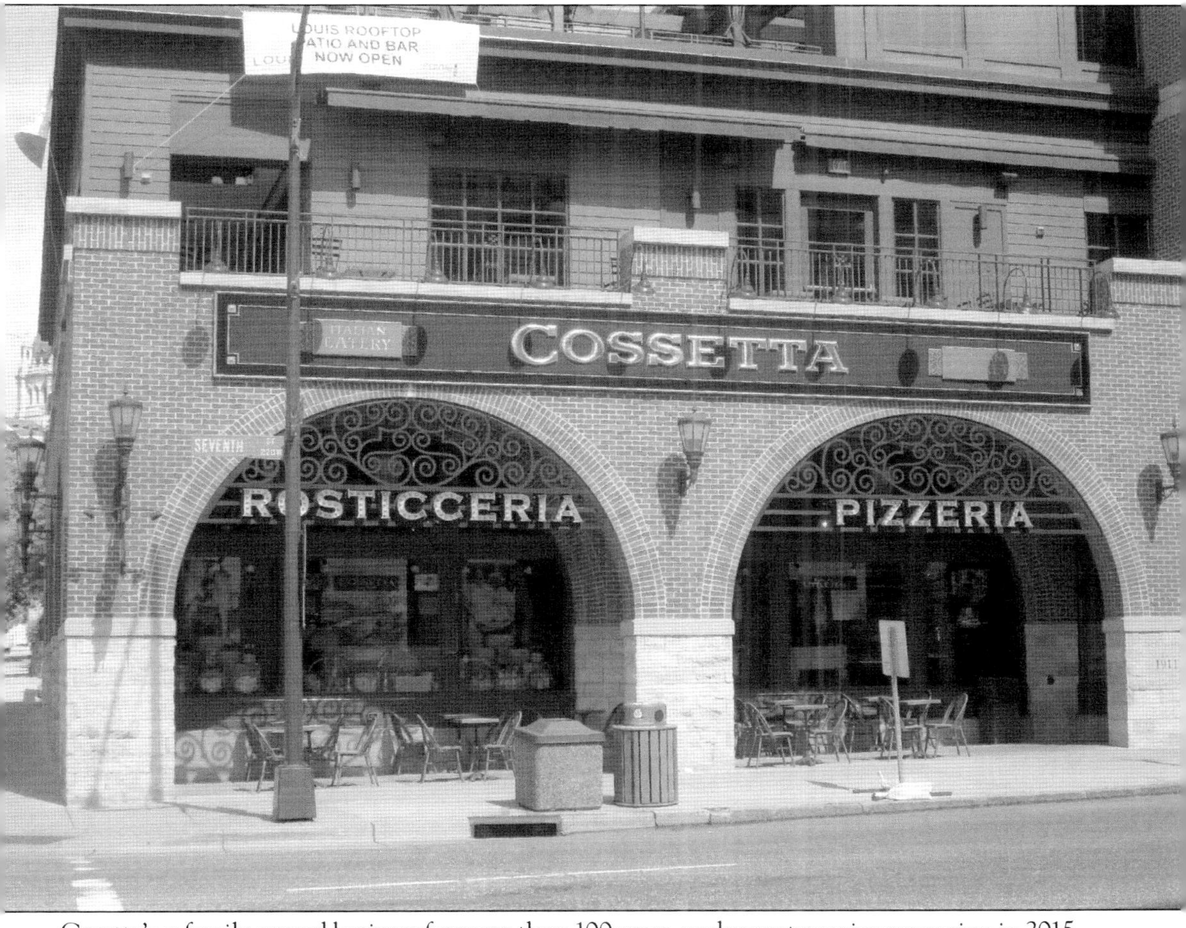

Cosetta's, a family-owned business for more than 100 years, underwent a major expansion in 2015. Earlier, the popular Italian restaurant and market relocated from its original Irvine Park location to West Seventh Street. The new Cosetta's features a rooftop patio with a commanding view of downtown St. Paul. (Author's collection.)

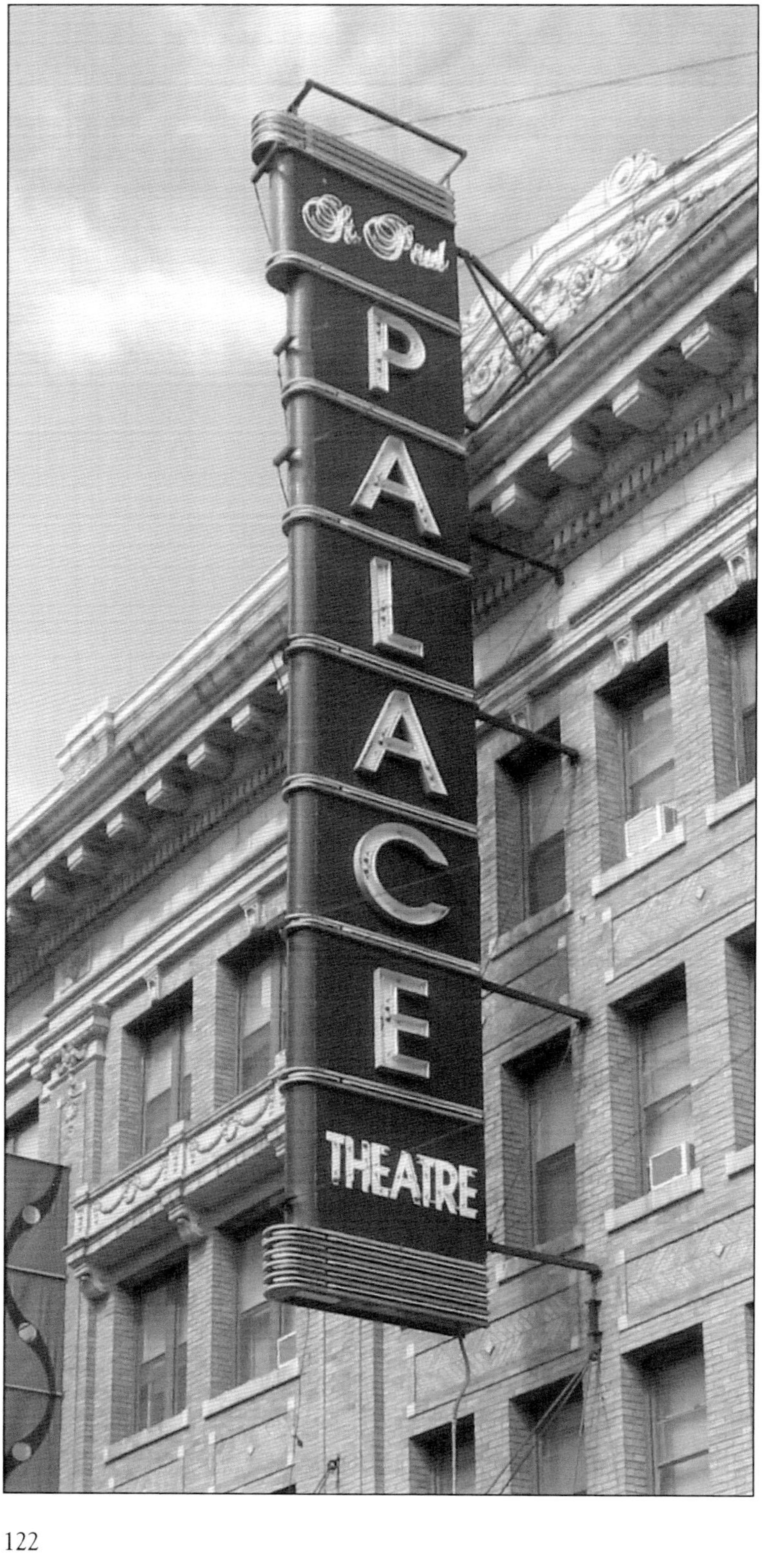

The Palace Theatre began life in 1916 as a vaudeville house that hosted famous showbusiness personalities including Charlie Chaplin, George Burns, and the Marx Brothers. Mainly vacant for the last 40 years, the Palace was purchased by the City of St. Paul and rehabbed as a popular music venue. The theater reopened in March 2017. (Author's collection.)

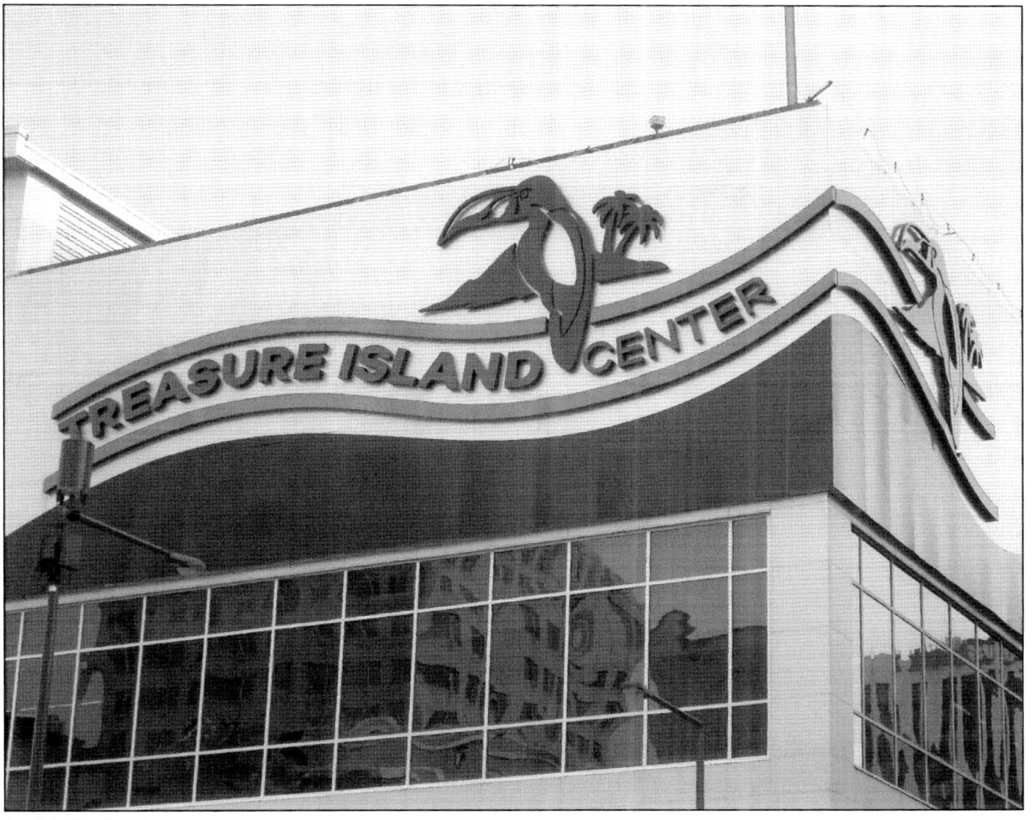

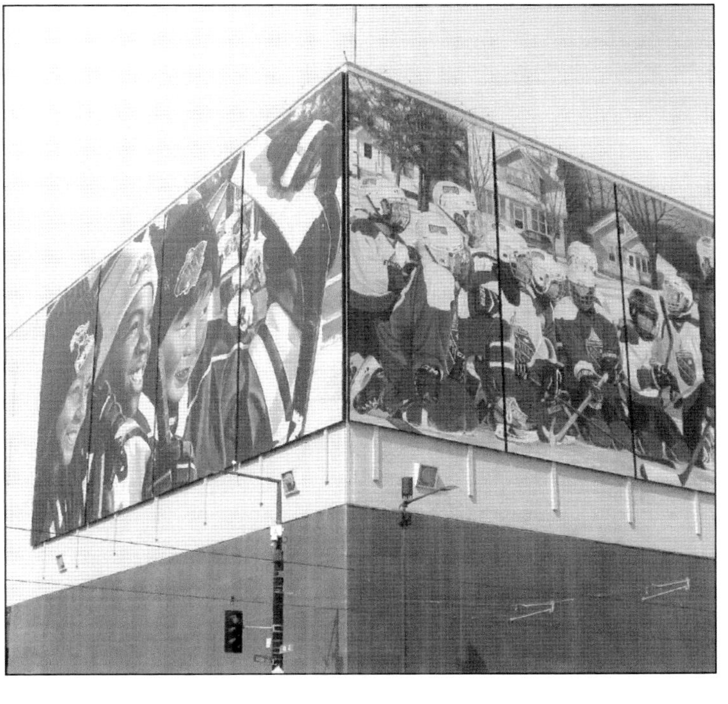

In 2018, the former Macy's department store at Fourth and Wabasha Streets was converted to a mixed-use commercial building that includes a practice facility for the Minnesota Wild. College and community hockey teams are able to use the ice rink on the top level of the building. In exchange for a sizeable investment in the downtown project, the Prairie Island Indian community received naming rights for its Treasure Island Resort and Casino. (Both, author's collection.)

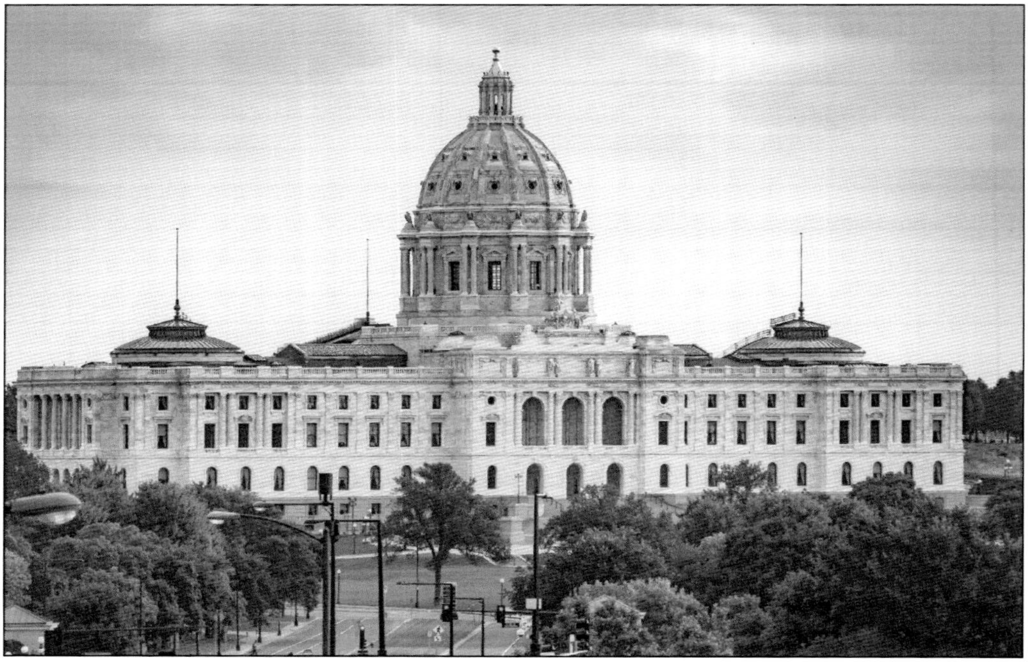

The Minnesota State Capitol was a busy construction zone during a four-year period from 2013 to 2017 while it underwent a major overhaul and modernization. Much of the work occurred behind the scenes as heating, electrical, and plumbing systems were repaired and replaced. The building's numerous murals and other artworks were also restored. The capitol's grand opening occurred during a three-day celebration in August 2017. (Courtesy of Visit St. Paul.)

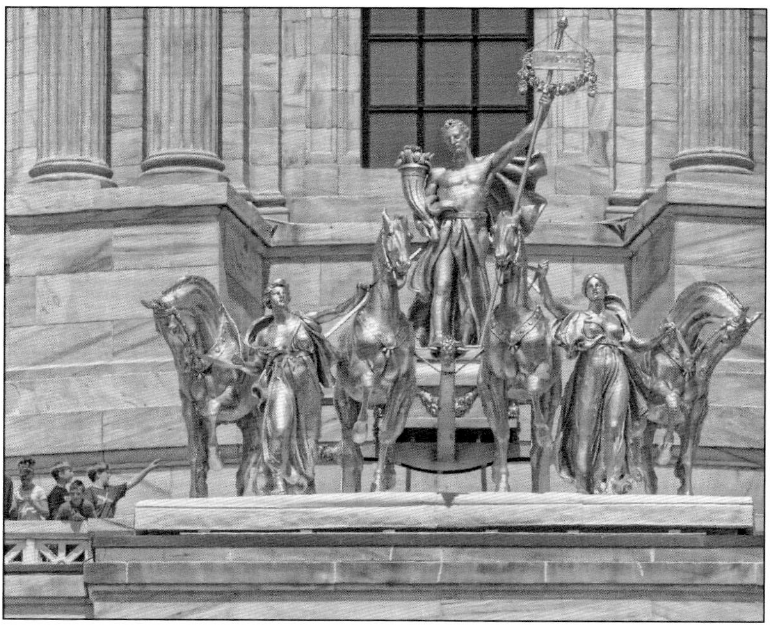

The *Quadringa* was refinished with gold leaf as part of the capitol renovation effort. Weather permitting, visitors to the capitol are able to climb a narrow, winding stairway to the base of the dome and view this dramatic sculpture up close. The vantage point at the capitol's upper level provides an expansive view of St. Paul. (Courtesy of Visit St. Paul.)

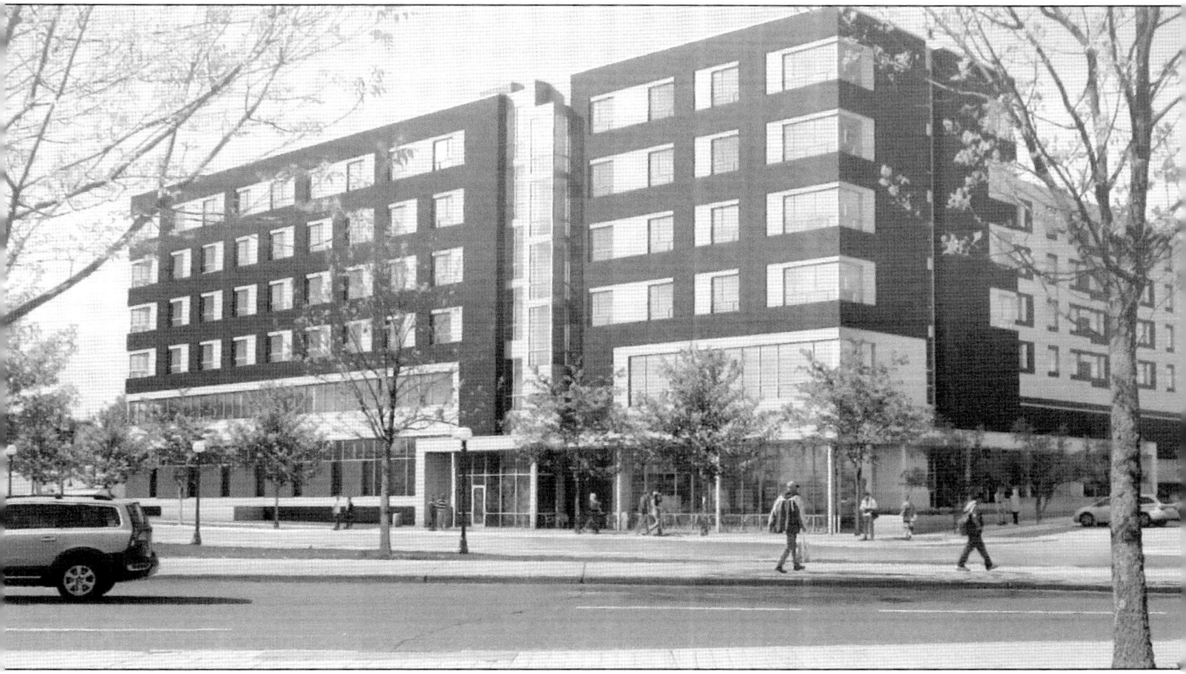

The St. Paul Opportunity Center will occupy the first floor of this facility, developed by Catholic Charities of St. Paul. The center will connect people facing social challenges with services that can move them toward self-sufficiency. The building's upper floors, known as the Dorothy Day Residences, will provide 171 units of affordable housing. The building is adjacent to Catholic Charities' Higher Ground Center, which provides emergency shelter and permanent housing for people dealing with homelessness. (Author's collection.)

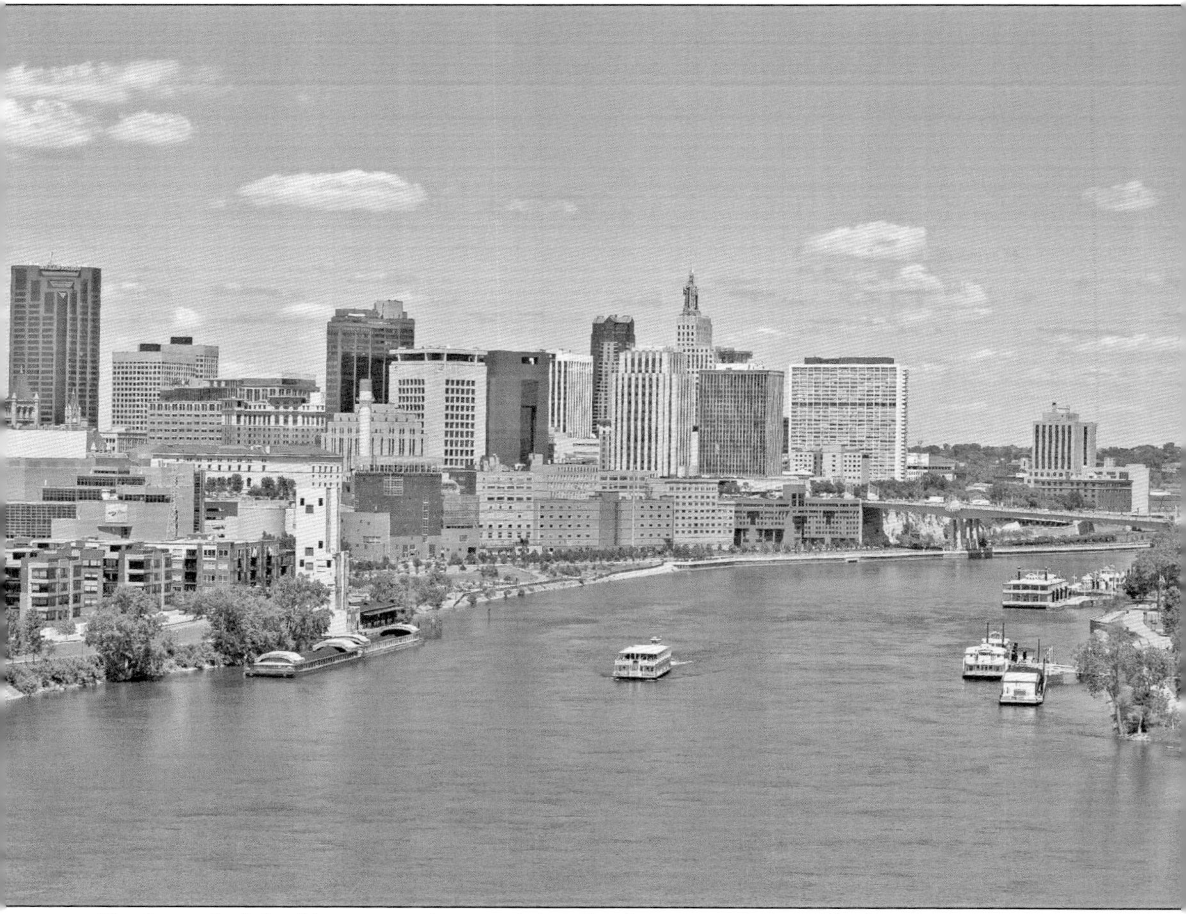

By the end of the 21st century's second decade, downtown St. Paul had overcome many of the economic challenges that threatened the capital city's historic commercial core. No longer a major retail hub, downtown has refashioned itself as a cultural and entertainment center. With a thriving economy and a new identity as an urban residential neighborhood, downtown St. Paul can look forward to a bright future. (Courtesy of Visit St. Paul.)

BIBLIOGRAPHY

Anderson, David. *Downtown: A History of Downtown Minneapolis and St. Paul.* Minneapolis, MN: Nodin Press, 2000.

Diers, John W. *St. Paul Union Depot.* Minneapolis, MN: University of Minnesota Press, 2013.

Diers, John W. and Aaron Isaacs. *Twin Cities by Trolley: The Street Car Era in Minneapolis and St. Paul.* Minneapolis, MN: University of Minnesota Press, 2007.

Kenney, Dave. *Twin Cities Picture Show: A Century of Moviegoing.* St. Paul, MN: Minnesota Historical Society Press, 2007.

Kunz, Virginia Brainard. *St. Paul: The First 150 Years.* St. Paul, MN: The Saint Paul Foundation, 1992.

Lindley, John M. *Celebrate Saint Paul: 150 Years of History.* Encino, CA: Cherbo Publishing Group, 2003.

Millett, Larry. *AIA Guide to the Twin Cities.* St. Paul, MN: Minnesota Historical Society Press, 2007.

———. *Twin Cities Then and Now.* St. Paul, MN: Minnesota Historical Society Press, 1996.

Trimble, Steve. *Historical Photos of St. Paul.* Nashville, TN: Turner Publishing Company, 2008.

———. *Remembering St. Paul.* Nashville, TN: Turner Publishing Company, 2010.

Williams, J. Fletcher. *A History of the City of St. Paul to 1875.* St. Paul, MN: Minnesota Historical Society Press, 1983.

Wingerd, Mary Lethert. *Claiming the City: Politics, Faith and the Power of Place in St. Paul.* Ithaca, NY: Cornell University Press, 2001.

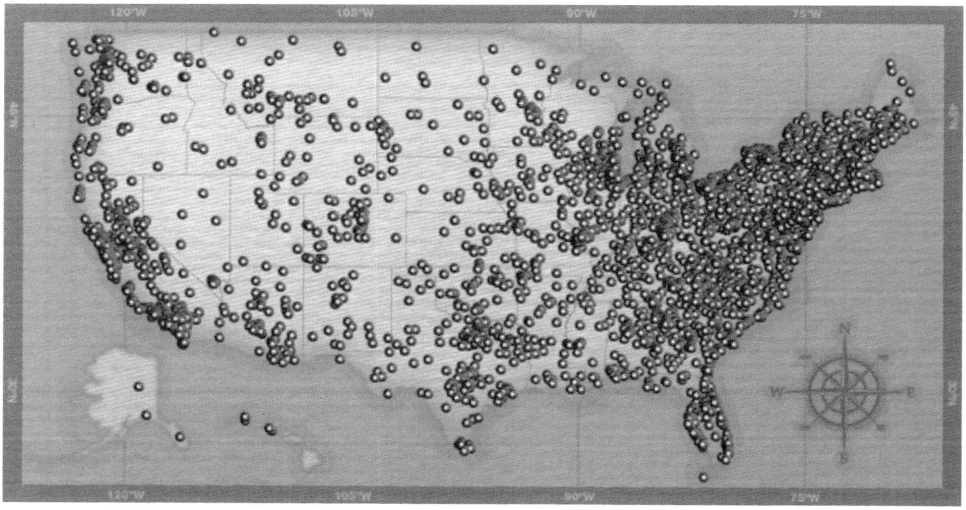